ANOMIE

ANOMIE

History
and Meanings

MARCO ORRÙ

University of South Florida

Boston
ALLEN & UNWIN
London   Sydney   Wellington

Allen & Unwin, Inc.,
8 Winchester Place, Winchester, Mass. 01890, USA
the U.S. company of
UNWIN HYMAN LTD

PO Box 18, Park Lane, Hemel Hempstead, Herts HP2 4TE, UK
40 Museum Street, London WC1A 1LU, UK
37/39 Queen Elizabeth Street, London SE1 2QB, UK

Allen & Unwin (Australia) Ltd,
8 Napier Street, North Sydney, NSW 2060, Australia

Allen & Unwin (New Zealand) Ltd in association with the Port
Nicholson Press Ltd,
60 Cambridge Terrace, Wellington, New Zealand

First published in 1987

Library of Congress Cataloging-in-Publication Data

Orrù, Marco, 1954–
    Anomie : history and meanings.
Bibliography: p.
Includes index.
1. Anomy.   I. Title.
HM291.O77 1987   303.3'72   86-32144
ISBN 0-04-301267-1 (alk. paper)

British Library Cataloguing in Publication Data

Orrù, Marco
    Anomie : history and meanings.
1. Anomy
I. Title
303.4'5   HM291
ISBN 0-04-301267-1

Typeset in 10 on 11 point Goudy by
V & M Graphics Ltd, Aylesbury, Bucks
and printed in Great Britain by
Billing & Sons Ltd, Worcester

Ai miei genitori

Salvatore Orrù e Angela Salis

CONTENTS

PREFACE

My interest in the topic of anomie developed during my graduate work in sociology at the University of California at Davis, when a French colleague often remarked that American sociologists had totally misinterpreted Durkheim's notion of anomie. As I began researching the topic, I had no idea that my seemingly idle curiosity would have kept me busy for so many years.

Searching for the correct meaning of anomie I started following all possible leads: Durkheim's early writings led me to the work of Jean Marie Guyau; Robert Merton's footnotes and passing comments sent me to read seventeenth-century English Biblical and legal texts; my knowledge of classical Greek threw me in the midst of Platonic and sophistic philosophy, and of Biblical texts in Greek. In the following years I took up each topic systematically, as I started to research the anomie literature period by period: nineteenth-century France, Renaissance England, Ancient Greece, late Judaism and early Christianity, and twentieth-century socio-logical literature.

To this day I am not sure that I have found the real meaning of anomie (in fact I know I haven't) but this monograph is the result of my journey through twenty-five centuries of anomie literature. Throughout my research I received continuous encouragement and moral support from my teacher and colleague, Gary G. Hamilton. Many of the ideas in this book developed out of our regular conversations over the years, and I thank him very much for his generosity in time and in sound advice.

I am also grateful to Judith Stacey and Neal W. Gilbert who read various drafts of this work and helped improve the manuscript in both substance and form. A special word of thanks goes to Robert K. Merton who reviewed the manuscript and provided extensive comments throughout; the final product was much improved thanks to his suggestions.

Less tangible but crucial support was provided by colleagues and friends. I particularly thank Bernadette Tarallo, Beverly Lozano, Diane Bjorklund and, most of all, Jeff Hoey.

Some of the chapters in this book have appeared, in slightly different form, in professional journals. Chapter 1 appeared in the *Archives européennes de sociologie* (vol. 26, pp. 3–28); Chapter 3 in the *Journal of the History of Ideas* (vol. 47, pp. 177–96); Chapter 4 in *The British Journal of Sociology* (vol. 34, pp. 499–518). They are reprinted here with the publishers' permission.

Davis, California

INTRODUCTION

SOCRATES: Then, Hermogenes, I should say
that this giving of names
can be no such light matter' as you fancy,
or the work of light or chance persons.
And Cratylus is right in saying
that things have names by nature,
and that not every man is an artificer of names,
but he only looks to the name
which each thing by nature has,
and is able to express the true forms of things
in letters and syllables.

Plato *Cratylus* 390E

This study describes the history and meanings of a key concept of modern sociology, anomie. The popularity of the concept is quite recent – a few decades old – but its roots go back a long way, more than twenty-five centuries.[1] Despite its modern appeal and past fortunes, very little is known about the sociological and pre-sociological roots of the concept of anomie.

Most contemporary discussions of anomie assume the following: (1) that Durkheim was the first to introduce anomie in sociology, (2) that he first discussed anomie in the third book of his *Division of Labor*, (3) that seventeenth-century Englishmen used the word in much the same way as modern sociologists, and (4) that anomie is the French and anomy the English spelling.[2] This study will show all these assumptions to be mistaken, but this is only of secondary import. Philological and historical accuracy are obviously desirable, but they are not essential to construct a sound theory of anomie. What is indispensable, however, is to be aware of the theoretical and ethical dimensions that underlie the concept of anomie. Such awareness, I claim, can best be obtained by looking at anomie in historical perspective; accordingly, my aim is to provide a systematic description of the literature that will give the reader the needed historical information about anomie.

It will immediately ask: what is anomie? Despite the widespread adoption of the concept, it is difficult, if not impossible, to come up with an agreed definition. For some writers, anomie is the absence of cultural restraints on human aspirations, for others it denotes a conflict of belief-systems in a society; anomie also

1

describes the imbalance between cultural goals and institutional means at either the social or the individual level, or a psychological condition of self-to-other alienation.[3] Certainly, the etymology of the word is straightforward – anomie means, literally, "the absence of laws or norms."[4] And yet, if one is asked to specify what kinds of laws or norms or customs are absent in a condition of anomie, the ambiguity reappears. Does anomie refer to the absence of positive laws? Does it characterize the lack of shared beliefs and customs? Does it describe the inconsistency of norms?

The problem of defining anomie is not an unusual one in the social sciences; the concept of alienation, to name a close relative of anomie, is subject to similar ambiguities. Some writers believe that the confusion about anomie simply mirrors the low scientific level of sociological research – a problem that will be solved as soon as sociology finds its Lavoisier.[5] The confusion, however, cannot be dismissed so lightly. If it is true that a definition determines the use of a word, it is also true that the use of a word defines its meaning. Anomie is easily defined etymologically, but not semantically. The etymological definition of anomie is fixed and is obvious to anyone who knows its Greek origin, *anomia* – absence of law. But such a definition is so broad as to be almost useless. The semantic definition, instead, is obtained from the contextual use of the word at different historical times – it is more specific, but also varies greatly throughout the literature, reflecting specific concerns of different epochs and cultures. Anomie means ruthlessness and *hybris* in Euripides, anarchy and intemperance in Plato, sin and wickedness in the Old Testament, unrighteousness or unwritten law in Paul's letters, irregularity or formal transgression in Bishop Bramhall's treatises, a positive characteristic of modern morality in Jean Marie Guyau's books, and a human condition of insatiability in Durkheim.

In reviewing the literature, we never find a univocal meaning of anomie, and the reason is simple. At the descriptive level, our background knowledge determines the use we make of our concepts: a philosopher discusses anomie in philosophical terms, a theologian discusses it in religious terms, a sociologist in sociological terms, a jurist in legal terms. However, this is only one source of variation. The concept of anomie has not only a factual, descriptive meaning, but also an evaluative, normative meaning. When we label something anomic, we do not simply describe it as normless, we also describe it as desirably or undesirably normless. Such an evaluative dimension is very obvious in pre-sociological writings; it is still present, although often unacknowledged, in contemporary social science research. In its historical use, anomie has been commonly characterized in a negative way, but there is an alternative historical tradition in which anomie is seen in a positive way – most explicitly in the work of Jean Marie Guyau, but also in ancient sophistic philosophy and in contemporary social thought. The variation in descriptive and evaluative aspects of anomie makes a univocal definition unlikely in future research; at any rate, an attempt to achieve one should not ignore the previous history of the concept.

The variation of meanings in the anomie literature might well discourage the rising Lavoisier, but it makes an historical investigation such as this all the more justifiable and worthwhile. I am not, here, after a final, long-lasting definition of anomie. Nor am I concerned with separating a true from a pseudo anomie. Instead, I want to show the variety of uses and meanings of the word in Western culture, and to point out how this variety matched the needs of different societies at different historical times. In following the fate of anomie throughout the centuries, one comes across a wide range of topics: discussions about nature, justice, culture, sin, freedom, evil, necessity, rationality, social order, human nature, morality, means and ends of action, individualism, alienation, and despair. The variety of topics reflects the prominence of different themes in different epochs; such themes were conveyed by the concept of anomie as the broad etymological meaning acquired semantic specifications.

The historical excursus on anomie would look like a collage of loosely related topics of discussion, were it not for anomie's underlying ethical dimensions. Throughout the anomie literature, parallel to the diversity of themes, there runs a continuity of common concerns. Whether the writers are engaged in philosophical disputes, in Biblical exegeses, or in sociological theorizing, there are a number of unstated assumptions which remain constant throughout the anomie literature. All the discussions of anomie share a common set of ethical and cognitive features.

At the ethical level, the anomie literature reveals two antithetical approaches to social phenomena and individual behavior. One approach emphasizes the social nature of morality and its externality to the individual actor – this is, for instance, Durkheim's position. The other approach stresses the individual nature of morality and its relative autonomy from the social sphere – this is the position of sophistic philosophers for whom there was no uniform, external law that could be imposed on the individual, except in a conventional transitory way. At the cognitive level, the anomie literature shows a similar opposition of emphases. On the one hand, some writers favored the holistic, organismic view of social phenomena, as in Durkheim's rule: "Treat social facts as things." On the other hand, other writers favored the atomistic view of social phenomena, stressing the role of voluntary individual action at the expense of its social determinants.

The two ethical postures can be described, for lack of any better labels, as the transcendental versus the immanent view of morality.[6] We speak of a transcendental view of morality, when the source of moral judgment is considered to be external to the individual and located in the socio-cultural values of the group or in its religious beliefs. The source of morality is either God or society. An immanentistic view of morality, on the contrary, locates the source of moral judgment in the individual actor, and considers social morality to be the product of interacting moral actors. The anomie literature offers evidence of both approaches to ethics. Plato, Philo of Alexandria, and Emile Durkheim, among others, discussed anomie from a transcendental perspective. Sophistic philosophers, Thomas Hobbes, and Jean Marie Guyau wrote about anomie from individual-based ethics.

At the cognitive level, the ethical dualism is paralleled by the tendency to emphasize a realistic or a nominalistic approach to social and psychological phenomena. The realists assume that ideas exist independently of the reality they describe; the nominalists claim that only individuals exist, and that theories and ideas are simply devised for the solution of practical problems. In the anomie literature, again, we find writers whose assumptions fall either in the nominalistic or in the realistic camp, although it is often the case that elements of both are found in the same author. The realists, like Plato or Durkheim, consider anomie as a corrupted and pathological condition of the ideal or normal social system; the nominalists, like the sophists or Guyau, only entertain instrumental notions of social order. Such notions are derived from historical social forms and cannot exist independently from the actual social conditions which generate them. Anomie is, for the nominalist, the product of interacting individuals who constitute the social group; such a group does not have any referent outside its constituting members.

Often, in the anomie literature, the ethical and cognitive dichotomies come to the surface in discussions of parallel, derived themes. We find diatribes on organicism and atomism, liberty and necessity, idealism and positivism, reason and senses, individualism and collectivism, objectivity and subjectivity, culture and nature, ends and means. In ancient Greece, Plato argued against the sophists about the superiority of culture over nature; in the Biblical literature, Paul's writings emphasized the freedom of the

4

spirit, in contrast to the coercive teachings of legalistic Judaism; in seventeenth-century England, Anglicans argued for a human reason capable of moral judgment against the Puritans' view of a sensual, corrupted human nature; in nineteenth-century France, Durkheim stressed the collective source of moral life and criticized Guyau's idea of an individualistic, anomic morality. The apparent diversity of topics was clearly paralleled by a shared set of concerns.

This study describes discussions of anomie in their historical context, highlighting their specificity; it also identifies shared moral and philosophical assumptions behind the apparent variation of themes. Beyond the continuing confrontation between opposing views of the social order, beyond the constant conflict between immanentism and transcendentalism, it is possible, in different epochs, to identify a dominant mode of thought. If nineteenth-century French sociology leaned toward transcendental realism, contempory American sociology leans toward the immanent, voluntaristic nominalism. The pattern of oscillation between these two poles goes back a long way. In ancient Greece, the nominalist position of the sophistic philosophers prevailed during the Periclean era; in the fourth century, with Plato and Aristotle, it shifted toward transcendental realism. In the Biblical literature, the Old Testament emphasized the transcendental view of a collective bond between the Jewish people and their God, playing up the paramount role of the written law, the Torah, as the guide to the good life. The New Testament, instead, proclaimed the supremacy of the one-to-one relationship with God, playing down the role of the written law and emphasizing the law of the spirit residing in the individual's heart. The examples could be multiplied, but suffice it here to say that the movement between facts and ideas, between individual and society, between nominalism and realism, has been a typical pattern of Western thought since the epoch Karl Jaspers defined as "the axial period."[7] The tension between immanence and transcendence is not so much the expression of two different ways of thinking about the world, as it is a *single* way of thinking which is subject to an internal tension regarding the location of reality. The outcome of such a tension is either an emphasis on thought at the expense of the reality it seeks to understand, or an emphasis on the experientially real at the expense of the thought which makes it intelligible.

The anomie literature offers an instance of such a dilemma. One speaks of anomie in relation to historically set social phenomena while entertaining an idea of non-anomic social or individual conditions; at the same time, the idea of a well-regulated society

5

emerges from one's experience in a "real" social form. Simply, experience is determined by thought just as thought is determined by experience; the two are in a continuous, dialectical tension. The literature on anomie reflects the tension of material and historical conditions of existence on the one hand, and the cognitive framework which informs these conditions on the other. As a result, one finds opposing perspectives on a same historical phenomenon and similar perspectives on different historical phenomena. For instance, Plato and the sophists are in disagreement about the same social reality, whereas Plato and Durkheim are in basic agreement about historically different social realities. The two sources of variation, material conditions and cognitive frameworks, can be studied from two distinct points of view.

The sociology of knowledge offers one approach which can relate economic and socio-political conditions to specific patterns of thought. I do not wish to endorse, here, a deterministic causal relation between economic structure and cultural phenomena – a position which would be rejected even in a sociology of knowledge approach. Rather, I want to explore possible links between the economic and the cultural sphere. Although amenable to many specifications and caveats, we can detect from this angle a broad pattern where immanentistic and materialistic outlooks on social reality parallel periods of economic prosperity and of socio-political growth. In fifth-century Greece, the golden age of the Athenian economy and of Periclean democracy paralleled the development of sophistic thought, of rhetoric, and of empirical sciences; in seventeenth-century England, maritime expansion and economic growth together with the strengthening of a constitutional monarchy stimulated the birth of modern science and of utilitarianism; after the Second World War, the United States witnessed economic growth and increased international power, coupled with an expansion in its materialistic cultural hegemony. This is a very simplistic scheme, but it allows us to entertain the notion that periods of economic progress are accompanied by innovation in the cultural and moral spheres. Likewise, situations of economic and political decline can be matched with the tendency to entertain idealistic and other-worldly views of the same social reality. The collapse of the Athenian empire coincided with the rise of Platonic philosophy; the Jewish diaspora after the destruction of Jerusalem allowed for the Mosaic law to become the cornerstone of Judaism; the political crises of nineteenth-century France were coupled with Durkheimian social realism. This view of the sociology of knowledge is, admittedly, a crude one – it does not do justice to an approach which is, in reality much more sophisticated than I have made it appear. However, it serves our purpose by isolating one direction of the causal flow: from material conditions to cultural forms.

The history of ideas offers an alternative approach which emphasizes the independence of cognitive structures and systems of thought, and their influence on both material conditions and on subsequent theoretical developments. From this angle, one can appreciate the progressive emphasis on individualism which runs from sophistic philosophy to Hellenistic philosophy and early Christianity, to seventeenth-century English Puritanism, and to twentieth-century American social thought. Parallel and opposite to such a current of individualism is the collectivism of Platonic philosophy, of post-exile Judaism, of medieval scholasticism, and of Durkheimian sociological thought. When considered from the perspective of the history of ideas, these streams of thought can be analyzed independently of the material and social conditions which in part determined them; moreover, they can be considered as facilitating or hindering one or another form of economic or political development. Again, one cannot emphasize an exclusively deterministic view at the expense of an idealistic view of reality, or vice versa. A more plausible approach, instead, is one that will account for both directions of the causal flow – from experience to thought and from thought to experience.

In my analysis of the anomie literature I have tried to combine the materialistic and the idealistic sides, looking simultaneously at the socio-historical conditions which informed specific discussions of anomie and at the internal logic of various ideas on anomie. In practice, as the reader will detect, the history of ideas approach dominates the sociology of knowledge approach. The history of ideas approach is inevitably espoused because it provides coherence to a study which spans some twenty-five centuries, but it also reflects my methodological preference for an approach in which ideal interests have a status independent of their socio-cultural determinants. Also, since raising a social scientist's self-awareness is a main purpose of this work, it follows that looking at the past to understand the present means comparing ideas across time, rather than emphasizing the socio-cultural constraints of the literature analyzed in each epoch.

The general remarks and distinctions I outline extend well beyond the narrow investigation of the history of anomie; nonetheless, they are essential in putting such history in a proper perspective. The concept of anomie is a central one in social thought because it looks at the relation between the individual and society. In discussing anomie, one offers an assessment of the historical conditions of the individual–society relationship, while entertaining, implicitly or explicitly, a view of the desirable, ideal condition. Should social norms dictate individual behavior and goals of action, or should individuals formulate their own aims? Can we only choose between total conformism and utter anarchy and chaos or can we envision alternative forms of social life which escape both extremes? How much social change is desirable and when does rapid change become a source of maladjustment in the individual? These are some of the issues which discussions about anomie have raised since classical times.

To most social scientists, these questions might appear foreign to their activities – more like philosophical dilemmas than issues of sociological research, but such is not the case. Sometimes, because of the excessive concern with the tree in front of us we lose perspective of the forest as a whole. The social scientist who studies the anomic effects of geographical relocation on elderly people might find the discussions of Greek philosophers about social conventions and natural principles to be utterly unrelated to the research at hand, but the superficial differences hide shared similarities. The broader question that both Greek philosophers and modern social scientists ask is, in the end, a common one. They study social reality to assess its shortcomings and to propose ways to overcome them. They ask: What is wrong with our society? What should we do about it? The two questions are not independent of each other. Our idea of the good society influences our perception of social problems just as our historical experiences forge our image of the ideal society. At the empirical, observational level, our instruments for studying social phenomena are, to be sure, much more sophisticated than the ones of the ancient Greeks; we know much more about social reality and its complexity. At the evaluative, normative level, however, we are in as much disarray as the philosophers of fifth-century Greece. At the empirical level, we have discarded Aristotelian physics and Ptolemaic cosmology, but at the normative level we cannot disregard the ethical theories of Greek philosophers. Natural sciences can, perhaps, live without a theory of what "ought to be," but human sciences cannot. A general theory of human nature always underlies our research of historically situated phenomena. Plainly, no matter how much factual knowledge we gain about social reality, it will not, *per se*, tell us explicitly what ought to be done and why. In fact it is often our idea of what ought to be done, our normative belief, that determines what we want to know about social phenomena. It is the normative, moral dimension of anomie which makes its historical investigation a worthwhile project.

Faced with rapid social change and fast-fading traditional values, societies at large and their members feel that anomie is here, and that the old reliable laws are gone. By and large, there has been unanimity on such evidence since Euripides' times; however, it has been far from evident whether rapid social change is desirable or undesirable, whether anomie is a pathological or a normal phenomenon in modern societies, whether we should applaud growing individualism and the anomic life or try to bring back the good old-fashioned ways.

These issues are the constant in the history of anomie, and they were discussed in ancient Greece just as they are discussed today. The usefulness of this study, then, is not that it will offer the final answer which twenty-five centuries of discussions have not been able to provide. Instead, it will be useful in generating an awareness of where we stand in relation to the past, and in relation to ourselves.

This monograph is divided into five parts which cover, chronologically, five distinct treatments of anomie in Western thought. The first chapter presents the ancient Greek literature on *anomia*: it describes how the concept was first coined and used, and how it took on new meanings when it was discussed with increasing frequency in fifth-century Greece. There, *anomia* was related to the issues and debates on nature and culture, on justice and the laws. In this chapter I will focus specifically on the opposition between sophistic thought and the theories of Socrates and Plato, and on their respective notions of *anomia*, pointing out some similarities with the modern anomie debates.

The second chapter deals with the concept of *anomia* in Biblical literature. Starting with the Greek translation of the Old Testament around the third century BC, I describe the range of meanings *anomia* and its grammatical variations had in the Scriptures, and in the exegetic commentaries of the Jewish scholar, Philo of Alexandria. I then focus on the eschatological, apocalyptic literature of late Judaism, where the concept of *anomia* had clear prominence. I compare the Jewish apocalyptic literature and the discussions of *anomia* in the New Testament, showing elements of continuity and of change as they are found in the writings of Matthew, Paul, and John. I conclude this chapter by comparing Biblical and sociological anomie.

A study of the literature on *anomy* in sixteenth- and seventeenth-century England constitutes the material of the third chapter. After its temporary abandonment during the Middle Ages, the concept re-entered Western culture with the stimulus of Renaissance classical scholarship and with the renewed interest in Greek Biblical texts brought about by the Reformation. In seventeenth-century England *anomy* (or *anomie*) was discussed in the context of religious disputes among Anglicans, Puritans, and Roman Catholics, or Rhemists as they were called. The concept was not entirely confined to religious quarrels; the discussion of *anomy* was relevant to the issues of freedom and necessity, natural law, and rational morality.

Chapter 4 describes the entry of the anomie concept into sociological discourse, pointing out some inaccuracies which have persisted for a long time in the history of sociology. Here I show that a different notion of anomie was formulated before Durkheim himself adopted the concept in his sociological writings. I present Jean Marie Guyau's claim that anomie is a positive feature of modern morality, and show the historical usefulness of his concept, comparing and contrasting it to Durkheim's.

Chapter 5 provides a description of the main themes which have emerged in the contemporary literature on anomie: Merton's theory of anomie, Srole's anomia scale, opposing evaluations of Durkheim's theory of anomie, and recent theories and findings in anomie research. In the contemporary literature I identify a substantial shift away from the Durkheimian tradition, toward an instrumental use of the concept; in this regard, I try to uncover the significance of such a departure at the cognitive and ethical levels, bridging the gap between explicit theories of an anomie of means, and implicit assumptions about an anomie of ends.

In the conclusion, I address some of the broad issues emerging from this study: the variability of discussions about anomie in Western culture, the definition of distinct ethical systems underlying the anomie literature, and the characterization of contemporary anomie research and its normative assumptions. Besides specifying historical trends, I outline a scheme of interaction between cognitive and ethical dimensions in anomie literature. I also propose a reappraisal of contemporary anomie research, where the lack of a unified paradigm on anomie should not be perceived as a stumbling block, but as a positive feature of the contemporary literature.

The requirement of value-freedom in social science research has often been interpreted in a negative way, as simply entailing the withholding of value-judgments. I believe that such an interpretation of value-freedom is a shortsighted one; it does not recognize that the withholding of value-judgments points to a clear value position – value-relativism. The study of the anomie literature illustrates the connection between value-freedom and value-relativism on the one hand, and between value-commitment and value-absolutism on the other. Besides providing the reader with a wealth of information about discussions of anomie in Western culture, I hope that this study will also help modern social scientists to become aware of the moral implications of their scientific stance.

Notes

1 The anomie literature only began to flourish in the late 1940s and early 1950s in the United States, but discussions of anomie are found as early as the seventh century BC.

2 See, for instance, George Simpson, *Emile Durkheim on the Division of Labor in Society* (New York: Macmillan, 1933), ix; Talcott Parsons, *The Structure of Social Action* (1937; reprinted New York: Free Press, 1968), 334; Sebastian de Grazia, *The Political Community* (Chicago: University of Chicago Press, 1948), xii, 195; Robert K. Merton, *Social Theory and Social Structure* (revised edn New York: Free Press, 1957), 135n, 161; Robert M. MacIver, *The Ramparts We Guard* (New York: Macmillan, 1950), 77, 139; Robert K. Merton, "Anomie, anomia, and social interaction," in *Anomie and Deviant Behavior*, ed. Marshall B. Clinard (New York: Free Press, 1964), 214, 226.

3 See, for example, Emile Durkheim, *Suicide*, trans. John A. Spaulding and George Simpson (New York: Free Press, 1951), 254–8; de Grazia, *Political Community*, 71; Merton, *Social Theory and Social Structure*, 135; Leo Srole, "Social Integration and Certain Corollaries," *American Sociological Review* 21 (December 1956):711.

4 Anomie comes from the Greek noun, *anomia*; *anomia* itself was derived from the Greek adjective, *anomos* (*a*, without and *nomos*, law). Cf. Chapter 1 below.

5 Cf. Merton, "Anomie, anomia," 225–6.

6 A distinction between transcendental and immanentistic views of morality is found in Alfred Fouillée, *Critique des systèmes de morale contemporaine* (1883; reprinted, Paris: Felix Alcan, 1912), 389–408; see also, more recently, John Horton, "The Dehumanization of Anomie and Alienation," *British Journal of Sociology* 15 (December 1964):288–92.

7 Karl Jasper writes: "This axis of history is to be found in the period around 500 B.C., in the spiritual process that occurred between 800 and 200 B.C." *The Origin and Goal of History*, trans. Michael Bullock (New Haven: Yale University Press, 1953), 1. For a recent discussion of the axial period themes, see "Wisdom, Revelation, and Doubt: Perspectives on the First Millennium B.C.," ed. Benjamin I. Schwartz, *Daedalus* 104 (Spring 1975).

CHAPTER 1

Anomia and Social Theory in Ancient Greece

From browsing through Alvin Gouldner's *Enter Plato*, one might hastily conclude that social theory proper did not exist before Plato. Gouldner argues in his monograph that "Plato is the first great social theorist in the Western tradition, and so much of what comes later derives directly or indirectly from him."[1] While one would acknowledge Plato as a towering figure in Western thought, it would be misleading to identify him or Socrates as the first social theorists in Western culture. Anyone with a basic knowledge of ancient philosophy knows of the pre-Socratics, but not many are aware of the crucial role of these thinkers in opening to theoretical discussion many key issues in Western social theory. To be sure, Gouldner does mention the pre-Socratics in his work, but as it is often the case, their ideas are only presented as a backdrop against which Plato's theories remain altogether unchallenged.

The philosophical literature of ancient Greece testifies to the existence, before Platonism, of lively social thought and of articulated discussions about *anomia*. At the center of such intellectual activity were, in the fifth century BC, the so-called sophists. In their writings we find topics which are still debated and discussed today. Of the sophists, G. B. Kerferd writes that "They taught and discussed grammar, linguistic theory, moral and political doctrines, doctrines about the gods and the nature and origin of man, literary analysis and criticism, mathematics, and at least in some cases the elements of physical theory about the universe."[2] The sophists also discussed *anomia*.

At first glance, the writings about *anomia* seem to be hopelessly scattered throughout the Greek literature; however, if we recover the literary and social context surrounding them, these writings document an ancient society in transition, and the moral crisis prompted by economic and political changes. The fifth-century Greek debates about *anomia* not only reflect the breakdown of traditional norms of behavior, but they testify to the attempt of tragedians, historians, and philosophers to find an answer to the social problems of their own time in a systematic fashion. There we find the founding ideas of Western human sciences.[3]

Recovering the Greek literature on *anomia* is relevant to modern sociologists because it offers a comparative perspective in which contemporary discussions of anomie can be revisited. It is not my claim that what happened in Greece in the fifth century BC is an instance of Vico's *corsi e ricorsi* if compared with the discussions of anomie in modern sociology; I am not arguing for a perennial idea of anomie hovering through the centuries in Western civilization. Rather, it is my claim that a study of *anomia* in the literature of ancient Greece allows us to place the present sociological debates into a historical perspective.

My argument will develop in four steps. First, I will describe the earliest instances about *anomia* that are found in Greek literature, and highlight the different meanings they convey. Second, I will discuss the perception of fifth-century historians and tragedians concerning the social conditions of their own times, and sketch the economic, political, and social themes of the period. Third, I will present the theoretical discussions prompted by the moral and political crisis: the sophistic debates about nature and convention (*physis* and *nomos*), and the Socratic dialogues on law and justice (*nomos* and *dikē*). Fourth, I will compare the Greek theories about society, morality, and human nature with the contemporary sociological theories, highlighting similarities and differences in relation to the concept of *anomia*.

Fifth-century Greek debates and modern sociological quarrels about anomie share common features, of which one is most striking. The Greek literature on *anomia* witnessed two opposing perspectives: the transcendental perspective of Platonic social thought, which considered *anomia* as the essence of evil and the root cause of social disorder, and the immanentistic perspective of sophistic thought which regarded *anomia* as the contextual problem of a changing society, a problem to be addressed in a pragmatic fashion. The transcendental side criticized the cultural values of Athenian democracy because they allowed anarchic freedom and the breakdown of social norms; the immanentistic side celebrated Athenian democracy and focused, at all times, on the immediate consequences of social control and of *anomia* on individual freedom and conduct.[4]

Modern social theory, and its treatment of anomie, has developed a similar dualism. Reviewers of the literature have often pointed out the opposition between Durkheim's notion of anomie and that of mainstream American sociology, as first and most eloquently developed by Robert Merton.[5] Durkheim's perspective recognized social order as the ultimate and only moral goal of individuals and collectivities; anomie was accordingly recognized as "the contradiction of all morality."[6] For Merton and most American sociologists, the referent value is not the ideal social order, but what John Horton calls "the success and self-interest ethic of the American middle classes."[7] Anomie is only a problem insofar as it disrupts the regulated competition of individuals.

The parallelism between ancient Greek and modern social theories of anomie is clearly a limited one; the characterization of two separate, antithetic traditions in each period is more like an approximate typology than a faithful historical account. Yet it is, I hope, a useful guideline for a meaningful interpretation of the otherwise disorienting jungle of anomie literature.

Early Greek Thought and Anomia

Anomie is derived from the Greek noun *anomia*, which itself goes back to the adjective *anomos*, meaning "without law." But the etymology of the word would mislead us if we understood *nomos* in the narrow sense of written law. In his book, *Nomos and the Beginnings of the Athenian Democracy*, Martin Ostwald shows that it is not until the middle of the fifth century BC that the Greek *nomos* came to describe written laws or statutes.[8] Before this time, *nomos* had a broader meaning. As Ostwald argues,

> *Nomos* is a norm both in a descriptive and in a prescriptive sense, and although the origin of this norm may on various occasions be attributed to the gods, to a lawgiver, or to an enactment by a society as a whole, the crucial point is that, regardless of origin, it is recognized and acknowledged as the valid norm within a given milieu.[9]

Anomia, similar to *nomos*, carries a broader meaning than pure lawlessness; it describes the "asocial behaviour of an individual who defies law-and-order and who acts in contravention of any or all of the canons regarded as valid and binding by the society in which he lives."[10] As defined by Ostwald, *anomia* refers exclusively to a quality of the individual, not to a condition of the social group.[11] This was the case in earlier Greek literature, where only the adjective *anomos* is documented. The earlier adjectival form, indeed, was predicated on individual behavior; but with the appearance of the noun *anomia*, first documented in Herodotus' *Histories*, its meaning broadened to describe the normlessness of a social group.

Before turning to the evidence, it is appropriate to describe briefly the historical location of the *anomia* literature. Only one instance of the word is documented before the fifth century BC; the adjective *anomos* appears in Hesiod's *Theogonia*, written around 700 BC. All the remaining evidence belongs to the fifth century – more specifically, to the period after the Athenian constitutional reform of 462–461 BC. It is at this time that we find *anomia*, first sporadically in the writings of Aeschylus, Sophocles, and Herodotus, then with increasing frequency in Euripides, the sophists – outstanding among them is the Anonymus Iamblichi – and the Socratic dialogues.[12]

Given its concentration in a short time-span, to distinguish between an earlier and a later literature on *anomia* is a difficult task. On the one hand, with such a distinction, writers as far apart as Hesiod and Aeschylus belong together in the earlier tradition; on the other hand, writers like Sophocles and Euripides, who lived only twenty years apart, would belong to quite different traditions. Such a distinction is, however, a standard one.[13] The political and social events of early-fifth-century Greece were so far reaching that they became a turning point in Greek culture. Only in this perspective, moreover, can we understand the process that brought *anomia* to the mouths and pens of so many orators and writers in fifth-century Greece, especially in Athens. Alternatively, the distinction drawn between an earlier and a later literature on *anomia* does not preclude the permanence, in later periods, of themes developed in the earlier *anomia* literature. The evidence shows that, together with the changing focus of *anomia*, there was a continuation of the earlier tradition.

The characteristic feature of the earlier *anomia* is its exclusive use as an adjective.[14] In this form there are at least three distinguishable meanings of *anomos*. In some instances, *anomos* described the lack of human qualities in an individual, which would prompt terrible, violent, outrageous, and monstrous deeds. In other instances it referred to the disregard of religious norms or divine orders which would cause godless, impious, and unholy acts. And third, anomic behavior was one that expressed defiance of unwritten rules of justice or traditional social customs and norms of proper behavior. Each of these three connotations referred, implicitly or explicitly, to deflections from a specific standard of behavior – whether it be the conduct proper to human nature, the action in compliance with divine orders, or the behavior in agreement with socially enacted rules.

INHUMANNESS

Instances of *anomos* as describing inhuman behavior are first found in Hesiod. In the *Theogonia*, he describes Typhaon, the monster that is half-human and half-snake, as "terrible, overbearing and normless [*anomon*]."[15] A similar description of the Centaurs is found in Sophocles' *Trachiniae*, where "that monstrous host of double form" is characterized as "violent, lawless [*anomon*], and of surpassing might."[16] In both cases, the unruly character of the monsters is associated with violence (*bia*) and the riotousness arising from the pride of strength (*hybris*).[17] This association of violence and unruly conduct attributed to mythical figures was carried forward in the rhetorical literature of later times. For instance, Gorgias, in his *Defence of Helen*, recounts that Helen "was carried off with force, suffering violence lawlessly [*anomos*] and being injured unjustly."[18] Isocrates, in his *Encomium on Helen*, praises Theseus for having subdued the Minotaur of Crete, the monster half-man and half-bull, and so freed the city "from an obligation so lawless [*anomou*], so terrible and so ineluctable."[19] The orator Lysias, in his speech against Symonides, describes the defendant as having been subjected to a "lawless [*anomos*] and violent outrage."[20] Closely resembling the above instances and adding a twist of psychological theory, Plato, in the *Republic*, notes how in every human being we find "an unruly [*anomon*], terrible and fierce kind of desires."[21]

From these examples it can be argued that *anomia* was at first associated with excessive violence, pride and ruthlessness, and that these qualities were considered to be at odds with human conduct proper. Appropriately, then, the anomic condition was first postulated on non-human or semi-human creatures like the mythical monsters.

IMPIETY

Anomic is also the godless, impious, and unholy conduct of individuals; the behavior that, implicitly or explicitly, is at odds with the rules or will of the gods. In Sophocles' *Oedipus Colonus*, Oedipus comes out of the sacred grove where he was hiding, and addresses the elders of Colonus: "Regard me not, I entreat you, as a lawless [*anomon*] person."[22] This statement, Ostwald writes, "is best interpreted as a request not to infer from his having trespassed on sacred ground ... that he is a person who habitually defies norms of behaviour, especially in religious matters."[23] In *Andromache*, Euripides describes the murder plotted by Hermione against Andromache and her son, as a "godless, lawless [*anomos*] and wretched killing."[24] The godlessness of anomic acts is similarly reiterated in later literature with rhetorical and oratorical emphasis. Gorgias, in his *Palamedes*, exhorts the jury not to condemn the accused, as they would otherwise be responsible for a "terrible, godless, unjust, and lawless [*anomon*] action."[25] The orator Antiphon, then, argues that the value placed upon our lives by the gods is such that "whosoever slays his fellow unlawfully [*anomos*], both sins against the gods and confounds the ordinances of man."[26] Xenophon, in his *Constitution of the Lacedaemonians*, recounts how Lycurgus was able to command respect for his legislation by showing that to refuse obedience to the laws given by the Pythian god was not only unlawful (*anomon*) but also impious (*anosion*).[27] In these passages, the anomic behavior implies not only conduct unfit for humans, but also conduct that disregards standards and norms sanctioned by divine powers.

INJUSTICE

A third meaning of *anomos* characterized the behavior that defied the way "things should be," a behavior that disregarded the sense of justice and proportion, the *dikē*.[28] Greek writers, in their effort to chastise unruly conduct, used the notion of unjust (*adikos*) in their string of adjectives; in some of the literature, the parallel between unjust and normless behavior was more direct and emphatic. In Euripides' *Iphigenia in Aulis*, Agamemnon refuses to act against his own children, "doing to my offspring what is both unlawful [*anoma*] and unjust."[29] Also in Euripides' *Bacchae*, we find the coupling of *anomos* and *adikos*, when the Chorus proclaims: "Let justice visible walk, let justice sworded walk, stabbing home to the throat of the godless, the lawless [*anomon*], the unjust."[30] The rhetorical literature also capitalized on this third connotation of *anomos*, as earlier quotations have shown. The Anonymus Iamblichi, a fifth-century author, writes: "If one uses the present good for unjust purposes, and lawless [*anoma*] ones, such conduct is the worst of all."[31] By this time, however, the parallelism between injustice and *anomia* was becoming a central topic of discussion, with important theoretical and moral implications.[32]

Anomos was alternatively used to convey the notion of inhuman, godless and unjust conduct; such usage was documented not only in the earlier literature, but also in the writings of later orators, tragedians and philosophers.[33] The three meanings of *anomos*, however, were not equally important in the later writings. With time, the first two usages of *anomos* to describe inhuman and godless behavior receded in importance; the parallelism between *anomia* and injustice, on the contrary, became the main source of debate. Furthermore, the idea that anomic behavior was monstrous and impious was used, by orators and rhetoricians, more as an emphatic device to win the audience to their view, than to express their actual moral beliefs.[34]

In the earlier literature on *anomia*, however, regardless of which of the three meanings is stressed, there is a common pattern. The evaluation of individual behavior is relatively unproblematic. The evaluation of conduct does not imply a discussion of moral standards. Rather, such standards are openly accepted and taken at their face value. Whether normlessness is equated with violent conduct, or godlessness, or injustice, it is obvious that the source of *nomos*, of the condition of law-and-order, is to be found not in individuals, but in the external powers of the gods or in the customs of the community. In the last instance, the gods rewarded the just and pious, and punished the violent and godless; alternatively, the social group sanctioned all deflections from customary standards.

By the fifth century, however, the situation was rapidly changing at the economic, political, and social levels. At the economic level, following the defeat of the Persians, the Greek cities were experiencing an unparalleled prosperity. The large increase in the role of trade and commerce allowed Pericles to boast that "All the good things from all over the world flow in to us, so that to us it seems just as natural to enjoy foreign goods as our own local products."[35] Indeed, "Greece as a whole in the fifth century B.C. would appear to have surpassed all previous periods in the products of agriculture, industry and trade."[36]

At the political level, following Cleisthenes' first reforms in 508 BC, Athens perfected its democratic institutions, reaching the apex with Ephialtes' "unmixed democracy" in 462 BC.[37] In his famous funeral oration, reported by Thucydides, Pericles made an apology for the Athenian system:

> It is true that our government is called a democracy, because it is administered in the interest not of the few, but of the many; yet while as regards the law all men are on an equality for the settlement of their private disputes, as regards the values set on them it is as each man is in any way distinguished that he is

preferred to public honours, not because he belongs to a particular class, but because of personal merits.[38]

The notion of equality before the law, together with a meritocratic system of leadership selection, aimed at integrating the egalitarian and the competitive strands within the democratic political system.

At the social level, the democratic experience of Athens enhanced the free and open discussion of politics, while Athenian imperialism brought its citizens in touch with different cultures. Both factors prompted the scrutiny of cultural values which had been held, until then, to be fixed and unchanging. The rationalistic investigation of natural phenomena had already furnished a materialistic view with the physiocratic philosophy of the late sixth century. During the fifth century, the social world underwent a similar rationalistic critique at the hands of the sophists.[39] The new intellectual outlook had made one point clear: no invisible hand held societies together; the conscious effort of individuals did. At both the physical and the social levels, Protagoras' motto, "Man is the measure of all things," held true. A new view of the world was replacing Hesiod's *Theogonia*, and the effect of such a change was to be reflected in, as well as conveyed by, a shift in the meaning of *anomia*.

The Fifth-Century Crisis

The social and cultural change of fifth-century Greece is mirrored in the work of the great tragedians. If Aeschylus showed to his audience the certainty of divine justice and Sophocles described great characters who forge their own destiny, Euripides best portrayed the break from tradition by focusing on the moral problems of the new epoch.[40] The reliable hierarchy of values was coming under attack as the external standards of morality were giving way to a growing individualism.[41] For Euripides, the social position of an individual was no longer a guarantee of moral status, "For many noble-born are base in soul."[42] He questioned the prejudices of his own times; for him, slaves and aristocrats, men and women, all had equal moral worth.

In Euripides' writings *anomia* plays a larger role than it had ever before in Greek literature, and it reflects the change from a theocentric, to an anthropocentric view of the world.[43] Earlier writers, by and large, upheld the divine origins of laws and norms; Euripides departed drastically from such a traditional view. In

19

Euripides' tragedies the conduct of the gods is criticized, when Ion complains of them: "How were it just that you should enact for men laws, and yourselves be found guilty of *anomia*?"[44] The gods have become unreliable in their upholding of justice and *nomos*, and such unreliability on their part prompts humans to disregard the traditional norms. In the *Hercules Furens*, Lycus is described as one who "outpaces the law, indulging his anomic disposition."[45] It is Lycus who "violating the majesty of heavens with his *anomia*," dared to challenge the gods' might.[46] It is a boldness regarded in previous times as *hybris*, but no longer limited to the few, as it extended rapidly to the larger society: "Now rivers flow upstream and the established course of justice is reversed."[47] The chorus of *Iphigenia in Aulis* laments this state of things emphatically: "What is now the power of Modesty or Virtue? Godlessness is on the rise, mortals push Virtue aside, *Anomia* governs the Law, and no one is afraid any longer of the divine retribution."[48]

Together with Euripides' description of the "anomic tide" at the individual level there developed, in fifth-century Greece, a notion of socio-political *anomia*. Herodotus seems to have been the first author to employ the noun, and such use testifies to a broadening of the meaning of the term. In Herodotus *anomia* does not refer to the conduct of single individuals, but to the behavior of the social group.[49] He writes that "there was much *anomia* in the land of Media";[50] the autonomy that the Medes had gained in freeing themselves from the Assyrians was degenerating into social chaos, and a remedy was sought by establishing a monarchic regime. This was the Medes' rationale: "Thus will the country be well governed, and we ourselves shall turn to our business, and cease to be disrupted by *anomia*."[51] Herodotus' *anomia* describes a situation in which although laws and customs existed, their enforcement was lacking, and laws were therefore disregarded by society at large. This created *anomia* or lawlessness. The ultimate concern which prompted the Medes to be ruled by a king was not, however, a moral one; rather, it was a pragmatic and political move prompted by the need of orderly social interaction, so that individuals could pursue their own business peacefully.

Thucydides, in his description of the great plague of 430 BC in Athens, claims that "it introduced in the city a greater *anomia*,"[52] as the catastrophe undermined all reasonable norms of behavior:

> No fear of gods or law of men restrained; for, on the one hand, seeing that all men were perishing alike, they judged that piety and impiety came to the same thing, and, on the other, no one

expected that he would live to be called to account and pay the penalty of his misdeeds.[53]

Although it referred to a specific historical event, Thucydides' rationale for the Athenian *anomia* aptly identified its sources as (1) the decline of religious beliefs and (2) the lack of an adequate enforcement of norms. The plague, Thucydides points out, *worsened* the state of *anomia* which was already a generalized phenomenon in Athens at that time. The reason for the social chaos was only partially attributed to the plague; the problem was rooted, at a deeper level, in the socio-cultural changes of fifth-century Greece. Karl Popper argues that Thucydides, a conservative aristocrat, regarded the democratic experience of Athens as the root cause of all social anarchy.[54]

At the political level, the disregard for laws and agreements between the Greek cities had become a widespread phenomenon; *anomia* was not limited to Athens. Isocrates points out how, in their tyrannical rule over Athens, the Spartans "regarded the most lawless [*anomōtatous*] men as the most loyal,"[55] and Athenian citizens were "lawlessly [*anomōs*] being put to death;"[56] and overall, "they [the Spartans] so far outdid all those who lived before their time in lawlessness [*anomia*] and greed [*pleonexia*] that they ... ruined themselves and their friends and their own country."[57]

The anomic political condition was not, as Isocrates makes us believe, a prerogative of Sparta alone – even if it surpassed every other Greek city in disregarding all kinds of traditionally accepted political behavior. There was more to it than the Spartan *anomia*, as "every form of depravity showed itself in Hellas in consequence of its revolutions."[58] As Thucydides saw it, for the Greek cities "there was no assurance binding enough, no oath terrible enough, to reconcile men; but always, if they were stronger, since they accounted all security hopeless, they were rather disposed to take precautions against being wronged than able to trust others."[59] In the international arena, the philosophy of the Greek cities was becoming a stern "might is right."[60]

The breakdown of traditional morality at the individual level (which Euripides described in his tragedies) was paralleled by a similar crisis at the political level; the two went hand in hand. Inevitably the theoretical debates of the times included both aspects and often treated them simultaneously. The key speakers and writers on such theoretical debates were the so-called "sophists."

The Moral and Political Debates

It is difficult to assess the historical importance of the sophistic movement in fifth-century Greece. Our knowledge of the sophists is based on a few scattered fragments of their original writings, or on second-hand reporting of later philosophers who were hostile to the sophists' teachings – Plato and Aristotle most of all. Still, the importance of sophistic thought can no longer be denied or lightly dismissed.[61] As G. B. Kerferd writes, "The modernity of the range of problems formulated and discussed by the sophists in their teaching is indeed startling."[62] Despite the paucity of sources and the lack of a unified doctrine on their part, the sophists raised questions which still today are very much at the center of debates by moral philosophers and social scientists.[63] Throughout the numerous topics touched on by the sophists, Kerferd identifies "two dominant themes – the need to accept relativism in values and elsewhere without reducing all to subjectivism, and the belief that there is no area of human life or of the world as a whole which should be immune from understanding achieved throughout reasoned argument."[64] The sophists, in short, put the human condition squarely at the center of their philosophical investigation; they first provided a rational discussion of human nature, morality, and social life.

Fifth-century discussions of *anomia* tackled, from the outset, problems that were both moral and political. At the moral level, Euripides had questioned the nature of laws and norms of behavior, their divine origin, and the extent to which they should compel the conduct of individuals. At the political level, Greek historians and orators had pointed out the anomic effects of political autonomy of Greek cities.[65] They also criticized the unrestrained use of force as a means of achieving political power at the expense of mutual trust and cooperation.

The moral and political issues were intertwined as they became a central concern of fifth-century thought with the controversy on *nomos* (law or custom) and *physis* (nature or reality).[66] Guthrie reports:

> The *nomos–physis* antithesis ... will be found to enter most of the questions of the day. Discussion of religion turned on whether gods existed by *physis* – in reality – or only by *nomos*; of political organization, on whether states arose by divine ordinance, by natural necessity or by *nomos*; of cosmopolitanism, on whether divisions within the human race are natural or only a matter of

nomos; of equality, on whether the rule of one man over another (slavery) or one nation over another (empire) is natural and inevitable, or only by *nomos*; and so on.[67]

The sophistic philosophers were at the center of the *nomos–physis* debate. On the one side, they proclaimed the superiority of the unchanging dictates of human nature, or *physis*, and showed the conventionality and variation of social norms. On the other, they argued that the conventionality of social norms did not diminish, in any way, their role in allowing an orderly social life. The opposing arguments of *nomos* and *physis* were often used as rhetorical devices when arguing legal cases, so that the orators would play on one of the two themes depending on the results they were seeking. Callicles, a sophist, reproached Socrates himself for making use of such a device in his dialogues.[68] Aristotle acknowledged the role of the *nomos–physis* dichotomy in argumentative legal discourse,[69] or as "a means of trapping an opponent into paradox."[70]

Apart from the contingency of defensive arguments, the sophists expressed strong views on the side of *nomos* or *physis*. An extreme defender of *physis* against *nomos* was Callicles, who argued that "nature herself makes it plain that it is right for the better to have the advantage over the worse, the more able over the less."[71] Such an argument endorsed, at the practical level, the imperialistic scheme of Athenian democracy, as well as the meritocratic qualities of its political system. Defending the other side, Protagoras claimed the superiority of *nomos*, asserting that:

> He who appears to you to be the most unjust of those who have been brought up in laws and society would appear to be a just man and a master of justice if he were to be compared with men who had no education, or courts of justice, or laws, or any restraint upon them which compelled them to practice virtue.[72]

The controversy revolved on whether laws and social norms improved the inborn faculties of the human nature, or whether they created obstacles to the individual's potential; in the latter case, the laws had to be accepted reluctantly as inevitable devices for peaceful social interaction. The sophist Antiphon expressed just such a view in asserting that "the most profitable means of utilizing justice is to respect the laws when witnesses are present but otherwise to follow the precepts of nature. Laws are artificial compacts, they lack the inevitability of natural growth."[73]

The Anonymus Iamblichi,[74] a late-fifth-century sophist, on the contrary, extolled the advantages of "law-and-order" (*eunomia*)

23

against the deleterious effect of a general disregard for the laws (*anomia*), arguing:

> For if men are so constituted by nature that they are not able to live alone but associate with each other, yielding to necessity, and for the sake and in reference to this association all life is regulated, and all arts were invented by them, neither can society exist without the government of law, for the disregard of law [*anomia*] would bring a greater disadvantage and penalty to them than a solitary life – wherefore, by reason of these necessary causes, law and justice rule among men, and these are in nowise changed or become extinct, for these are permanent by nature.[75]

For the Anonymus Iamblichi the innate qualities of the individual had to be perfected in the interest of law and justice, since only respect for the established laws could assure a peaceful coexistence in society. *Anomia*, the Anonymus reasoned, has many undesirable effects on the social life and on the members of the group: it causes distrust and asocial feelings in the individuals, so that people will only look after their private interests.[76] In a condition of *anomia*, furthermore, it is impossible to enjoy the gains of hard labor because we can never feel safe, because people plot at all times against each other's well-being.[77] Civil strife and war with neighboring people also arise from *anomia*;[78] and last, "tyranny, which is so great and such an evil, comes from no other source than *anomia*."[79] The Anonymus explains that it is wrong to think of tyranny as the product of the violence of an individual against the multitude; rather, "when law and justice have departed from the multitude, then the care and custody of these will pass into the hands of one."[80] It is the legal and moral vacuum created by the anomic behavior of the citizens, not the thirst for power of single individuals, that ultimately brings about a tyrannical regime. Given all these considerations, the Anonymus is able to conclude that, "If therefore *anomia* is the cause of such great evils, and law-and-order [*eunomia*] causes such great goods, it is not possible otherwise to acquire happiness unless one considers law as the guide of his whole life."[81]

The political consequences of *anomia* had already been pointed out by Herodotus when describing the autonomy of the Medes as having degenerated into social chaos. The Anonymus offers a theoretical argument in defense of law-and-order, and subsequent writers reiterated the point. Isocrates argued against the Peloponnesian democracies that "instead of securing autonomy they have been plunged into much and terrible *anomia*";[82] and in praise of Athens' rule over Greece, Isocrates remarks that "Finding the

Hellenes living anomically, and oppressed by tyrannies, and perishing through anarchy, she [Athens] delivered them from these evils."[83] Plutarch, in his *Moralia*, also associates autonomy and *anomia*: "Good heavens! What end will there be to the license that is subverting our town? Now already autonomy is on the way to *anomia*!"[84]

The political outlook of the *nomos–physis* debate was rather straightforward since it relied on the concrete, observable implications of *anomia* at the social and political levels. Understandably enough, no one could advocate a *bellum omnium contra omnes*, a war of all against all, in the face of its destruction of all forms of social life. Yet the broader problem to be addressed was, to what extent should the norms of an ordered social life be allowed to dictate rules of behavior to the individual? This amounted to introducing the moral considerations into the *nomos–physis* discussion, and at this point the issues were not as clear-cut.

The moral side of the debate evaded the straightforward alternative between a desirable social order and an undesirable social *anomia*; in fact, the political judgment itself had to be re-evaluated in the light of its moral consequences, showing how closely the political and moral elements were linked together. The *nomos–physis* issue can be seen, in part, as an attempt to strike a balance between the public and the private spheres, between the "natural freedom" of the individual and the "artificial restraint" imposed by the social group.[85] On the one hand, to the apoligists of *physis*, social norms amounted to a corruption of the superior morality of nature, as the sophist Hippias argued: "By nature like is akin to like, but convention, the tyrant of mankind, often compels us to do many things which are against nature."[86] On the other hand, to the defenders of *nomos*, human nature appeared to be corrupt and in need of improvement, as the Anonymus peri nomon[87] maintained: "Nature is disorderly and varies with the individual, whereas the laws are common, agreed, and the same for all. Nature may be corrupt, and often has base desires, and men with such a nature will be found doing wrong; but the laws aim at what is just, good and beneficial."[88]

It is evident, from the arguments on either side, that nature and convention, *physis* and *nomos*, were inversely related: upholding one meant downgrading the other; the values of individuality were pitted against the values of social life, the moral concerns against the political reality. The issue, then, was how much autonomy and freedom of action could be allowed in a given situation before the disadvantages at the social level outweighed the advantages to the individual. The sophists' defense of opposite views, however, was

25

grounded on the shared assumption that their arguments were instrumental to practical, contingent purposes. Whichever view they espoused, it was not the result of a metaphysical interpretation of the social world, but of immediate, action-oriented concerns in the areas of politics, rhetoric, military science, law, etc.[89]

Parallel the *nomos–physis* dichotomy was the one between *nomos* and *dikē* (law and justice). We saw earlier how anomic behavior was associated in the early literature with unjust conduct. The identity of the two was a shared notion which came under close scrutiny at the hands of the sophists. Once the conventionality and variability of laws and customs had been recognized, the relationship between the just and the lawful had become questionable. Laws and customs could now be identified as either just or unjust depending on the parameters applied. The relationship between positive law and morality had become problematic.[90]

Some sophists denied that the just was in any way identical with the legally sanctioned, as Hippias observed: "Laws, or their observance, can hardly be thought of much account, since the very men who passed them often reject and amend them."[91] The notion of justice, for Hippias, went beyond the legally enacted rules, as it appealed to a universal moral law. Positive law was only a temporary and contingent agreement which had no bearing on the ultimate notion of justice. A similar view was expressed by Antiphon, whose "own consistent standpoint is that a morality enforced by law and custom is contrary to nature, and nature's way is to be preferred."[92] The sophist Protagoras, on the other hand, advocated the identity of what is lawful with what is just. As Guthrie paraphrases it,

> [It] is Protagoras's conviction that *dikē* [justice] exists for the preservation of social order, and that therefore the maintenance of existing laws, even though they are not the best, is just and laudable because the alternatives of disobedience or subversion would destroy the "bond of friendship and union" on which our very life depends.[93]

The position of Protagoras is similar, in this context, to the Socratic equation of law and justice, and of *anomia* and unrighteousness. But whereas Protagoras justifies his position on sociohistorical grounds, Socrates claims that law and justice coincide by definition;[94] and conversely, *anomia* was one and the same with injustice.[95] Protagoras' argument was a practical one – injustice disrupted the social life. Socrates' reason for equating law and justice was that it was in the interest of the common good, for the prosperity of the social group: "Those cities whose citizens abide by [the laws] prove strongest and enjoy most happiness; but without agreement no city can be made a good city, no house can be made a prosperous house."[96] According to Socrates, however, by reason of membership in society, the individual owes obedience to the laws of the city, even when these laws go against one's own interest. "You must do whatever your city and your country command, or else persuade them in accordance with universal justice."[97] With Socrates, the laws were more than a convenient solution to contingent problems of social order; they best embodied the principles of justice. They were just by definition.[98] Xenophon, who had attributed to Socrates the equation of law and justice, reiterated the point in his description of Cyrus' training in justice: "Since what is in accordance with the laws is just and what disregards them [*anomon*] is violent, he bade the judge always render his verdict on the side of the law."[99]

In Plato's *Minos* the topic of law and justice is also treated, when Socrates tries to convince his companion that law and justice are the same: "The law abiding are just, and the lawless [*anomoi*] unjust";[100] still, his interlocutor, an unnamed sophist, is in doubt:

> In your present way of putting it, Socrates, the same things appear to be accepted as lawful both by us and by the rest of the world, always: but when I reflect that we are continually changing our laws in all sorts of ways, I cannot bring myself to assent.[101]

Socrates' attempt firmly to establish a definition of law and justice was functional to his ethical goals. He envisioned the possibility that careful reasoning would provide lasting definitions of law, justice, and other virtues.[102] The sophists started from a quite different premise, in that they advocated the conventionality of moral discourse and its variability across societies; accordingly, their aim was simply to solve contingent and practical problems, not to offer a "grand theory" of morality. Socrates' crucial aim was, by and large, to establish the autonomy of the individual as a moral subject; he did not uphold a passive conformity to social norms, but an enlightened, critical acceptance of them. In this regard, he was closer to the sophistic outlook than to that of his famous follower, Plato.

Socrates' view was perfected in Plato's writings as the latter anchored the moral reality to the ideal Good.[103] For Plato, the obedience and respect of the laws was not open to critical discussion; rather, it was a moral imperative in its own right. Accordingly, *anomia* is by Plato characterized as undesirable, not in relation to specific social consequences, but in its very essence.[104] In this regard, Gouldner remarks:

> If, in the Platonic view, there is the assumption that justice and conformity with law (*nomos*) have certain communalities, there is also the corresponding assumption that injustice is linked with the unlimited, unbounded, or lawless and that the unjust man is the *anomos* man and injustice is *anomia*. Plato uses *anomos* as a synonym for anarchy, or lawless and disorderly social organization.[105]

Plato indeed saw *anomia* as a threat to society; but his notion went beyond the equation of *anomia* with injustice, to characterize a wider range of conditions. In his writings, Plato identifies *anomia* with injustice;[106] but he also equates *anomia* with godlessness,[107] impiety and iniquity,[108] the less beneficial,[109] terrible and fierce desires,[110] cruelty,[111] anarchy,[112] and disorder.[113] The range of meanings points out that Plato identified *anomia* as a vice in general terms, the vice *par excellence*, a condition of "intemperance, a lack of emotional discipline,"[114] which is, in Plato's view, typical of human nature as such.[115]

Plato's position can be interpreted as an attempt to overcome the moral relativism of sophistic teachings with a new teleological view of the world; a view in which everything had a justification in terms of the ultimate end, the world of moral absolutes. In a way, the *Theogonia* of Hesiod had found a new synthesis in Plato's idealistic social theory. If Hesiod had grounded his view of order in the gods, Plato, in the *Laws*, anchored his notion of law-and-order in the ideal society, the perfect city–state. In both views, however, there was little room left for the individual: just as the *dikē* of the Hesiodean world was externally set by the gods, so the *dikē* of the Platonic world was set by the state.

Anomia, the disregard of written or unwritten laws, accordingly was chastised by Plato. Gouldner comments:

> Clearly, what Plato seeks is not so much liberty but the elimination of *anomia* and the establishment of social order and restraint, in political as well as in other matters. "Anarchy," he insists with the fervor of a Pythagorean, "must be extirpated from the entire life of all mankind and from all the breasts of men."[116]

The relativization of values upheld by the sophists had been defeated with Plato's "grand theory." It was not until the Hellenistic period that the individualistic and materialistic outlook of the sophists re-emerged – with the Epicurean and Stoic philosophies. *Anomia*, however, did not receive any attention at this later point;[117] only in our time has the interest in anomie matched and surpassed that of the fifth-century Greeks. For this reason, if for no other, the study of their discussions can help us make sense of our own "love affair" with anomie.

Anomie and Social Theory: Then and Now

In contempory social theory anomie has become a popular concept. Especially in American sociology, Robert Merton helped popularize the concept with his classical article, "Social Structure and Anomie,"[118] which has been described as "probably the most widely quoted paper in sociology."[119] Indeed, the literature on anomie, both theoretical and empirical, has been thriving since the early 1950s, and all signs indicate that such a trend will continue. One is bound to ask: why the love affair of modern sociology with anomie? How does the modern concept compare with the one of the classics? The historical case of ancient Greece is of great help in addressing both issues.

The first question was posed by Merton, as he felt compelled to ask: "Why the resonance [of anomie] in contemporary society?"[120] The answer is at once simple and complex. It is simple because, quite obviously, we are confronted in contemporary society with various phenomena which we deem appropriate to describe as resulting from anomie. The answer becomes complex, however, because it is within the historical boundaries of nineteenth- and twentieth-century social theory that we describe these phenomena as anomie. That is, we recast problems of social order, which by and large existed before the social sciences developed, in *a new perspective*. Such a perspective, I maintain, resembles in many ways the perspective of the Greek sophists and of Greek tragedians and historians.

In his book *The Liberal Temper in Greek Politics*, Eric A. Havelock speaks of the pre-Socratics in these terms:

> Reaching across those barriers in the mind artificially set up by the systems of Plato and Aristotle they seem to find intellectual company in unexpected quarters. These affinities are very diverse. Their vision of evolution conducted on a cosmic scale might have been approved by Darwin, Huxley and Spencer. But the conception proposed by Democritus of human government as a contract would have been understood best by the pre-feudal

societies of northern Europe. Antiphon's violent attack on the tyranny of custom law would have been appreciated by Bentham. The pragmatism and empiricism of Protagoras would have won sympathy from Hume, James and Dewey.[121]

It is especially in the sophists' approach that we find a clear anticipation of the attitude characterizing modern sociological work. Gouldner readily asserts: "[The sophists] are more commonly engaged in transmitting neutral technical skills than in clarifying and evaluating the ends to which these are to be applied."[122] And later on he argues:

> While the sophists often use sense data as the starting point and test of their reasoning, Plato distrusts the senses and the data they provide ... In this sense, the modern empirical study of men shows more continuity with the standpoint of the sophists than that of the Platonists.[123]

Gouldner's comment is on the mark, except that he sees both the sophists and modern sociologists as unduly ignoring the more important issue of ultimate values – the one Plato addressed. But this is only apparently so. The sophists were very much concerned with moral and political issues, as we have had the opportunity to see in their discussions of *anomia*. However, their view of morality is not of a realm which is altogether different from other realms of human life – for them, the world of values is not a separate one, but it is an integral part of the real world. As Havelock writes, paraphrasing the sophists' view, "morality, social and personal ... is a great human invention which, like agriculture or metallurgy, fills the concrete need of human beings and so yields them profit. That need is for group security and then for a civilized way of life."[124]

For better or worse, modern sociologists are the legitimate heirs of sophistic thought. Just as the sophists recast the problem of social order and questioned the advantages and disadvantages of social norms and individual aspirations, so do we continuously re-evaluate and weigh the pros and cons of changing social arrangements. Just as Euripides, a tragedian with a sophistic outlook, saw the inconsistencies of the old social order and exposed the anomic qualities of both gods and humans, so do we sense that anomie is all around us at the social (divine) and at the individual (human) level. Very much in the sophistic spirit, our starting point is the historically defined social reality and our own individual experience within it. We cannot shy away from such reality, nor can we try to overcome its limitations with a metaphysical wish. At the same time, our abandonment of transcendental explanations does not signify that we are any less committed to a search for truth. It rather signifies the commitment to a truth which is grounded in historical practice.

Gouldner wrote about the sophists what could easily be said of modern sociologists:

> The diversified customs and beliefs they encounter lead some sophists to conclude that when men disagree about institutions, laws, or customs, it does not necessarily follow that some of them must be right and others wrong; and that there is not necessarily any one unvarying standard of truth by which the validity of social beliefs can be judged. Institutions and laws, from this standpoint, have to be evaluated in terms of the differing conditions that prevail in different communities.[125]

My positive assessment of the anomie literature in the light of earlier historical evidence is not a claim, implicitly or explicitly, that all is well with sociology. Nor do I claim that our sophistic bent will solve the problems of contemporary society any better than religious beliefs solved the problems of earlier times. Rather, I claim that the modern discussions about anomie can be better understood in historical perspective, and that they can be applied, reflexively, to our own work on anomie.

Not only is anomie around us, it is also within us.[126] Plato explicitly chastised the sophists' use of knowledge: "Do you not remark how great is the evil that dialectic has introduced? Its practitioners are infected with *anomia*."[127] In more recent times, John Horton has made a similar point: "Paradoxically, from either a Marxian or a Durkheimian perspective, contemporary uses of the concepts of anomie and alienation would be examples of alienation and anomie."[128] We need to look no further than our own "sociological backyard" to know exactly what we mean by anomie *in sociology*.

It is apparent that the second question I raised, of how the modern concept of anomie compares with the one of ancient Greece, is closely related to the first question about the popularity of the concept of anomie. If our love affair with anomie expresses the anomic climate of modern sociology, it also expresses the underlying assumptions of such a climate. I have already sketched, in the introduction, a dichotomy that is apparent in both classical Greek social theory and in contemporary sociology: the transcendental view of social reality espoused by Plato and Durkheim on the one hand, and the immanentistic view espoused by the sophists and most American sociologists on the other.

The dominant feature of sophistic thought was its radical relativism in the realm of values. To a sophist it was almost self-evident that "If the same thing were to all men by nature fair and wise, there could be no disputes or quarrels among us. But as it is there is no consistency or impartiality where mortals are concerned."[129] If the Greek sophists claimed their own assumptions to be value-relative, many modern social scientists claim them to be value-free. The positions are, by and large, identical. Guthrie makes this very point:

> The positivist rejects the view that positive law must set out from the ideal of a natural, i.e. universally valid, standard of right: there is only a relative right or goodness, which is derived from the positive law prevailing at a particular time. The positivist knows that the search for goodness is a chimaera-hunt. ... He is in fact repeating the sophists' assertions in the controversy of the fifth and fourth centuries B.C. Value, for him as for Archelaus, exists by *nomos* only, not by *physis*.[130]

The claim to value-freedom is, at least in part, a claim to value-relativism. For the sophists, the link between teaching value-neutral techniques and upholding the relativism of ultimate values is shown in Protagoras' argument: "The fact is that good is a variable, complex and complicated ... A thing physically good for human beings externally can actually be very bad internally. That is why doctors always prohibit the sick to use olive oil when it is intended to be taken internally."[131] For Protagoras evaluative judgments are intertwined with technical judgments; his view of morality is instrumental and relative. Morality changes as conditions of existence and knowledge change.

The equation of value-freedom and value-relativism also applies to mainstream contemporary sociology. In his critique of a value-free sociology, Gouldner admits that "The value-free doctrine ... enhanced a freedom from moral compulsiveness ... The value-free principle strengthened Reason (or Ego) against the compulsive demands of a merely traditional morality."[132] Value-freedom, then, widens the moral possibilities. At the same time, the acceptance of the relativity of values amounts to their positive endorsement; that is, they are at any given time *the only values*.[133] Value-relativism, then, can result in conformism. It deprives the social theorist of a critical edge, of a fulcrum of leverage outside the world. The main target of Socrates' philosophy was, in this regard, to rescue the individual from a blind social conformism by pointing to the liberating effect of knowledge at the moral level. This brings us to the other side of the dichotomy in social theory, the transcendental view of social reality, which claims to offer a fulcrum of leverage for social criticism.

Plato's and Durkheim's social theories are by no means identical, but they reflect a similar transcendental outlook which is also apparent in their respective notion of anomie. The source of values is, for both authors, to be sought outside the individual. For Plato, the supreme Good resides in the world of moral absolutes; for Durkheim, the moral fact is likewise to be found outside the individual, at the societal level. By locating the source of values in transcendent realms both Plato and Durkheim are able to criticize the historically specific values of fifth-century Athens and of nineteenth-century Europe. They are in the position of assessing the evil effects of anomie from a social–transcendental vantage point. For Plato, the ideal State is the only source of justice and of the laws; for Durkheim, society alone is endowed with moral vision. Accordingly, for both authors anomie is the *essence* of evil because it is the force antithetical to the ideal social order.[134]

My comparison between a transcendental and an immanent concept of anomie and their underlying social theories is, for obvious reasons, a partial and one-sided assessment – after all, it is only possible to assess from a perspective. The hint is that the issues are definitely more complex than we might wish. Durkheim's and Merton's anomie are not diametrically opposite to each other, nor are Plato's and Gorgias'. The political overtones of Durkheim's social theory, likewise, are not necessarily opposite to the ones of most American sociologists – the latter often echo the former. It would be naive to think that value-relativism or -positivism are, as such, progressive elements of social change; witness Socrates' criticism of the sophists and the sociologists of knowledge's criticism of positivism.[135]

What is clear is that in spite of seemingly divergent perspectives we have much in common with *both* Plato and the sophists; I emphasized our neglected relation with the latter. The lesson to be learned by looking back for anomie in history is not, and cannot be, a black and white view of the world. More modestly, borrowing Gouldner's words, I would claim this to be a way "to raise the sociologist's self-awareness of a new historical level."[136]

Notes

1   Alvin W. Gouldner, *Enter Plato: Classical Greece and the Origins of Social Theory* (New York: Basic, 1965), 172.

2   G. B. Kerferd, *The Sophistic Movement* (Cambridge: Cambridge University Press, 1981), 174.

3   Kerferd writes: "What seems to me impressive however is the clear indications that survive of a range of technical doctrines under discussion in what we would now call the spheres of philosophy and sociology." *The Sophistic Movement*, 175.

4   This opposition of perspectives is vigorously upheld by Karl Popper in *The Open Society and its Enemies*, Vol. 1 (1945; revised ed London: Routledge & Kegan Paul, 1957). I do not share, however, the conclusions which Popper draws in his work.

5   See, for example, John Horton, "The Dehumanization of Anomie and Alienation: A Problem in the Ideology of Sociology," *British Journal of Sociology* 15 (December 1964):294–5; Marvin B. Scott and Roy Turner, "Weber and the Anomic Theory of Deviance," *Sociological Quarterly* 6 (Summer 1965):233–5; François Chazel, "Considerations sur la nature de l'anomie," *Revue française de sociologie* 8 (April–June 1967):154–6; Philippe Besnard, "Merton à la recherche de l'anomie," *Revue française de sociologie* 19 (January–March 1978):23–35.

6   Emile Durkheim, *The Division of Labor in Society*, trans. George Simpson (1933; reprinted New York: Free Press, 1961), 431.

7   Horton, "The Dehumanization of Anomie," 294.

8   More specifically, Ostwald writes that the change took place at some point between 511/10 and 464/3 BC, that is, during the democratic reform of Cleisthenes in Athens. See Martin Ostwald, *Nomos and the Beginnings of the Athenian Democracy* (Oxford: Clarendon, 1969), 59. On the origins of *nomos* and of its grammatical variations, see E. Laroche, *Histoire de las racine NEM-en grec ancien* (Paris: Librairie C. Klincksieck, 1949); on *nomos* see also Marcello Gigante, *Nomos Basileus* (Naples: Edizioni Glaux, 1956).

9   Ostwald, *Nomos and the Beginnings*, 21.

10   ibid., 85.

11   Ostwald states that *anomia* described a quality of individual conduct, and *dysnomia* described a social or political condition. For both, he adds the opposite term was *eunomia* (ibid., 62–95). I find Ostwald's distinction questionable because, as he points out, "*Dysnomia* is found only twice in Greek literature (Hesiod and Solon)" (ibid., 85n). This means that *dysnomia* and *anomia*, as nouns, appeared at different times in Greek literature and could not compete for the same meaning. Moreover, various commentators on Herodotus' use of anomie (especially on Herodotus 1.96 and ff.) point to its meaning as *a condition of a social group* and not, as Ostwald skillfully tries to argue, as defining "the asocial conduct of individuals" (ibid., 89–90). See, for instance, H. J. Erasmus, "Eunomia," *Acta Classica* 3 (1960):58, and J. A. S. Evans, "Despotes Nomos," *Atheneum* n.s. 43 (1965):145–6. I believe the difference in interpretations to be largely a matter of perspectives:

it is difficult to establish at what point the behavior of single individuals becomes a "social condition." At any rate, it would be misleading to interpret *anomia* as *only* describing a quality of individual behavior. For a discussion of this topic in modern sociology, see Richard Schacht, "Doubts about anomie and anomia," in *Alienation and Anomie Revisited*, ed. S. Giora Shoham (Tel-Aviv: Ramot, 1982), 73–4.

12 *Anomia* and its grammatical variations appear twice in Aeschylus, twice in Sophocles, seven times in Herodotus, thirteen in Euripides, fourteen in Plato, and fifteen in Isocrates. The count can obviously vary somewhat, and is, in any case, only a partial indicator.

13 Cf. Chester G. Starr, *A History of the Ancient World* (New York: Oxford University Press, 1965), ch. 5.

14 The examples offered in this section will include instances of the adverb, *anomōs*, which follows the same patterns of the adjective.

15 Hesiod *Theogonia* 307. In parentheses I give the transliteration of the term as it appears in the Greek texts, with its gender, number and case.

16 Sophocles, *Trachiniae* 1095–6.

17 On the notion of *hybris* in Greek literature and its use by the writers mentioned in this study, see Carlo del Grande, *Hybris: colpa e castigo nell'espressione poetica e letteraria della Grecia antica–da Omero a Cleante* (Naples: Riccardo Ricciardi editore, 1947).

18 Gorgias fr. 11.7 (the standard reference is Diels-Kranz, *Die Fragmente de Vorsokratiker*; hereafter, DK).

19 Isocrates, *Helen* 28–9.

20 Lysias 3.18.

21 Plato, *Republic* 572B.

22 Sophocles, *Oedipus Colonus* 142.

23 Ostwald, *Nomos and the Beginnings*, 87.

24 Euripides, *Andromache* 491.

25 Gorgias fr. 11a.36 in DK.

26 Antiphon 4.1.2.

27 Xenophon, *Lacedaemonians* 8.5.

28 On the meaning of *dikē* and *dikaiosynē* in Greek culture, see A. W. H. Adkins, *Moral Values and Political Behavior in Ancient Greece* (London: Chatto & Windus, 1972).

29 Euripides, *Iphigenia in Aulis* 399.

30 Euripides, *Bacchae* 995 and 1015.

31 Anonymus Iamblichi fr. 3.1 in DK.

32 Cf. Adkins, *Moral Values*, 103–6.

33 On the shared themes of tragedians and orators see A. Douglas Thomson, *Euripides and the Attic Orators: A Comparison* (London: Macmillan, 1898).

34 The sophist Protagoras was considered the first to capitalize on rhetorical methods of persuasion, "to make the weaker argument the stronger" (Aristotle, *Rhetoric* 1402A).

35   Thucydides 2.38.

36   Kerferd, *The Sophistic Movement*, 15.

37   Chester G. Starr writes: "In 508 B.C. Clisthenes had reorganized Athenian political groupings so as to break the strength of the clans. He had also lodged the main constitutional power in the hands of the assembly, but its range of action was still checked both by the elected archons, almost always of aristocratic origin, and by the council of the Aeropagus. During the next 50 years these checks were removed one by one; 'equality of rights' (*isonomia*) yielded to 'rule of the people' (*demokratia*)." Starr, *A History*, 299.

38   Thucydides 2.37; trans. Charles Forster Smith.

39   W.K.C. Guthrie comments: "The influence of the Eleatics on Protagoras and Gorgias is undeniable, as is that of Heraclitus on Protagoras, and Gorgias is said to have been a pupil and follower of Empedocles. One of the most powerful influences for humanism is to be found in the theories of the natural origins of life and society which were a feature of Ionian thought from Anaximander onwards." Guthrie, *A History of Greek Philosophy*, Vol. 3 (Cambridge: Cambridge University Press, 1969), 14.

40   For a general introduction to Euripides see Gilbert Murray, *Euripides and his Age* (2nd edn Oxford: Oxford University Press, 1946).

41   For a detailed account of Euripides' treatment of ethical topics, see R. B. Appleton, *Euripides the Idealist* (London: Dent, 1927), ch. 4.

42   Euripides, *Electra* 551.

43   For a discussion of Euripides' views on religion see Appleton, *Euripides the Idealist*, ch. 8.

44   Euripides, *Ion* 442–3.

45   Euripides, *Hercules Furens* 779.

46   ibid. 757.

47   Euripides, *Medea* 410–11.

48   Euripides, *Iphigenia in Aulis* 1089–97.

49   See note 10 above.

50   Herodotus 1.96.

51   Herodotus 1.97.

52   Thucydides 2.53.1.

53   Thucydides 2.53.4; trans. Charles Forster Smith.

54   Popper, *The Open Society*, Vol. 1, 178–84. On Thucydides' cultural background see Victor Ehrenberg, *From Solon to Socrates: Greek History and Civilization During the Sixth and Fifth Centuries BC* (London: Methuen, 1968), 363–71.

55   Isocrates, *Panegyricus* 111.

56   ibid., 168.

57   Isocrates, *Panathenaicus* 55; trans. George Norlin.

58   Thucydides 3.83; trans. Charles Forster Smith.

59   ibid.

60   Such was, for instance, the view held by Callicles: "It is natural justice, that the cattle and other possessions of the inferior and

weaker belong to the superior and stronger." Plato, *Gorgias* 484C; trans. W. D. Woodhead.

61   For an overview of the shifting interpretations of sophistic thought see Kerferd, *The Sophistic Movement*, 4–15, and Guthrie, *A History*, Vol. 3, 9–13. More recent books on the topic are H. D. Rankin, *Sophists, Socratics and Cynics* (Totowa, NJ: Barnes & Noble, 1983); Martin Dreher, *Sophistik und Polisentwicklung* (Frankfurt: P. Lang, 1983).

62   Kerferd, *The Sophistic Movement*, 1.

63   Cf. Guthrie, *A History*, Vol. 3, 1.

64   Kerferd, *The Sophistic Movement*, 2.

65   Cf. Herodotus 1.96; Isocrates, *Archidamus* 65; Plutarch, *Moralia* 755B.

66   The standard reference on the topic is Felix Heinimann, *Nomos und Physis* (Basle: Schweiz. Beitr. zur Altertumsw., 1, 1945). See also Guthrie, *A History*, Vol. 3, ch. 4; Kerferd, *The Sophistic Movement*, ch. 10; Popper, *The Open Society*, Vol. 1, ch. 6.

67   Guthrie, *A History*, Vol. 3, 57–8.

68   Callicles charges: "And you have discovered this clever trick and do not play fair in your arguments, for if a man speaks on the basis of convention, you slyly question him on the basis of nature, but if he follows nature, you follow convention." Plato, *Gorgias* 483A; trans. W. D. Woodhead.

69   Cf. Aristotle, *Rhetoric* 1.15.

70   Guthrie, *A History*, Vol. 3, 58; Aristotle, *De Soph. Elenchis* 173A.

71   Plato, *Gorgias* 483 D; trans. W.D. Woodhead.

72   Plato, *Protagoras* 327CD; trans. Benjamin Jowett.

73   Antiphon fr. 44A in DK.

74   For an overview of the different attempts to identify the Anonymus Iamblichi, see Guthrie, *A History*, Vol. 3, 314–15. For an assessment of the Anonymus' influence on later writers, see Andrew Thomas Cole, Jr, "The Anonymus Iamblichi and his Place in Greek Political Theory," *Harvard Studies in Classical Philology* 65 (1961):127–63.

75   Anonymus Iamblichi fr. 6.1 in DK; trans. T. M. Johnson.

76   ibid., 7.8.

77   ibid., 7.9.

78   ibid., 7.10.

79   ibid., 7.12.

80   ibid., 7.14.

81   ibid., 7.17. This passage is not included in the Diels-Kranz collection, but it appears in Mario Untersteiner, *Sofisti. Testimonianze e frammenti*, Vol. 3 (Florence: La Nuova Italia, 1967), 139.

82   Isocrates, *Archidamus* 65.

83   Isocrates, *Panegyricus* 39.

84   Plutarch, *Moralia* 755B.

85   The sophists were attempting to produce a plausible social theory.

For an overview of this aspect of their thought see Guthrie, *A History*, Vol. 3, ch. 5, and Kerferd, *The Sophistic Movement*, ch. 12.

86 Plato, *Protagoras* 337D.

87 The attribution of this passage to an unnamed sophist, an "Anonymous on the Laws," is controversial. For a discussion of the problem see Gigante, *Nomos Basileus*, ch. 20; Guthrie, *A History*, Vol. 3, 75; Untersteiner, *Sofisti*, fasc. 3, 192. Untersteiner, at any rate, includes the fragment in his collection of sophistic writings.

88 Anonymus peri nomōn fr. 15–16; tr. W. K. C. Guthrie.

89 Callicles argues the point: "For philosophy, you know, Socrates, is a pretty thing if you engage in it moderately in your youth; but if you continue in it longer than you should, it is the ruin of any man … Such men know nothing of the laws of their cities, or of the language they should use in their business associations … and so when they enter upon any activity public or private they appear ridiculous." Plato, *Gorgias* 484D; trans. W. D. Woodhead.

90 On this problematic in sophistic thought see Guthrie, *A History*, Vol. 3, 173–5; Popper, *The Open Society*, Vol. 1, 64 ff.; Adkins, *Moral Values*, ch. 5.

91 Xenophon, *Memorabilia* 4.4.14.

92 Guthrie, *A History*, Vol. 3, 112.

93 ibid., 175. Cf. Plato, *Protagoras* 322C.

94 Cf. Plato, *Minos* 314CD and Xenophon, *Memorabilia* 4.4.13.

95 Xenophon, *Memorabilia* 4.4.13.

96 ibid., 4.4.16; trans. E. C. Marchant.

97 Plato, *Crito* 51C; trans. Hugh Tredennick.

98 On the significance of definitions in Socrates' ethical philosophy, see Guthrie, *A History*, Vol. 3, 425–42.

99 Xenophon, *Cyropaedia* 1.3.17.

100 Plato, *Minos* 314D.

101 ibid., 316B; trans. W. R. M. Lamb.

102 "The problems he discussed were, What is godly, what is ungodly; what is beautiful, what is ugly; what is just, what is unjust; what is prudence, what is madness; what is courage, what is cowardice; what is a state, what is a statesman; what is government, and what is a governor." Xenophon, *Memorabilia* 1.1.16; trans. E. C. Marchant.

103 In Guthrie's words, Plato "wished to give a theoretical or metaphysical backing to the mainly practical and ethical teachings of Socrates about the good." *A History*, Vol. 3, 506. Obviously, this operation resulted in a tension between Socratism and Platonism. Gouldner writes, "There is a tension between an earlier stress on the liberating dialectic, when men have already within them a potential for knowledge and self-attained understanding, and a later stress on the controlling laws, which see men as plastic material that need to be molded through a deliberate conditioning." *Enter Plato*, 176.

104 Clearly, because of the emphasis on definitions in both Socrates'

and Plato's philosophy, the notion of anomie was but a "residual category" of the notion of lawfulness; that is, for Plato, anomie and all evil in general was not a reality in itself, but simply a *deformation* of the positive value. Describing Plato's anomie as the "essence" of evil, I mean anomie to be evil *by definition*.

105 Gouldner, *Enter Plato*, 221.

106 Plato, *Minos* 314D and 317C.

107 Plato, *Epistle VII* 336B.

108 Plato, *Republic* 496D and *Laws* 885B.

109 Plato, *Greater Hippias* 285A.

110 Plato, *Republic* 572B.

111 Plato, *Laws* 823E.

112 Plato, *Republic* 575A.

113 Plato, *Alcibiades II* 146B.

114 Gouldner, *Enter Plato*, 221.

115 Cf. Plato, *Republic* 572B.

116 Gouldner, *Enter Plato*, 221; Plato, *Laws* 942C.

117 No instances of *anomia* are found in the Epicurean literature. In the early Stoic literature there are two instances in which *anomia* appears; both reflect the cosmological character of Stoic ethics. For instance, Crysippus, describing the administration of the universe and the kinship between natural order and human creatures, states: "He who honours and upholds this policy and does not oppose it in any way is law-abiding [*nomimos*], devout and orderly [*cosmios*]; he, however, who disturbs it, as far as that is possible to him, and violates it or does not know it, is lawless [*anomos*] and disorderly [*acosmos*]." *Stoicorum Veterum Fragmenta* (Stuttgart: Teubner, 1964), Vol. 3, ch. 6, n. 335; trans. J. W. Cohoon.

118 Robert K. Merton, "Social Structure and Anomie," *American Sociological Review* 3 (June 1938): 672–82.

119 Marshall B. Clinard, *Anomie and Deviant Behavior* (New York: Free Press, 1964), v.

120 Robert K. Merton, *Social Theory and Social Structure* (Glencoe: Free Press, 1949), 378.

121 Eric A. Havelock, *The Liberal Temper in Greek Politics* (New Haven: Yale University Press, 1957), 17–18.

122 Gouldner, *Enter Plato*, 186.

123 ibid., 192–3.

124 Havelock, *The Liberal Temper*, 185.

125 Gouldner, *Enter Plato*, 190.

126 See, for instance, Gouldner's illuminating comment: "The message seems to be that anomic normlessness is no longer merely something that the sociologist studies in the social world, but it is something that *he inflicts upon it* and is the basis of his method of investigation." Alvin Gouldner, *The Coming Crisis of Western Sociology* (New York: Basic, 1970), 393–4.

127 Plato, *Republic* 537E.

128 Horton, "The Dehumanization of Anomie," 295.

129 Euripides, *Phoenissae* 499–501; trans. W. K. C. Guthrie.

130 Guthrie, *A History*, Vol. 3, 164–5.

131 Plato, *Protagoras* 334B6–C2; trans. Eric A. Havelock.

132 Alvin W. Gouldner, "Anti-Minotaur: The Myth of a Value-Free Sociology," *Social Problems* 9 (Fall 1962): 203–4.

133 This is, *in nuce*, the criticism that the classical sociology of knowledge levels against positivistic sociology.

134 That is, anomie is evil *by definition*. On the subject, see Gouldner, *The Coming Crisis*, ch. 11.

135 In this respect, Popper's views in *The Open Society* are myopically one-sided.

136 Gouldner, *The Coming Crisis*, 489.

CHAPTER 2

Anomia in the
Biblical Literature

Most social scientists are unaware that the concept of *anomia* has a relevant role in Biblical literature; moreover, even if aware, most might still suspect that Biblical and sociological anomie would have very little, if anything, in common.[1] Yet, not only is *anomia* a key word in the Greek Scriptures and in related writings, but also Biblical and sociological concepts of anomie are surprisingly similar.

In 1902, in the second preface to *The Division of Labor*, Durkheim wrote: "It is this anomic state that is the cause, as we shall show, of the incessant recurrent conflicts, and the multifarious disorders."[2] In the Qumran manuscripts of the first century BC, we read: "To the spirit of *anomia* belong greed, injustice, impiety and lying, pride and the inflation of the heart ... [The world] is drawn to unholiness by the power of *anomia*."[3] Religious overtones aside, the similarity between the two statements is striking. Both Durkheim and the writers of late Judaism consider anomie to be an evil force, a cause of disorder and of all forms of vice. Whether the referent values are religious or sociological makes little difference, for both statements postulate a dualistic view of human nature and morality. This dualism envisions good and evil as separate, antithetic forces struggling against each other. Anomie is a product of the forces of evil.

In this chapter I will analyze the meanings of *anomia* in Biblical writings. The analysis is useful on two accounts. First, it provides a fresh look at the literature on *anomia* in Judaism and early Christianity, and second, it clarifies the sociological notion of anomie by teasing out some of its hidden religious features.

From a sociological perspective, the discussions about *anomia* in the Judaic and Christian writings show elements of continuity between the two traditions; yet, they also show a clear radicalization of religious thought in late Judaism and early Christianity.

41

This radicalization is illustrated in the eschatology of both traditions. In the apocalyptic literature, *anomia* plays a prominent role: it embodies the forces of evil which govern this world, rules the children of darkness, and fights against the forces of righteousness and the children of light of the future world. *Anomia* reflects the internal development from Judaic thought to Christianity; but it also reflects the influence of Greek thought – especially neo-Platonism and stoicism – on Biblical literature. Elements of Greek philosophy are apparent in the writings of the Jewish commentator, Philo of Alexandria, but also in the New Testament authors.

Recovering the Biblical notion of *anomia*, however, is not merely a matter of curiosity for historically remote cultural events; the Judeo-Christian religious ideas are a crucial component of Western thought at large. In relation to broader theoretical themes and to the use of specific concepts like *anomia*, religious and sociological traditions have a great deal in common. The apocalyptic *anomia* of the Judeo-Christian tradition prefigured, in many ways, the apocalyptic anomie often described by modern sociologists. On this account, the rediscovery of Biblical *anomia* is relevant to modern social theory because it recasts the link between sociology and its religious roots – it allows sociology to recover some of its repressed subconscious.

In this chapter, my argument is presented under five headings. First, I describe the entry of the word *anomia* in Biblical literature with the translation of the Old Testament into Greek by the Jews of Alexandria. There, I highlight the range of meanings taken by *anomia* and its central distinguishing features. Second, I describe the general characteristics of Hellenism and focus on the Old Testament commentaries of Philo of Alexandria, pointing to the theoretical convergence, in his writings, of Judaic religious thought and Greek philosophical thought. Third, I review the *anomia* literature of the New Testament and the Pauline emphasis on the Law of the Spirit over the Mosaic Law – on the ethics of ultimate ends over the ethics of responsibility. Fourth, I discuss the role of *anomia* in the apocalyptic literature of late Judaism (especially in the Qumran manuscripts) and of early Christianity (especially in Matthew, Paul, and John), drawing out the elements of continuity and change between the two traditions and their relative views on *anomia*. I also briefly describe the transition of the word *anomia* from Greek into Latin culture. Fifth, and last, I compare the Biblical apocalyptic and its concept of *anomia* with modern sociological thought, highlighting some hitherto unperceived similarities.

Modern discussions of anomie claim to be free of ethical or

religious constraints; I maintain that there is more to sociological research on anomie than scientific objectivity. Much of our "scientific view" of the social world finds it roots in Judaism and Christianity – especially in their shared eschatological dualism of good and evil. To claim the existence of ethical presuppositions in modern sociology is not to brand its work as theoretically flawed or worthless. Rather, it is to give it an added historical dimension. It is to claim that anomie theories too are a reflection of our cultural heritage.

The Greek Old Testament

In the Greek Old Testament the word *anomia* is the translation for about twenty different Hebrew words which corresponded to such English terms as wickedness, ungodliness, impiety, injustice, wrong, depravity, evil and, above all, sin and iniquity.[4] In the sense of sin and iniquity, *anomia* was used interchangeably with the Greek word *hamartia*; the two terms were used in the plural to indicate specific acts of sin.[5]

Throughout the Greek Old Testament, specifically in the Septuagint, *anomia* and its grammatical variations appear more than 300 times. As early as the Book of Genesis (19:5) we find that the Angel says to Lot: "Arise … and go forth; lest thou also be destroyed with the iniquities [*anomiais*] of the city [Sodom]." Similarly, in the Book of Exodus (34:9), Moses proclaims that the Lord "shalt take away our sins [*hamartias*] and our iniquities [*anomias*]." Here, to render *hamartia* and *anomia*, sin and iniquity appear hand in hand in the same passage. The Book of Psalms, where the Greek *anomia* is most frequently found, offers several examples of a symmetric use of *anomia* and *hamartia*.[6] Psalm 50: 1–3, for instance, reads:

Have mercy upon me, O God, acccording to thy great mercy;
and according to the multitude of thy compassions
blot out my transgressions [*anoméma*].
Wash me thoroughly from mine iniquity [*anomias*],
and cleanse me from my sin [*hamartias*].
For I am conscious of mine iniquity [*anomian*];
and my sin [*hamartia*] is continually before me.

The English rendering of *anomia* with iniquity and of *hamartia* with sin, is clearly indebted to the Vulgate, the official Latin translation of the Bible, where *anomia* is *iniquitas*, iniquity, and *hamartia* is *peccatum*, sin.[7] In the Old Testament the two words were synonymous, but by the time the Greek Septuagint was translated into Latin, *anomia* had developed a special meaning of its own. In the writings of late Judaism and of the New Testament, in fact, *anomia* is used in the singular form to indicate something more than mere acts of transgression. Ignace de la Potterie writes:

> *Anomia*, which can be translated here at "iniquity," corresponds to the Hebrew *áwel* or *áwlah*. It is always used in the singular, for it no longer signifies individual sin but a collective state. It is essentially an eschatological term that designates the hostility and revolt of the forces of evil against the kingdom of God in the last days of the world.[8]

Influenced by this latter development in the meaning of *anomia*, the Latin Fathers of the Church dwelled on the distinction between *iniquitas* and *peccatum* in relation to passages from the Old Testament where the two terms appeared hand by hand.

Hilarius, commenting on Psalm 129:9, "And he shall redeem Israel from all his iniquities [*tón anomión*]," wrote: "Iniquity differs from sin ... in fact, iniquity is every transgression of the divine law, which is more serious than sin ... it is a sin of iniquity whatever is done outside the law, like the crimes of the Gentiles."[9] Hieronimus wrote in a similar vein, referring to Osea 8:13, "Now will he remember their iniquities, and will take vengeance of their sins." He commented: "Between *anomia*, that is iniquity, and sin this matters, that iniquity is outside the law, and sin is after the law."[10]

For Hilarius and Hieronimus, *anomia* and *hamartia*, iniquity and sin, were not synonymous. *Anomia* had a broader meaning than *hamartia* because whereas the latter described only a transgression of the written law, *anomia* encompassed actions that were done outside of the law – "like the crimes of the Gentiles." *Anomia* was a violation of general moral principles, not of any written code of Judaism. Even more important, *anomia* was considered the root cause of specific transgressions; it was a sort of moral condition of the individual. Ambrosius wrote that "sin is the work of iniquity, and iniquity is the doer of the fault and crime."[11] Isidorus, then, remarked that "Iniquity refers to the harshness of the soul, whereas sin refers to the fall of the body; therefore iniquity precedes, and sin follows; but iniquity is the worse."[12]

Anomia and its Latin counterpart, *iniquitas*, were, for the Latin Fathers, broader terms than sin and transgression. *Anomia* lacked specific legalistic boundaries, it had no connection with the written law, but referred to broader unwritten guiding principles of human conduct – a sort of natural law. Hence, *anomia* was perceived to be a general moral term: *anomia* was the polar opposite of the moral law, it was the force of evil pitted against the force of good, it was the devil against God. Indeed there are a few instances when the Greek *anomia* of the Old Testament translated the Hebrew name of Satan, *Belial*.[13] However, by and large, the Greek Septuagint offers a characterization of *anomia* in strictly religious terms by relating it, more or less closely, with sin and transgression. Being the translation of a sacred text, the Septuagint does not allow a broader discussion of *anomia*'s ethical implications.

The development in the meaning of *anomia* from its use in the plural form indicating actions of sin, to its use in the singular form describing a broader immoral condition, was not an independent, internal development of Judaism. Rather, it was, at least partially, the product of Hellenistic influences on the late Jewish thought of the second and first century BC, and on early Christian thought. The ethical overtones of *anomia* are, in fact, documented clearly in the works of the foremost writer of Hellenistic Judaism, Philo of Alexandria.

Philo of Alexandria's Hellenistic Judaism

Before analyzing Philo's thought it is necessary to describe briefly the historical period that we call Hellenism, since Hellenistic culture had a strong influence not only on Philo's own writings, but also on the subsequent Judeo-Christian literature – the writings of the New Testament and the Greek and Latin patristic writings. Arnaldo Momigliano writes:

> Insofar as our inheritance goes back to antiquity, it is essentially Greco-Latin-Jewish *because* it is essentially Hellenistic. The notion of Hellenistic civilization defines both the time (323–30 BC) and the space (Mediterranean zone) in which these three cultures converged and began to react on one another. It follows that it is not superfluous to investigate the circumstances in which a new special relationship was established between Jews, Greeks and Romans in the Hellenistic age.[14]

The interaction of Hellenistic cultures was highly uneven. In fact, whereas Jews and Romans went out of their way to learn the Greek language and culture, the Greeks practically ignored the Judaic and Latin cultures altogether. Momigliano points out that "The dialogue with the Greeks happened because the Romans and the Jews wanted it."[15] The interest of Jews and Romans in things Greek was not dictated by any sense of inferiority towards Greek learning – far from that. For both Romans and Jews, Greek learning was a way to define their own identity in contrast to the dominant Greek culture. Momigliano comments: "Both Jews and Romans decided to learn Greek in order to compare their own ways with those of the Greeks and to shape their intellectual life in relation to the Greeks."[16] On this ground, both Romans and Jews were able to acquire a sense of national identity. Accordingly, Cicero could divide the world into three parts: Italy, Greece, and the barbarians. Similarly, Philo distinguished among Jews, Greeks, and barbarians.[17]

The Hellenistic period was characterized by particular political, economic and social conditions.[18] Although Hellenistic culture revolved around the Greek cities, these had lost the political power that Sparta and Athens enjoyed in the classical period. After the death of Alexander, there developed three major powers in the Hellenistic world: the Ptolemies, the Seleucids, and the Antigonids. Behind these three dynasties stood a complicated system of states, monarchies and leagues of city–states. The cities were no longer autonomous, but depended on the various kings for their political stability. The monarchs, then, needed the loyalty of the cities to preserve their power. The political structure was, overall, very precarious; incessant wars broke out among the different kings, and by 200 BC, the Hellenistic monarchs had battled each other to a standstill. Understandably, the interest of individuals turned away from the political arena, toward the problems of identity generated by a cosmopolitan, fragmented society. Stoic philosophers, especially, developed the idea that one was no longer a citizen of the city–state, but the inhabitant of a larger world. In such a condition, one had to feel at home anywhere in the world by gaining a sense of individual autonomy together with a notion of universal equality. The world was *oikoumenē*, a community whose unifying principle was the law of nature and of universal reason.

Economically, the Hellenistic age witnessed an increase in commerce and trade, along with the development of a centralized system of government – especialy in Egypt, where the Ptolemies ruled. By the end of the third century BC, however, the economic growth was severely curtailed by the continuous wars among kingdoms.[19] At the social level, then, the political and economic instability generated conflicts and uprisings which added to the general sense of uncertainty of the era. F. W. Walbank writes: "Economic distress and great extremes of poverty and wealth were a recipe for class conflict and led to threats of social revolution in Greece proper and in the lands around the Aegean."[20]

A situation of political, economic and social instability was accompanied, in intellectual circles, by a retreat from the political life and by a cultivation of individual qualities. Looking for a point of reference in such uncertain times, intellectuals developed a strong interest in religious doctrines and esoteric cults. In relation to the large amount of forged religious documents during this period, Momigliano remarks that such a phenomenon "indicates the need for a revealed, authoritative religious knowledge of a kind that was not easily available in the Greek tradition."[21]

The translation of the Old Testament into Greek had the combined effect of offering the Hellenized Jews an element of national identification, and of providing the Greeks with an example of a defined, homogeneous religious system absent in their own culture. The Greek Old Testament marked the encounter of Judaic and Greek thought. There, Jerusalem and Athens did not stand in opposition to each other, but blended together. This blending was clearly demonstrated in Philo's work. E. R. Goodenough writes of Philo: "He used to say that Plato had cribbed his ideas from Moses, but his biblical interpretations often read as though he thought Moses had been trained by Plato."[22]

A Jewish writer of the first century BC, Philo of Alexandria provided the broader ethical perspective missing in the Greek Old Testament. Philo's commentaries on the Pentateuch offer, in fact, a religious outlook which is anchored to the religious Jewish tradition, the Scriptures, and to Greek classical philosophy. Philo employed the latter as an instrument of Biblical interpretation, thereby broadening the moral outlook of the Scriptures; Philo was, indeed, the first writer for whom philosophy was *ancilla theologiae*, the handmaid of theology.[23]

In Philo's writings *anomia* and its grammatical variations appear consistently in the classical Greek sense of "lawlessness," "disorder" and "anarchy"; but the context in which they appear testifies to the overarching religious message Philo wants to convey. For him *anomia* expresses a condition of the human soul, which "being made of matter, is errant, disorderly, and irrational; but more than mere body, it is a force; it is active in its errancy and not merely passive; it is not easily overcome by the immanent reason."[24] For Philo, the struggle between the irrational and the rational is constant in all human beings: from the victory of reason come "goodness, virtue, wisdom, and righteousness"; from the victory of irrationality come wickedness, impiety and sin.[25]

Philo uses the notion of *anomia* to draw, from the Old Testament writings, a sharp distinction between good and evil. To accomplish this, he borrows from the Platonic and Stoic notions of *anomia* and applies them to the Biblical texts. In Philo, *anomia* is constantly contrasted to its opposite. Discussing the evil character of sensual pleasures symbolized by the serpent in the garden of Eden,[26] Philo compares them to a tyrant opposed to the righteous rule of reason: "the one [reason] being the author of laws, the other [the senses] of *anomia*."[27] In another context, commenting on Cain and Abel, Philo confronts the good Abel, who loved God, with the evil Cain, who loved himself. God abandoned Cain and, as when a ruler abandons his city, Cain "becomes prey of two very great evils, anarchy and *anomia*."[28] The city that Cain has built is inhabited by "devotees of impiety, godlessness, self-love, and arrogance."[29] Its laws are "various forms of *anomia* and injustice, unfairness, licentiousness, audacity, senselessness, self-will, immoderate indulgence in pleasures, unnatural lust that may not be named."[30] For Philo, *anomia* is the source of evil for both social life and for the individual. At the political level, *anomia* throws the city in a condition of anarchy; at the individual level, the rejection of God is cause of *anomia* in the "city of the soul" – *anomia* is the tyranny of the senses.

Philo capitalized on his knowledge of Greek philosophy, especially Plato's ethical theory and notion of *anomia*, to interpret the Scriptures and clarify their moral thrust. As Philo sees it, on the side of God is light, truth, and the law; on the side of the devil is darkness, falsehood, and *anomia*. The contrast of opposite moral conditions runs throughout Philo's writings, and the law becomes the discriminating element between good and evil.[31] In his work *On Drunkenness*, Philo writes that "it is the special task of law and instruction to 'distinguish' the profane from the sacred and the impure from the pure."[32] The law separates good from evil; it promotes the former and rejects the latter. *Anomia*, then, is undesirable exactly because it prevents this first step of the law, the one of discriminating between good and evil: "It is the way of *anomia* and indiscipline to mix and confuse everything and thus force under the same head things which are in conflict with each other."[33]

The law that Philo describes is not a positive, written law; it is, instead, the unwritten law of nature. The law of nature is the product of the immanent Logos, "the totality of the powers of God existing within the world itself."[34] Philo describes the Logos as "the cutter [*tomeus*], who never ceases to divide";[35] and it is through the Logos that good can be distinguished from evil, law from *anomia*.

Philo's ethical theory and his concept of *anomia* blended classical Greek philosophy with Jewish religious thought – both had a crucial role in Philo's moral outlook. In the Old Testament we find the opposition of good and evil and the opposition of the moral law and *anomia*; these notions, however, were mostly undeveloped in the Biblical text. With his Hellenistic background, Philo was able to tease out the ethical implications of the Scriptures, and offer a concept of *anomia* that was reminiscent of Platonic philosophy, yet consistent with the Judaic tradition. Both elements become essential components of Philo's thought.

The encounter of Greek and Judaic thought in the Hellenistic age greatly enhanced the ethical significance of the Scriptures, and the New Testament writings were to elaborate further on the moral meanings of the sacred texts. We must consider, now, to what extent the Old Testament views on *anomia* persisted in early Christianity, and to what extent they underwent any significant modification.

Anomia, *The New Testament, and the Law*

When one compares the Old with the New Testament in terms of their underlying ethical message, it is easy to overemphasize the legalistic legacy of the Mosaic tradition against the liberating message of the New Testament. Undoubtedly a change occurred with the New Testament's emphasis on an "ethic of ultimate ends," to borrow Max Weber's characterization of it.[36] However, such emphasis on the personal attitude is not necessarily antagonistic to the Mosaic law; it rather seeks to improve on it by going beyond the letter of the law. The New Testament's ethics reunites the written law with the spirit of the law, they do not oppose one against the other.[37]

The concept of *anomia* as it appears in the New Testament is subject to this same caveat. The new ethical elements which *anomia* conveys are well rooted in the Old Testament tradition, they are not in opposition to it. This claim is supported by an overview of the pertinent passages where *anomia* appears. *Anomia* and its grammatical variations appear in twenty-one New Testament passages; of these, one-third are literal quotations from the Old Testament.[38] Only in four instances, in the whole of the New Testament, does *anomia* convey an attack to the excesses of Judaic legalistic ethics.[39] In all the other passages, *anomia* is used according to, or at least not against, the Old Testament's notion. Let us examine the exceptions first.

Paul's letters are at the epicenter of the New Testament's

criticism of Judaic legalism; as one might suspect, it is there that we find *anomia* in the new meaning of "without law." Summarizing Paul's ethical stance, Stanislaus Lyonnet writes:

> The Christian animated by the Spirit is freed in Christ not only from the Mosaic law insofar as it is Mosaic, but also from the Mosaic law insofar as it is law, in fact, from any law which constrains man from without (I do not say, which obliges him), without his becoming an amoral being, above and beyond good and evil.[40]

The Christian freedom is, essentially, a freedom from external, legalistic constraint; the law, Paul writes, is a cause of sin: "Where there is no law, neither is there transgression."[41] The law, being an external force, cannot improve the individual's conduct, it can only sanction one's deflection. For this reason Paul writes that "The law is not made for a righteous man, but for the lawless (*anomois*) and unruly, for the ungodly and sinners, for the unholy and profane."[42] As Lyonnet comments, "If all Christians were just, there would be no need to constrain them with the law. As a general rule, the law intervenes only to repress an existing disorder."[43]

If Paul's point is that *anomia* brings about the need for an external law, it stands to reason that such a law would be superfluous if there were no *anomia*. Where there is no *anomia*, however, there is another kind of law – not an external law but an internal one – the law of intention, the law of the Spirit. It is exactly in following the law of the Spirit that the Christian becomes free from external laws, as Augustine remarked with his aphorism: "Love, and do as you please."

The ethical disposition of Paul allows him to abandon the narrow legalistic view, so that in 1 Corinthians (9:20–1) he can write:

> And to the Jews I became as a Jew, that I might gain the Jews; to them that are under the law, as under the law, not being myself under the law, that I might gain them that are under the law; to them that are without law [*tois anomois*] as without law [*anomos*], not being without law [*anomos*] to God, but under law to Christ, that I might gain them that are without law [*anomous*].

Paul argues his point by distinguishing the external law from the ethics of intention; the latter he calls "the law of Christ,"[44] which Chrysostom defines as the "law of the spirit and of grace." Paul's emphatic rejection of narrow legalism, then, is in no way an endorsement of *anomia*; on the contrary, he wants to resolve the real problem of *anomia* which consists in disregarding the general moral law, the "law of the Spirit." The absence of a legal constraint, accordingly, does not do away with sin, unless the written law is superseded by the ethics of intention. Paul makes this point clear in Romans (2:12): "For as many as have sinned without the law [*anomōs*], shall also perish without law [*anomōs*]." The absence of the Judaic law does not exempt the individual from following the moral law: they will be justified who show "the work of the law written in their hearts."[45] From the tenor of these passages where Paul invests *anomia* with a new meaning, it can be argued that he does not stand in opposition to the Scriptural tradition; rather, he recasts the latter in a new perspective by going beyond, not against, the traditional teachings.

As I pointed out earlier, the quotations from the Old Testament account for one-third of the New Testament's passages where *anomia* and its grammatical variations appear. Paul, more than anyone else, quotes the Old Testament, showing himself to be at once the most innovative and the most traditional in his usage of *anomia*.

Paul's claim that he became a Jew with the Jews holds true in his letters; in fact, in Hebrews we find most of the Old Testament passages regarding *anomia*. There, Paul quotes Psalm 44:7, "Thou hast loved righteousness [*dikaiosunēn*], and hated iniquity [*anomian*]"; in the same Epistle he also quotes, twice, Jeremiah 38:34, "And their sins [*hamartiōn*] and their iniquities [*anomiōn*] will I remember no more." Paul's quotations from the Old Testament do not contradict his views of *anomia* as expressed in the earlier passages we examined; on the contrary, they add to our understanding of his position with respect to the Old Testament. In the Old Testament *anomia* carries mostly the meaning of "iniquity," and bears no relationship with the notion of written law. With this meaning of the term, Paul and the Old Testament tradition are in total agreement.

In the New Testament, the concept of *anomia* appeared either in the context of a critique of the Judaic excesses of legalism, or as literal quotations from the Old Testament. A third use of the concept, however, surpassed in relevance and scope the two mentioned above. This is the meaning *anomia* acquired in eschatological contexts.

Anomia *in the Eschatological*
Tradition

In the previous section, I covered about half of the New Testament discussions of *anomia*; the remaining discussions are found in the context of apocalyptic and eschatological themes of the Judeo-Christian literature. In the literature of late Judaism we find a rich eschatological tradition. The so-called Qumran manuscripts (or Dead Sea Scrolls) are an outstanding example of such literature, and they offer a first discussion of *anomia* – more specifically, of *anomia*'s Hebrew counterpart, *áwel* and *áwlah*.[46] One of the manuscripts, the *Manual of Discipline*, reads:

> In the fountain of light is the origin of truth, and in one of darkness is the origin of iniquity [*anomia*]. In the hand of the Prince of Light is the control over all the sons of justice ... and in the hand of the Angel of Darkness is the complete control over the sons of iniquity ... Until then [the final judgment] the spirits of truth and iniquity [*anomia*] will struggle over the hearts of men.[47]

In this context, de la Potterie interprets *anomia* as "an eschatological term that designates the hostility and revolt of the forces of evil against the kingdom of God in the last days of the world."[48] Here, iniquity is no longer synonymous with sin, but acquires a new, special meaning. *Anomia* "is the secret quality, the spirit, the tendency that inspires and provokes [sins]."[49] The Qumran manuscripts identify *anomia* as an "abomination of the truth"[50] which is at the origin of specific acts of transgression. Furthermore, the same manuscripts not only describe iniquity *per se*, but they also make reference to the "children of iniquity," the "descendants of iniquity," the "men of iniquity," so that "one may speak correctly of iniquity as a cosmic principle."[51] Philo of Alexandria, whose writings I discussed above, offers further support for the notion of eschatological *anomia*. Philo's notion of *anomia* stressed the opposition between the principles of good and evil: on the one side is light, justice, and law, on the other side is darkness, injustice, and *anomia*. Indeed, Philo was writing at the height of Judeo-Christian eschatology.[52]

The New Testament constantly echoes, in its discussions of the apocalyptic *anomia*, the themes found in late Judaism. In Matthew's Gospel, *anomia* is always used in the context of the last judgment. At this time, Matthew writes, the Lord will address the damned ones, saying, "Depart from me, ye that work iniquity [*anomian*]."[53] Matthew also remarks that in the last days, "many false prophets shall arise, and shall lead many astray. And because iniquity [*anomia*] shall be multiplied, the love of the many shall wax cold."[54]

Evidence of the eschatological *anomia* is also found in Paul's letters. In 2 Corinthians (6:14–15) the apostle writes: "What fellowship have righteousness [*dikaiosunē*] and iniquity [*anomia*]? or what communion hath light with darkness? And what concord hath Christ with Belial? or what portion hath a believer with an unbeliever?" This, Raymond E. Brown comments, is "a dualistic NT passage that closely resembles Qumran theology."[55] Of a similar nature is a passage of Mark's Gospel: "This age of iniquity [*anomias*] and unbelief [*apistias*] is under the domination of Satan, who prevents whoever is under the yoke of impious spirits from receiving the truth and power of God."[56]

The second Epistle to the Thessalonians (2:8) offers another instance of the apocalyptic *anomia*. There, Paul writes of the Antichrist,

> For the mystery of lawlessness [*anomias*] doth already work … And then shall be revealed that lawless one [*ho anomos*], whom the Lord Jesus shall slay with the breath of his mouth, and bring to nought by the manifestation of his coming.[57]

In the eschatological literature, *anomia* had clearly acquired a special meaning. *Anomia* was no longer the equivalent of sin or transgression; it described, instead, the evil forces opposing "the plan, the will of God." Such divine plan, de la Potterie argues, "is not 'the law,' but 'the truth.'"[58]

The special meaning of *anomia* in the eschatological context is easily detected in the passages that have been examined; yet, this is not the case for a passage from John's first Epistle regarded as "a difficult, yet important verse."[59] As I pointed out earlier, *anomia* and *hamartia* had, in the Old Testament, a close and often interchangeable meaning. The seeming identity of the two concepts becomes a stumbling block in 1 John 3:4, which reads: "Every one that doeth sin [*hamartia*] doeth also lawlessness [*anomian*]: and sin [*hamartia*] is lawlessness [anomia]." Standard interpretations of this passage have considered *anomia* in its etymological Greek sense, to mean lawlessness (indeed this is the rendering of the Revised Version).[60] The exegetes argued that John had in mind, here, the antinomians who "thought that the Law had no significance and who lived lives of licentiousness."[61] Such an interpretation, however, is faulty because, as Brown argues, "If the opponents were permissive about lawlessness, one would have expected the author to say, 'Lawlessness is sin,' not 'Sin is lawlessness.'"[62] Yet, it cannot be posited that John meant the same thing by the two terms *hamartia* and *anomia*: his statement would then be a meaningless tautology. De la Potterie comments: "The formula itself ... presupposes a progression of thought; the second term should have a new meaning, which is not contained in the first."[63]

The eschatological *anomia* offers a most plausible answer for the exegesis of the passage; it fits in the context of John's letter and it offers a way out of the seeming tautology. The passage can be seen as part of a logical unit, which R. E. Brown identifies in the verses 2:28–3:10. There, John makes nine antithetical statements which, side by side, characterize two groups of people: the children of God and the children of the devil.[64] Each statement consists of two parts: a description of a type of conduct and a description of the spiritual condition that accompanies such conduct. The first proposition of each pair describes "the Christian's way of living," and "the profound · reality that motivates and inspires such conduct."[65] The second proposition of each pair describes the conduct which is antithetical to the Christian way, and "indicates each time the spiritual state ... the sinner is not of God, has neither seen nor known him, is of the devil, and commits iniquity."[66]

From the overall structure of the text, de la Potterie writes, it can be argued that *anomia* "belongs to a series of expressions that describe the spiritual reality of the sinner, his situation, his interior state, and not so much the evil act he commits."[67] Going even further, de la Potterie claims that John had here in mind a specific and serious sin, since the literal Greek reads "Everyone who commits *the* sin, commits *the* iniquity [*anomian*]." According to the eschatological tradition, this specific sin can be identified with "the typical sin of the 'Antichrists,' who reject Christ, the son of God."[68] This is the sin of unbelief mentioned in Mark's apocalyptic passage: "This age of iniquity [*anomias*] and unbelief [*apistias*]."[69] The overall sense of John's statement is, then, recast in a new perspective. De la Potterie comments:

> In explaining *hamartia* by *anomia*, the author ... wishes to invite his fellow Christians to extend their moral point of view to the theological and religious spheres, and to consider the seriousness of non-belief and the refusal of light.[70]

The parallelism is clear: whoever commits the sin of unbelief does the work of iniquity and is of the devil. The devil is, in short, "the Iniquity," just as the Old Testament's Belial was *Anomia*. With such identification, the concept of *anomia* comes full circle.

The eschatological *anomia* constitutes the single most important meaning of the word in the New Testament; this is also the case in other writings of the early Christian period. In the *Didache*, the Teaching of the Twelve Apostles, we read: "For in the last days the false prophets and corrupters will come in swarms; the sheep will turn into wolves, and love will turn into hate. When lawlessness [*anomia*] is on the increase, men will hate and persecute and betray one another."[71] The passage is a clear echo of Matthew 24:12; however, the eschatological dualism is more forceful in the Epistle of Barnabas, who proclaims:

> There are Two Ways of instruction – as there are two powers – that of Light and that of Darkness. And there is a great difference betwen the Two Ways: the one is controlled by God's light-bringing angels, the other by angels of Satan. And as the latter is the Ruler of the present era of lawlessness [*anomia*], so the former is Lord from eternity to eternity.[72]

Clearly, the eschatological tradition was not limited to the New Testament writings, but encompassed early Christian thought in general; so much so, that the new meaning of *anomia* obscured the earlier meaning the word had in the Old Testament. When the Latin Fathers of the Church translated the Greek Bible and offered their exegetical commentaries in Latin, *anomia* was systematically translated with *iniquitas*, giving the word a broader meaning than the one it originally had in the Old Testament. To be sure, the two meanings were not antithetical ones; iniquity represented, instead, a broadening of the meaning of *anomia*. From simply indicating individual actions of sin in the Old Testament, *anomia* came to signify a broader moral condition which accounted for the specific transgressions. The changes in the meaning of *anomia* in Biblical literature parallel the changes which occurred in Greek thought, where *anomia* was first predicated of individual behavior, and then of a social or individual condition.[73] In both instances, *anomia* went from describing an act of transgression to indicating a formal pre-condition of transgressions.

With the ascendancy of Latin culture and the decline of the Greek language, *anomia* was slowly replaced by its Latin counterpart, *iniquitas*. Why, one would ask, was *iniquitas* chosen to render the Greek *anomia*? The answer is simple: *iniquitas* is the word that most closely resembles *anomia* both etymologically and semantically. I pointed out in the first chapter that the Greek root of *anomia*, *nomos*, had a broader meaning than the narrow one of "written law." *Nomos* was also the unwritten norm, both at the level of religious commands and at the level of socially approved behavior. In Latin, the unwritten norm, the ordering principle, was called *aequitas*, equity. Especially under the influence of Stoic philosophy and of its notion of a universal law of nature, *aequitas* came to be regarded, in Latin, as the ultimate standard of law and justice.[74] *Iniquitas* was, etymologically, the lack of *aequitas*, just as *anomia* was the lack of *nomos*.

In the Latin classics, *iniquitas* had a variety of meanings depending on the context in which the term was used. *Iniquitas* meant inequality, unevenness, difficulty, misfortune, but also injustice, unfairness, and unreasonableness. The Fathers of the Church capitalized on the latter meanings of the work to render the Greek *anomia*. In the Vulgate, the Latin version of the Bible, *iniquitas* meant abnormality, lawlessness, sin, opposition to the divine law, sinfulness, and iniquity.[75]

Although the religious meaning of *iniquitas* entered the Latin language rather late, it soon became the dominant meaning of the word. The English word iniquity, then, is clearly indebted to the Latin Bible for the dominant religious connotation of the word. Iniquity is a descendant of the Latin *iniquitas* and, therefore, of the Greek *anomia*. The religious overtones of *iniquitas*, after centuries of Latin culture, ended up obscuring the original meaning of "lawlessness," or "lack of equity," in favor of the notion of sin or transgression. During the Middle Ages, the concept of *anomia* all but disappeared, only to resurface in Western Europe during the Renaissance and the Reformation.[76] The rediscovery of *anomia* in this era will be discussed in the next chapter.

Apocalyptic, Sociological Thought and Anomie

The apocalyptic literature of late Judaism and early Christianity had a far-reaching effect on many religious movements in Western European history.[77] We can list the Montanism of the second century, the movement that developed around AD 1000 and came to be known as millenarism, the Franciscan Spirituals and the visions of Joachim of Floris in the thirteenth century, and the literature which identified the Pope of Rome with the Antichrist, during the Reformation. Yet, the spread of apocalyptic ideas went beyond the religious sphere, influencing Enlightenment thinkers, Romanticism writers, and the early socialists, among others.

In his article, "The Intellectuals and the Powers," Edward Shils argues that the revolutionary thrust of intellectuals can be referred back to "the *apocalyptic* or millenarian tradition." He comments:

> The disposition to distinguish sharply betwen good and evil and to refuse to admit the permissibility of any admixture, the insistence that justice be done though the heavens fall, the refusal to compromise or to tolerate compromise – all the

features of the doctrinaire politics, or the politics of the ideal – which are so common among modern intellectuals must be attributed in some measure at least to this tradition.[78]

The millenarian roots are self-evident in revolutionary Marxist theory, but they are just as much a component of other forms of not-so-revolutionary social theory. In fact, just as Marx's theory considers alienation to be the outcome of the evils of capitalism, Durkheim's theory envisions anomie as the characteristic sickness of modern industrial societies. As John Horton comments, both concepts are "ethically grounded metaphors for an attack on the economic and political organization of the European industrial middle classes."[79] The apocalyptic tone of Marx and Durkheim towards modern society is even more striking if we consider that the origins of the apocalyptic tradition are first found in late Judaism, and that both authors had access to this tradition. Marx's family belonged to the rabbinical elite in Germany; Durkheim's rabbinical ancestry in France went back eight generations and he was to become a rabbi himself. Marx's and Durkheim's social theories developed in opposite political directions, but they shared a common tradition of radicalism. For both, the modern this-worldly reality had deeply distorted the ideal relation between individual and society; the maladies such distortion produced were anomie and alienation.

Of the two authors, Durkheim is the one who most strikingly echoes the Judaic eschatological literature; Durkheim's sociological theory and his concept of anomie reflect his rabbinical background.[80] As Harry Alpert wrote, Durkheim "was fully conscious of his own predominantly ethical and religious preoccupations and frequently had occasion to recall to his colleagues of the *Année Sociologique* that he was, after all, the son of a Rabbi."[81]

At the theoretical level, Durkheim supported the notion of a human nature divided in itself between body and soul.[82] Each one of us, Durkheim argued, is a *Homo duplex* – partly sensual, partly rational. As far back as Plato we find the idea of a duality of human nature, but Durkheim remarks that no one has yet been able to offer an explanation for the opposition of body and soul. He comments:

> Doubtless, one can admit that because of the excellence that is attributed to it the world of ideas and of good contains within itself the reason for its existence; but how does it happen that outside of it there is a principle of evil, of darkness, of non-being?[83]

Human dualism, Durkheim claims, can be explained sociologically. He writes: "The duality of our nature is only a particular case of that division of things into the sacred and the profane, that is at the foundation of all religions."[84]

Durkheim's social theory in general rests on a constant dualism and opposition of antithetical elements. His description of *Homo duplex* contrasts the soul to the body and the sacred to the profane, but we find many more opposites. Steven Lukes points out that Durkheim's key sociological concepts "presuppose a number of central dichotomies, chief among them those between psychology and sociology, and between the social and the individual."[85] Lukes lists the opposition between moral rules and sensual appetites, concepts and sensations, sacred and profane, and normal and pathological.[86] These binary oppositions, I claim are the by-product of a basic eschatological dualism of good and evil. On the side of good are society, moral rules, concepts, the sacred, and the normal; on the side of evil are the individual, sensual appetites, sensations, the profane, and the pathological. If for Philo of Alexandria the *Logos* was the greater divider, for Durkheim it was society that created a distinction between sacred and profane in all aspects of life.

Not only is Durkheim's system of thought reminiscent of his Judaic background, his concept of anomie is also a by-product of such *Weltanschauung*; Durkheim's descriptions of anomie are highly suggestive in this regard. Anomie represents the polar opposite of morality; it is, in Durkheim's words, "the contradiction of all morality."[87] Human nature is anomic, irrational, insatiable and egoistic, whereas society is the source of norms, rationality, contentment and altruism. Anomie is, for Durkheim, the product of materialism and utilitarianism, of the profane and the this-worldly just as *anomia* was, for the Qumran authors, the product of the kingdom of darkness. Philo's doctrine of the conflict between the rational and the irrational in the human soul can be easily paraphrased to describe Durkheim's opposition of the individual to society. From society come goodness, virtue, wisdom, and righteousness, from the individual come wickedness, unrighteousness, and anomie. Durkheim's 1902 preface to *The Division of Labor* reiterates his radical ethical view: "anomy is an evil," he writes.[88]

The similarity between Durkheim's sociological theory and the themes of Judaic religious thought should not be surprising. It is in fact quite clear that in Durkheim's thought society takes the place of God as the source of moral rules for the individual. In *Moral Education*, Durkheim explains: "The parallel [between God and society] is indeed so complete that in itself it already constitutes a first demonstration ... that divinity is the symbolic expression of the collectivity."[89] In his book on Durkheim, Dominick La Capra stressed emphatically how for Durkheim, "Some quasi-religious basis was necessary for all morality and social solidarity."[90] Understandably, then, Durkheim's concept of anomie echoed the religious connotations of the word.

But we might ask at this point: if Durkheim's quasi-religious notion of anomie echoes his Judaic background, what about later usages of the word? Is there a religious counterpart to, say, Robert Merton's concept of anomie? The available literature would suggest that while Durkheim's theory of society (and of anomie) is clearly indebted to religious themes, Merton's theory is, instead, eminently secular. Whereas for Durkheim society is the religious entity which imposes itself on the individual in a god-like fashion, for Merton society exists only as a relationship of individuals to their culture – society does not have, for Merton, a supra-individual quality. In this sense we can link Merton's notion of anomie to a non-religious tradition, like the one of sophistic philosophy.

And yet there is a sense in which Merton's anomie echoes themes already developed in the religious literature we have examined. As Merton sees it, anomie can be observed at two levels: as either a condition of imbalance within the social structure, or as a rule-breaking behavior on the part of individuals. The rule-breaking behavior is seen as a consequence of the imbalance between the cultural ends and the institutional means. The apocalyptic writers and the Fathers of the Church distinguished betwen *anomia* as a condition of lawlessness and *anomia* as the act of transgression which ensues from the condition. Merton echoes them by distinguishing between the social condition which creates a pressure toward deviant behavior, and the individual modes of adaptation to such pressure. Clearly, the Biblical writers saw with religious eyes what Merton sees with sociological eyes.

Modern sociology is not all of a piece. The emphasis Durkheim put on society as a godly entity and on anomie as the evil enemy is at odds with Merton's more instrumental non-religious notions of society and anomie. However, it is reasonable to suggest that both traditions are indebted, to a greater or lesser extent, to some religious view. Our knowledge of the Biblical literature on anomie, then, cannot but improve our understanding of what anomie means to us today.

1   An exception is the recent article by Stjepan G. Meštrović, "Anomia and Sin in Durkheim's Thought," *Journal for the Scientific Study of Religion* 24 (June 1985):119–36. However, Meštrović offers a very superficial reading of the Biblical literature on *anomia*, and consequently he postulates a relationship between the Biblical and Durkheimian concepts which is marred with oversimplifications and inaccuracies.

2   Emile Durkheim, *The Division of Labor in Society*, trans. George Simpson (1933; reprinted New York: Free Press, 1964), 2.

3   *Manual of Discipline* 4:9 and 4:19; trans. Ignace de la Potterie. For most of the material on anomie in late Judaism and in some New Testament passages, I have relied on the excellent article by Ignace de la Potterie, "Sin Is Iniquity," first published in *Nouvelle Revue Theologique* 78 (1956):785–97. My source for this article is Ignace de la Potterie and Stanislaus Lyonnet, *The Christian Lives by the Spirit*, trans. John Morris (Staten Island: Alba House, 1971), 37–55. On the same topic see also Stanislaus Lyonnet and Leopold Sabourin, *Sin, Redemption, and Sacrifice* (Rome: Biblical Institute Press, 1970), pt 1.

4   Cf. John F. Schleusner, ed., *Novus Thesaurus Philologico-Criticus*, Vol. 1 (London: R. Priestley, 1822), 232–6.

5   Gerhard Kittel, *Theologisches Woerterbuch zum Neuen Testament*, Vol. 4 (Stuttgart: W. Kohlhammer, 1953–5), 1078.

6   See, for instance, Psalms 31:1, 58:4, 102:10.

7   T. V. Shorter writes: "The first person to publish the Bible in English was John Wiclif, in 1380. His translation was made from the Vulgate, as he was unacquainted with the original languages." *History of the Church of England* (London: Parker, 1838), 374. The first English translation from the Greek did not appear until 1539; by then, the English rendering of the Vulgate was already deeply rooted in the English language.

8   De la Potterie, "Sin Is Iniquity," 42.

9   Hilarius, *Tractatus super psalmos* Ps. 129:8. I have translated the quotations from Latin works.

10   Hieronimus, *Commentarius in Oseam prophetam* 8:13–14.

11   Ambrosius, *De apologia prophetae David* ch. 13, para. 62.

12   Isidorus, *Differentiarum* bk 1, para. 299.

13   Cf. Deuteronomy 15:9; 2 Samuel 22:5; Psalms 17:4.

14   Arnaldo Momigliano, "The Fault of the Greeks," in *Daedalus* 104 (Spring 1975):10.

15   ibid., 12.

16   ibid., 13.

17   For a description of the Hellenization of Judaism see Martin Hengel, *Jews, Greeks and Barbarians* (Philadelphia: Fortress Press, 1980).

18   For an overview of Hellenism see F. W. Walbank, *The Hellenistic*

World (Brighton: Harvester, 1981); Moses Hadas, *Hellenistic Culture* (New York: Columbia University Press, 1959).

19 Cf. Walbank, *Hellenistic World*, 159–75.
20 ibid., 167.
21 Momigliano, "The Fault of the Greeks," 17.
22 Erwing R. Goodenough, *An Introduction to Philo Judaeus* (1940; reprinted Oxford: Blackwell, 1962), 10.
23 Cf. Harry A. Wolfson, *Philo*, Vol. 1 (Cambridge, Mass.: Harvard University Press, 1948), 17–27 and 87–163.
24 ibid., 426.
25 ibid.
26 Genesis 3.
27 Philo, *Allegorical Interpretations* bk 3, 80.
28 Philo, *The Worse Attacks the Better* 141.
29 Philo, *The Posterity and Exile of Cain* 52.
30 ibid.
31 Cf. Wolfson, *Philo*, Vol. 1, 332–47.
32 Philo, *On Drunkenness* 143; trans. F. H. Colson and G. H. Whitakes.
33 ibid.
34 Wolfson, *Philo*, Vol. 1, 327.
35 ibid., 333; Philo, *Who Is the Heir* 130.
36 Max Weber, "Politics as a vocation," in H. H. Gerth and C. Wright Mills, *From Max Weber* (1946; reprinted New York: Oxford University Press, 1980), 120–1.
37 See, for instance, Matthew 5:17: "Think not that I came to destroy the law or the prophets: I came not to destroy, but to fulfil." On the topic see also Alexander Sand, "Die Polemic gegen 'Gesetzlosigkeit' im Evangelium nach Matthaeus und bei Paulus," *Biblische Zeitschrift* 14 (1970):112–25.
38 They are: Matthew 7:23; Romans 4:7; Hebrews 1:9, 8:12, 10:17; Mark 15:28; Luke 22:37.
39 In these cases, the adjective and the adverb are used, rather than the noun.
40 Stanislaus Lyonnet, "Christian freedom and the law of the spirit according to St. Paul," in de la Potterie and Lyonnet, *The Christian Lives by the Spirit*, 146.
41 Romans 4:15.
42 1 Timothy 1:9.
43 Lyonnet, "Christian freedom," 164.
44 Galatians 6:2 and 1 Corinthians 9:21.
45 Romans 2:15.
46 Both words translate iniquity; the first noun is masculine, the second feminine.
47 *Manual of Discipline* 3:18–21 and 4:23.
48 De la Potterie, "Sin Is Iniquity," 42.
49 ibid., 43.
50 *Manual of Discipline* 4:19.
51 De la Potterie, "Sin Is Iniquity," 44.

52 Cf. Wolfson, *Philo*, Vol. 2, 407–26.
53 Matthew 7:23.
54 Matthew 24:12.
55 Raymond E. Brown, *The Epistles of John* (Garden City: Doubleday, 1982), 400.
56 This passage is found at the end of Mark's Gospel in the Washington manuscript. Cited in de la Potterie, "Sin Is Iniquity," 45.
57 For a discussion of this passage in seventeenth-century England by the Laudian Robert Shelford, see Chapter 3 below, p. 77.
58 De la Potterie, "Sin Is Iniquity," 46.
59 ibid., 37.
60 For Renaissance discussions of John's passage see Chapter 3 below.
61 Brown, *The Epistles of John*, 399.
62 ibid.
63 De la Potterie, "Sin Is Iniquity," 46.
64 The nine parallel statements are:

Everyone who acts justly has been begotten by God
Everyone who has this hope based on Him makes himself pure
Everyone who acts sinfully is really doing iniquity
Everyone who abides in him does not commit sin
Everyone who does commit sin has never seen him
The person who acts justly is truly just
The person who acts sinfully belongs to the devil
Everyone who has been begotten by God does not act sinfully
Everyone who does not act justly does not belong to God
(Cf. Brown, *The Epistles of John*, 418).

65 De la Potterie, "Sin Is Iniquity," 48.
66 ibid., 48–9.
67 ibid., 49.
68 ibid., 50; cf. 1 John 2:22–3.
69 End of Mark's Gospel in the Washington manuscript.
70 De la Potterie, "Sin Is Iniquity," 52.
71 *Didache* 16:3–4; trans. James A. Kleist.
72 Barnabas 18:1–2; trans. James A. Kleist.
73 See Chapter 1 above, "Early Greek Thought and *Anomia*."
74 Milton R. Konvit writes: "The leading [Roman] jurisconsults were closely associated with Greek philosophy, especially with Stoicism, and it was they who came to see in the *jus gentium*, the law common to nations, an expression of the Stoic law of nature; and it was precisely through equity that the *jus gentium* and the law of nature touched and blended." Konvitz, "Equity in law and ethics," in *Dictionary of the History of Ideas*, ed. Philip P. Wiener, Vol. 2 (New York: Scribner, 1973), 151.
75 Cf. Franz Kaulen, *Sprachliches Handbuch zur biblischen Vulgata* (Hildesheim: Georg Olms Verlag, 1973), 54.
76 See Chapter 3 below, "Greek Learning in the Northern Renaissance."

77   Cf. Walter Schmithals, *The Apocalyptic Movement*, trans. John E. Steely (Nashville: Abingdon Press, 1975), 213–48.

78   Edward Shils, "The Intellectuals and the Powers," *Comparative Studies in Society and History* 1 (January 1958):20.

79   John Horton, "The Dehumanization of Anomie and Alienation," *British Journal of Sociology* 15 (December 1964):285.

80   Cf. Jean-Claude Filloux, "'Il ne faut pas oublier que je suis fils de rabbin,'" *Revue française de sociologie* 15 (April–June 1976):259–66.

81   Harry Alpert, *Emile Durkheim and His Sociology* (New York: Russell & Russell, 1939), 15.

82   Emile Durkheim, "The dualism of human nature and its social conditions," [1914], trans. Charles Blend, in Kurt H. Wolff, ed., *Emile Durkheim, 1858–1917* (Columbus: Ohio University Press, 1960), 325–40.

83   ibid., 333.

84   ibid., 335.

85   Steven Lukes, "Prolegomena to the Interpretation of Durkheim," *Archives Européennes de Sociologie* 12 (1971): 193.

86   ibid., 193–205.

87   Emile Durkheim, *Division of Labor* (note 2 above), 431n.

88   ibid., 5. A view of Durkheim's antinomies and of his concept of anomie similar to the one presented here is found in Dominick La Capra, *Emile Durkheim Sociologist and Philosopher* (Ithaca: Cornell University Press, 1972), 281–91.

89   Emile Durkheim, *Moral Education*, trans. Everett K. Wilson and Herman Schnurer (New York: Free Press, 1973), 104–5.

90   La Capra, *Emile Durkheim*, 288.

CHAPTER 3

Anomy and Reason in the English Renaissance

In the fourth chapter of *An Elegant and Learned Discourse of the Light of Nature*, published in 1652,[1] Nathaniel Culverwell set himself the task to define "the just notion of a *Law in general*":

> The Apostle *Paul*, to staine the pride of them that gloried in the Law, calls such things by the name of Law as were most odious and anomalous. Thus he tells us of *nomos thanatou*, & *nomos hamartias* [the law of death and the law of sin], though sin be properly *anomia* [lawlessness] ... And yet this is sure, that a rational creature is only capable of a Law, which is a moral restraint, and so cannot reach to those things that are necessitated to act *ad extremum virium* [to the limit of their passion].[2]

A secondary figure in the neo-Platonist school of Cambridge, Culverwell is only one of many English Renaissance writers who defined anomy[3] as they discussed law, morality, and human reason; in his *Discourse* Culverwell argued that the existence of laws presupposed human reason and the freedom of the will, and that, consequently, *anomia* was also a specifically human phenomenon.

Renaissance English writers produced an extensive literature defending the reasonableness of morality and the rational foundations of natural law, and debated heatedly the problems of law and lawlessness to the extent of coining an English word rendering the Greek *anomia* to express the nature and characteristics of violations of normative standards. Their notion of anomy was, understandably, quite different from our own.

The theories of natural law built on the long-standing tradition of Stoic philosophy and Scholastic doctrine, taking up arguments which had existed through the Middle Ages. In the English Renaissance, these theoretical efforts offered a philosophical foundation for the strengthening of the English Commonwealth and of its newly formed national church. Their efficacy was, however, short lived: by the end of the seventeenth century, the natural-law theory had taken on a radically different meaning. In John Locke's philosophy, the natural-law principles were no longer used to justify social institutions and religious hierarchies; rather, they had become an instrument for the justification of the inalienable rights of individuals. In Locke, the social realism of the Anglican Aquinas, Richard Hooker, coexisted uneasily with the voluntaristic individualism of Thomas Hobbes. Anglicans and neo-Platonists had vehemently attacked and criticized Hobbes's atheistic materialism, but they had been unable to undermine Hobbes's influence on later political thought. In Locke's theories, Hobbes and Hooker appear side by side, creating a blend of empiricism and rationalism which makes Locke's thought philosophically ambiguous and highly complex. Through Locke, however, the old dilemma of social thought had been synthesized and recast in a new light, allowing for its transition into the social thought of the modern era.

This chapter provides historical evidence on the discussions surrounding anomy as they took place in sixteenth- and seventeenth-century England, and it emphasizes the extent to which such discussions expressed an attempt by different religious factions to uphold contrasting ideological and moral claims. Concerning the discussions of anomy and the related issues of law and human nature, I outline three distinct approaches of Roman Catholics, Puritans, and Anglicans. Within this last group an articulate discussion of morality, law, and anomy took place; the Anglicans, in fact, acting as the heirs of the Erasmian tradition, carried into seventeenth-century England the humanistic notion of the centrality of reason in moral discourse. After the Anglicans the project was continued by the neo-Platonists of Cambridge and at the turn of the century it was recast into a new ethical theory in the work of John Locke.

By showing how the querelles about anomy were directed to an historically contingent answer to specific religious and moral problems of Renaissance England, I hope to clarify not only their but also our own contemporary notion of anomy.

Greek Learning in the Northern Renaissance

As I pointed out in the previous chapter, the word *anomia* all but disappeared during the Middle Ages. Considering this fact, we must clear up, as carefully as we can, the entry of the Greek word into the English language, before we can investigate the range of meanings of anomy in the English Renaissance.

The route of *anomia* is less clear and univocal than we would expect, for a host of words appear to have been confused with, or considered to be synonyms of, *anomia*. In the Latin language, alongside *anomia*, we find *anorma*, *anormis*, *anomus*, *anomalus*, and *anormalus*, all words whose meanings overlap, partly or totally, with *anomia*.[4] In relation to the "pseudo-etymological perversion" of the word *abnormal*, the *Oxford English Dictionary* pointed out the confusion between the Greek word *anomalos* and the Latin word *abnormis*;[5] a more general confusion seems to have occurred, however, involving the Greek words *anomalos* (anomalous) which literally means uneven or unequal, and *anomos* (anomic), which means without rule or law.[6] The problem was probably due less to philological or semantic ignorance than to a combination of closeness of spelling and similarity in the meaning of the two words. In fact anomaly came to signify a deviation from the rule, or an irregularity, just as anomy was equated with lawlessness or irregularity.

The confusion between the adjectives "anomalous" and "anomic," and therefore betwen the nouns "anomaly" and "anomy," persisted, at any rate, during the Renaissance.[7] In the *Catholicon* of Giovanni Balbi, a medieval Latin dictionary published for the first time in 1460,[8] *anomalos* meant "without law" or "without rule," and *anomia* meant "iniquity" or "without law"; the *Ortus Vocabulorum*, published in England in 1500, listed *anomia*, *anorma*, *anomalus*, and *anormalus* as having essentially all a similar meaning;[9] John Rider's *Bibliotheca Scholastica*, an English–Latin dictionary printed in 1589, listed *anomia* as a synonym for *anorma*, to be rendered in English as irregularity, without rule, disorder, and confusion. Still, Rider considered *anomia* an obsolete word, as he explained:

> These words that be old and out of use, I put them downe, not that in writing any Latine exercise, having other choice, thou shouldst use them: for to prevent that I brand them in the forehead with the figure of 3. But when thou readest them in their several authors, thou shouldest be eased of a farther toile, in knowing here their signification.[10]

Rider's warning was to have little effect, for in that very year, 1589, we find the first documented use of a new English word: *anomy*.[11]

In the Latin literature *anomia* appears sparsely yet steadily throughout the centuries,[12] but the rediscovery of *anomia* is to be sought in the revival of Greek learning that began in fourteenth-century Italy and moved, sometime after 1450, to northern Europe starting what has been called "the northern Renaissance."[13] Two main areas of study developed from the ground-work of the Italian Renaissance: Biblical and legal scholarship. Both were, at the onset, unified in the peculiarly humanistic approach of philology: "It is the belief in the autonomy of the word which made possible the whole movement of Humanism, in which so much importance was given to the word of the ancients and of Biblical writers."[14]

The Roman arch-philologist, Lorenzo Valla (1400–57), was able to provide through the *passpartout* of language an innovative critical analysis of legal doctrines (in his *Epistola ad collegium iurisconsultorum neapolitanorum*),[15] as well as a groundbreaking philological criticism of crucial passages of the New Testament (in his *Annotationes*). But the leading exponent of classical humanism in northern Europe was Erasmus of Rotterdam. In his 1505 preface to the first printing of Valla's *Annotationes* (written *c.* 1448), Erasmus vehemently attacked those who in his time thought the grammarian had no place in the interpretation of the Scriptures:

> For it happens that all their straining and struggling to present themselves as very learned only makes them look very foolish in the eyes of those who know their languages, and all their uproar proves to be an empty balloon as soon as one Greek word enters into the discussion.[16]

Erasmus's enthusiasm for Valla's work led him, in a little over ten years, to prepare his own textual analysis of the New Testament, the *Novum Instrumentum*, published in 1516. This was to be the first Greek edition of the Scriptures, accompanied by Erasmus's own Latin translation and commentary.[17] Erasmus approached the Bible with a genuinely humanistic perspective as he recognized the value of philology and provided a unified interpretation of the Scriptures through the combined use of classical learning and human reason. He upheld the "primacy of the moral meaning of scripture"; his intent was not the creation of doctrinal conflicts, but the "upbuilding of the moral life."[18]

The Greek *anomia* and its grammatical variations first attracted the attention of Renaissance writers as they commented on selected Biblical passages. Coming across the passage from Romans 2:12, "For so many as have sinned without the law shall also perish without the law," Erasmus comments: "The Greek version is more pleasant with its adverb *anomos*, as saying, illegally or lawlessly, which in both parts is used. In fact, *exlegem* [illegal or lawless], is the rendering of the adjective *anomos*."[19]

Because of his Renaissance outlook Erasmus could indulge in

comments about the pleasantness of the adverb "anomically." It was, however, in a quite different mood that Martin Luther commented on the same passage from Romans:

> The Apostle crushes the pride of the heathen who gloried themselves in the excuse that they had not known the Law ... Paul tells them: "Oh no! They shall perish without law," just as also they are saved without the Law ... The human will (*by nature*) always goes against the Law; it would rather do the opposite (of its demands), if only it could, even if (outwardly) man does what the law commands.[20]

The philological concern was absent in Luther's reading of the Scriptures. He was no humanist; rather, he was overwhelmed by the notion of a totally corrupted human nature and by the idea that only faith in God (*sola fides*) could supply a way to salvation. Writing his commentary on John's first epistle in 1527, Luther needed to clarify the meaning of the Greek *anomia* as it appeared in 1 John 3:4; "Everyone who commits sin commits lawlessness [*anomian*], and sin is lawlessness [*anomia*]." Luther argued:

> A difficult passage. For John distinguishes sharply between sin (*hamartia*) and lawlessness (*anomia*). On the other hand, however, he uses the two words interchangeably ... "Sin" is a word used simply and in general to refer to all vices. "Lawlessness," however, is that which goes so far that one's neighbor is made to stumble.[21]

These early instances of comments about *anomia* show, from the outset, two distinct approaches to the Scriptures (that will continue in later English writings) of humanist scholars on one side and of doctrinaire theologians on the other. The former aimed at the harmonization of reason and religion; the latter upheld the unbridgeable gap between God and the human nature. The confrontation between these two positions took place when Erasmus officially attacked Luther's doctrine in *On the Freedom of the Will*, in 1524. A year later, with *The Bondage of the Will*, Luther "quickly produced an exceptionally violent reply, in which he developed a comprehensive statement of his own theological positions, and included a definitive presentation of his own anti-humanist and ultra-Augustinian doctrine of man."[22] It was in the context of conflicting theories about human nature, reason, and the freedom of the will that discussions of *anomia* were brought to the fore in defense of the different religious factions in Renaissance Europe.

Anglicizing Anomia

Biblical scholarship had the upper hand in the rediscovery of *anomia* as Renaissance writers examined the Scriptures very closely and were bound to acknowledge the Greek term *anomia* as having some specific meaning; yet Biblical scholarship was paralleled in its enterprise by the work of legal scholars. Although its direct effect on the actual rediscovery of *anomia* was minor, humanistic jurisprudence was crucial in providing the ground for a theory of law and morality in which reason and reasonableness would become leading elements.[23]

The outstanding scholarship of secular Greek learning was shown in, among others, Thomas Linacre's translations of Aristotle's works, Erasmus's Latin renderings of Plutarch, and Guillaume Budé's extensive *Commentarii Linguae Graecae* (1529). The most tangible contribution to the diffusion of Greek learning in a systematic fashion was offered by Henry Estienne (1531–98) who, as Sandys writes, literally "ruined himself over the publication of his *Thesaurus Linguae Graecae* (1572) ... the original work has been re-edited in modern times, and, as a Greek lexicon on a large scale, it is still unsurpassed."[24] It is with this solid background of Biblical, legal, and philological scholarship that writers in Renaissance Europe provided the groundwork for an articulate discussion about *anomia* and reason by English writers.

The Biblical writings are the chief source of discussion about *anomia*, but they are not the only source. In fact, the first documented use of the English word *anomy* is not from a Biblical but from a legal text, from William Lambarde's *Archeion*, completed in 1591 and published for the first time in 1635.[25] The author, an Elizabethan jurist, participated in the movement that followed the first wave of humanistic jurisprudence, when, from the critique of Roman law, legal scholars generated a new approach based on a historical method, the famous *mos gallicus* of Andrea Alciato (1492–1550). Quentin Skinner describes this phenomenon as follows:

> One suggestion which then arose, particularly amongst the jurists themselves, was that since the only indigenous forms of law known to northern Europe were the customary laws of each individual country, it followed that these should be systematised and applied as the only alternative basis for assessing the proper distribution of legal obligations and rights.[26]

Because of his concern about offering a historical justification for the English judicial system, Lambarde was called the "prince of legal antiquaries," the wealth of his sources ranging from the medieval jurists Henry Bracton, Ranulph de Glanville, and John Britton, to the modern historians Polydor Vergil and Matthew Paris.[27]

Lambarde's *Archeion* is considered to be the best account on the English High Courts in his time. The *Archeion's* crucial task was to show the historical and rational justifications of a peculiarly English system of law, which combined a tradition of Common Law with the High Courts' administration of Equity.[28] At a time when the reception of Roman Law had succeeded in Germany, when Cardinal Reginald Pole was describing the English Law as "barbaric stuff" and was asking that Roman Law be adopted instead,[29] Lambarde wanted to provide both a historical and a jurisprudential rationale for the preservation of Common Law and Equity. The "Conflicts Betweene the Law Absolute and Ordinarie" were not recent ones, Lambarde claimed, since they could be traced back to the Magna Carta, Henry VI, and Edward I.[30] Furthermore, the combination of common law and equity was justified not only on historical grounds but also on rational grounds.

> For ... it followeth by reason, that commonly and regularly the *positive Law* should bee put in ure, and that *Equitie* should not bee appealed unto but only in rare and extraordinary matters, least on the one side, if the *Iudge* in *Equitie* should take *Iurisdiction* over all, it should come to passe (as *Aristotle* saith) that a *Beast* should beare the rule ... And on the other side, if onely streight Law should bee administered, the helpe of GOD which speaketh in that *Oracle* of *Equitie*, should be denied unto men that neede it.[31]

For Lambarde, the excessive literalism of the law was as dangerous as the excessive use of Equity. His position reiterated Aristotle's teaching in the *Nichomachean Ethics*: "And this is the nature of the equitable, namely, a correction of the law insofar as the law errs because it is or must be stated universally."[32]

Discussing the role of the Star Chamber and the need of mediating between its abuse and its abolition, Lambarde defined *anomy*:

> What is then to be said? Shall the King and his *Councell* open a Court for all sorts of Pleas that be determinable by the course of Common Law? That were to set an *Anomy*, and to bring disorder, doubt, and incertaintie over all: Shall no helpe at all

bee sought for at the hands of the King, when it cannot be found in the Common Law? That were to stop his eares at the crie of the *oppressed*, and would draw wrath and punishment from Heaven. Betweene these two extremes, *Medio tutissimus ibis*, there lieth a meane, that will both uphold the *Majestie* of the King, maintaine the *Authoritie* of the *Common Courts*, and succour the distressed *Client* in his greatest necessitie.[33]

Anomy fed admirably into Lambarde's ideological justification of the "golden mediocritie"; his notion is not only the first, but also a sophisticated example of English Renaissance writings about anomy. For Lambarde anomy was the outcome of the lack of normative standards, the absence of shared norms from which disorder, doubt and uncertainty would ensue. He thought of anomy in a classical Greek sense as the *absence* of a reliable standard, and he foresaw the dangers entailed in the abolition of "ruled law and bounded jurisdiction."[34] Still, Lambarde's attempt to reconcile conflicting jurisprudential claims parallels the aims of English humanists in all areas of study, whether legal, Biblical, or moral; for he was united with them in searching, through knowledge, a reasonable, enlightened choice of action.

Apart from the jurist William Lambarde, Renaissance English theologians appear to have been the principal discussants of "anomy." In their writings anomy appears either with the -y or with the -ie ending; still, both versions are English, neither is French in its origin.[35] Moreover, the same writers use either English or Greek scripts of the word; or, as it is often the case, both English and Greek forms appear side by side in the same passage. But whatever spelling they used, English writers realized that anomy was a term with a specialized meaning.

The transition from a Greek script to an English one took place as the commentators of Biblical texts encountered the word *anomia* in the Greek Scriptures, especially in the key passage of 1 John 3:4, "Everyone who commits sin commits lawlessness [*anomian*], and sin is lawlessness [*anomia*]." In this regard, it would appear that the rediscovery of *anomia* hinged, essentially, on the fortuitous use of the Greek word *anomia* by John; this, however, is not the case. As I showed in the previous chapter, John's passage was meant as a definition of sin as the work of the forces of evil; seventeenth-century theologians, however, failed to locate John's statement in its eschatological context. Instead, they took *anomia* to indicate a transgression of the law or a deviation from it. This, in turn, entailed the need of a definition of what law was being transgressed and of what the formal requisites were for

71

such transgression to have the quality of sin. These were the crucial questions addressed by English theologians in their discussion about *anomia*.

In 1582 an English version of the New Testament was published by the English Catholics from their College of Rhemes (Reims) in France, who wanted to provide the public with an alternative to the numerous versions of the Scriptures disseminated by their Protestant counterparts.[36] Coming upon 1 John 3:4, the Rhemists offered their exegesis:

> *Sinne is iniquitie.* Iniquitie is not taken here for wickedness, as is commonly used both in Latin and in our language, as is plaine by the Greeke word *anomia*, signifying nothing els but a swarving or declining from the straight line of the law of God or nature. So that the Apostle meaneth, that every sinne is an obliquitie or defect from the rule of the law: but not contrarie, that every such swarving from the law should be properly a sinne, as the Heretikes untruely gather, to prove that concupiscence remaining after Baptisme is a very sinne, though we never give our consent unto it.[37]

The interpretation of the Rhemists was that anomy described a lack of conformity with the law, without however being a transgression of the law. Such definition was functional to two ideological claims put forth by the Roman Catholics: on the one side they wanted to provide Biblical support to their distinction between a venial and a mortal sin, where the former was a simple "swarving" from the law and the later a fully-fledged transgression; on the other side they wanted to refute the Protestant doctrine of total depravity and sinfulness of human nature. For the Rhemists a transgression of the law required the express consent of the individual in order for it to have the force of sin; their interpretation, understandably, was immediately challenged by the English Puritans.

A rebuttal came from the quarrelsome Puritan, William Fulke, who wrote a *Defense of the Sincere and True Translation of the Holie Scriptures* only a year after the appearance of the Rhemists' *New Testament*. Some years after his death in 1589, Fulke's more extensive rebuttal of the Rhemists' text was published; there, on 1 John 3:4, we read:

> If sinne be every transgression of the Law, it followeth that every transgression of the Law is sinne, and so meaneth the Apostle by the word *adikia*, as wel as by the word *anomia* ... Beda not only taketh all to be sinne, which is iniquitie, and is contrarie to the

equitie of Gods Law, but also he compteth even the corruption of innocencie, which is of infirmitie, to be sinne, therefore all concupiscence that is contrarie to the Law of God, which S. Paul expresly called sinne.[38]

Fulke's argument was built on a parallel reading of 1 John 3:4 and 5:17. Whereas the former passage read "*hamartia estin anomia,*" the latter read "*adikia hamartia estin.*" In the English translation, however, as in the Latin Vulgate, both *anomia* and *adikia* had been rendered with the same word: "iniquitas" in Latin, "iniquity" in English. On this ground, Fulke was able to claim the interchangeability of the two sentences of John; but the Rhemists's argument was based exactly on the use of two different Greek words by John, as they had written: "And though in the 5 chapter folowing vers. 17. the Apostle turne the speache, affirming every iniquitie to be sinne, yet, there the Greeke word is not the same as before, *anomia*, but *adikia*, by which it is plaine that there he meaneth by *iniquitie*, mans actual and proper transgression which must needes be a sinne."[39]

Fulke's criticism was not sufficient to undermine the Rhemists' version at the theological level, nor were the Puritans able to gain much political clout under the reign of James I. The diatribes over interpretations of the New Testament continued as the Puritan leaders deemed it necessary to publish posthumously, in 1618, Thomas Cartwright's *Confutation of the Rhemists' Translation*. There, Cartwright had written on that same passage from 1 John:

> The Apostle hereby aggravateth the nature of sin, for that it is against the law, of a breach thereof: and these wretches to maintain the guiltines of sin, and the impunity thereof make the breach of the law less heynous then sinne ... *Augustine* is flat against them, saying, *that the concupiscence of the flesh is both sinne, because there is disobedience against the rule of the minde, and the cause of sinne through his want that consenteth, and infection of him that is borne.* Whereunto agreeth *Augustines* definition of sinne, which amongst other sinnes maketh *concupiscence* sinne also.[40]

It is evident, from both Fulke's and Cartwright's comments, how far apart their interpretation was from that of the Catholics. On one side the Rhemists deemed it appropriate to interpret *anomia* through its philological meaning as a "declination" from the norm; on the other side, the Puritans recognized no other authority, in the interpretation of the Scriptures, than the Bible itself; consequently, they rejected the philological subtleties of the

Rhemists. The disagreement was not a matter of philological nuances, but a substantive divergence in the way each side addressed the issues of human nature, law, and reason. If, as the Puritans claimed, the individual was corrupt by nature and could not help but sin in anything he did, the attempt to enlighten one's moral choice through knowledge would be doomed to failure. On the other hand the Rhemists' notion that the condition of *anomia* was less serious than fully-fledged iniquity undermined the idea that the individual should strive to achieve higher moral goals at all times. The claim to the existence of an identifiable English Church, however, "required, above all things, a theology which should teach that the law which was expressed in Church discipline and Church organization, was the law of God, and therefore the law of reason."[41] The task of indicating a *via media*, a middle ground, fell to the Anglicans, especially to their ideological leader, Richard Hooker (1553–1600).

Anglicans, Neo-Platonists, Anomy, and Reason

Richard Hooker's majestic *Of the Laws of Ecclesiastical Polity* is much more than a legalistic statement of the Anglican *via media* against the extremes of Calvinism and Catholicism ... Presenting a picture of a rational man in a rational universe, he rehabilitates – in terms neither sentimental nor wishful – the classical Christian concept of right reason, and declares the ontological reality and harmony of nature, reason, and morality.[42]

It is appropriate, in discussing the context of Renaissance England's "moral discourse," to consider Hooker's *Laws* as the synthesis of the English tradition of Erasmian humanism, as well as the point of departure for a prolific line of thought which emphasized the role of reason in ethics and law. Hooker went beyond the crucial theological confrontation between Calvinists and Roman Catholics by raising the more general issue of the relationship between the religious sphere, the political society, and the individual. He had to begin, then, by proposing a systematic classification of "laws and their several kinds in general."

Human reason is at the center of Hooker's system of laws: his views on theology, salvation, justification and Church order are all

74

informed by the notion that only through reason is it possible to reconcile what otherwise would seem conflicting claims and insoluble contradictions. "No doubt if men had beene willing to learne how many lawes their actions in this life are subject unto, and what the true force of ech law is, all these controversies might have dyed the very day they were first brought forth."[43] Against the Calvinists and zealous Puritans on one side and the Roman Catholics on the other, Hooker wanted to point out how different spheres of legislation pertained to different areas of human conduct. The vehement polemics from both sides, he explained, stemmed from their inability to disentangle the religious from the political and the individual spheres.[44] Of the Calvinists, Hooker says: "For whereas God hath left sundry kindes of lawes unto men, and by all those lawes the actions of men are in some sort directed: they hold that one onely lawe, the scripture, must be the rule to direct in all thinges."[45] Hooker dissents from the Calvinists since their claim strips human reason of its ability to distinguish between good and evil. Rather, he writes, "The waies of well-doing are in number even as many as are the kindes of voluntary actions: so that whatsoever we do in this world and may doe it ill, we shew our selves therein by well doing to be wise."[46]

Likewise, Hooker rejected the radical position of the Puritan Cartwright that "Whatsoever is not done by the worde of God is sinne."[47] To Cartwright, Hooker replied that only if we can reasonably discriminate between good and evil can we willingly obey or transgress the law: "Amongst creatures in this world, only mans observation of the lawe of his nature is *Righteousness*, only mans transgression *Sinne* ... *take away the will, and all actes are equall*."[48] Hooker points out that an act lacking the will of the agent cannot be considered a sin or a transgression of the law.

> What we doe against our wills, or constrainedly, we are not properly said to do it, because the motive cause of doing it is not in our selves, but carrieth us, as if the winde should drive a feather in the aire, we no whit furthering that whereby we are driven.[49]

For Hooker, laws are based on human reason and presuppose the furtherance of a reasonable good; they also presuppose the freedom of the human agent. In this respect, Hooker could not be any farther apart from the Calvinists, who proclaimed the total depravity of human nature (including the intellect which can suffer from pride) and the irreparable gap between religious and human justification. Hooker stood in the tradition of Aristotle and Aquinas; he was, within the English Renaissance, the intellectual bridge between the early Oxford Reformers (Erasmus, Colet, and Thomas More) and the neo-Platonists of Cambridge (Whichcote, Smith, Cudworth, and Henry More).[50]

Hooker offered a paradigm on which the Anglican Church could rely in answering questions about the nature of laws, the relations between transgression, reason, and free will, and the nature of sin. The concept of anomy was to become useful for the ideological purposes of the Anglicans, since it allowed them to make critical distinctions concerning the moral relation between actions and rules. It is appropriate, therefore, that in their Biblical discussions Anglican writers should have been the first churchmen to use anomy in its English script.[51]

The first instance of such use is found in Bishop Joseph Hall's *No Peace with Rome*, published c. 1625. There, Hall "maintained that the Catholic Church, of which the Church of England formed a part, had fallen into corruptions, of which the Church of England had now purged herself."[52] Arguing against the Catholics' distinction between venial and mortal sin, Hall wrote:

> If we have respect unto the infinite mercy of God ... there is no sin, which, to borrow the words of Prudentius, is not venial: but in respect of the anomy or disorder, there is no sin, which is not worthy of eternal death ... St. John's word is *All sin* is *anomia*, transgression of the Law ... Our Rhemists, subtle men, can no more abide the proposition converted, than themselves. "All sin indeed," say they, "is *anomia, a transgression of the Law*; but every transgression of the Law is not sin." The Apostle, therefore, himself turns it for us: *All unrighteousness*, saith he, *is sin*.[53]

The approach of Bishop Hall exemplifies the *via media* pursued by those who adhered to the conciliatory position of the Anglican Church; if the Rhemists had defined *anomia* as a "swarving" from the law, and the Puritans had proclaimed everything done outside the faith in Christ to be *anomia* and sin, Hall pointed out the mistake of the Catholics without subscribing to the extreme view of Puritans and Calvinists. On this ground, Hall proposed a dual interpretation of anomy as both a *condition* of disorder and an *act* of transgression; he strongly rejected the Catholics' underestimation of *anomia*, by asking: "What manner of sins do they put in the rank of venial? Drunkenness, adultery, angry curses or blasfemy ... He must needs be shamelessly wicked, that abhors not this licentiousness."[54] On the other hand, he warned: "That there are certain degrees of evil, we both acknowledge and teach ... some offences are more heinous than others."[55]

In line with Hooker's intentions, the goal of the Anglicans was to mediate the sectarian differences of the English Church through reasonableness, but their mediation was rejected by the zealous doctrinaires.[56] With the advent of Charles I and his alliance with the English episcopacy, the unification of the Church of England was sought through political persecution and repression of Protestant dissenters. For William Laud, the Arminian prelate who in 1633 became Archbishop of Canterbury, the Church of England "was founded upon the twin pillars of the royal prerogative and the divine commission of the episcopacy."[57]

Many Anglican bishops were critical of Laud's uncompromising policy (among them Joseph Hall and James Ussher) and favored a more tolerant approach to the sectarian differences within the English Church. Still, there developed at the same time an Anglo-Catholic movement on Laud's side that upheld a position closer to the Roman Church and harshly critical of the Puritan and Calvinist groups. Among the Anglo-Catholics, known also as "Arminians," was a Suffolk priest, Robert Shelford, who argued on the Laudian side with "A Treatise showing the Antichrist not to be yet come," published posthumously in 1635. In his work, Shelford took up the verses from 2 Thessalonians in order to show, through their analysis, that the Antichrist could not be indentified with the Pope.[58] Such a position was sponsored by Laud against the Calvinist tradition: "No man can challenge me that I hold the Pope not to be Antichrist ... The Church of England hath not positively resolved him to be so."[59] Upon 2 Thessalonians 2:7, Shelford comments:

> Here is demonstrated Antichrists seed and originall, which is *iniquitie*. Iniquitie in the Greek text is *anomia, anomie* or a life without law ... and therefore their anomie S. Paul calls *a mysterie*. Anomie began in the Apostles dayes, and continued to Mahomets time.[60]

Then, commenting on the following verse, "And then shall that wicked be revealed," Shelford explains:

> *That wicked* in the Greek text is *ho anomos*, id est, exlex, that outlaw; for he shall live without law ... His will shall be his law, as if he were a God ... And lastly, because Antichrist is called of the Apostle *ho anomos, the man without law*: and the Turk hath no other law to rule his people by, but his own will.[61]

Shelford's position was symptomatic of the Laudian divines who "while rejecting papal claims and the more recent developments of Italian and Spanish theology ... still felt themselves and their church to be Catholic ... The English Church, for Laud, was Catholic yet reformed, the *via media* between Geneva and Rome."[62] Still, Shelford's readiness to compromise was criticized by more orthodox Anglicans, like Bishop Ussher (1581–1646) who complained about Cambridge "publishing unto the world such rotten stuff as Shelford hath vented in his five discourses."[63] For better or worse, the Laudian policy aimed at the unification of the English Church had the opposite effect of strengthening the Puritan opposition and bringing about their open revolt.[64] The Civil War gave the Puritans the upper hand; yet the so-called Latitudinarians and the Anglicans who fled abroad continued to promote in their writings the reasonableness of the *via media*.[65]

It is with the writings of one of the exiled Anglicans, John Bramhall, Bishop of Derry (called "the Irish Laud"), that anomy found its most sophisticated discussion in Renaissance England; again, the discussion of anomy was related with the key issues of human nature, reason, and free will. In 1645 Bramhall, exiled in Paris, was arguing against no less an opponent than Thomas Hobbes. Their debate on liberty and necessity became public[66] and has been described as "one of the best philosophical duels."[67] The subject of their controversy was Hobbes's radical determinism, which implied, at the moral level, the absence of freedom of the human will, and therefore the notion that God was the first cause of all good and evil in the world. Bramhall was concerned with the moral implications of Hobbes's deterministic theory, as he wrote:

> Though I honour T.H. for his person and for his learning, yet I must confess ingenuously, I hate this doctrine from my heart ... It makes the First Cause, that is, God Almighty, to be the introducer of all evil and sin into the world, as much as man; yea, more than man.[68]

Bramhall argued that even if God is the first cause of the law and the first cause of human action, still the transgression of the law is the outcome of individual will. He argued: if God were the cause of sin that would eliminate the formal reason of sin; "for if sin be good and just and lawful, it is no more evil, it is no sin, no anomy"[69]. To demonstrate his point, Bramhall offered an example:

> The prince is the author or cause of the law, and the prince is the cause of the judiciary action of the judge in general ... but the prince is not the cause of the irregularity, or repugnance, or non-conformity, or contrariety which is between the judge's action

and the law, but the judge himself ... he is the only cause of the anomy or irregularity.[70]

In his argument, Bramhall wanted to emphasize the *formal quality* of sin or anomy; the notion of sin entailed not only the existence of the law and of human action but also, crucially, the *relation between law and action* – a relation that would account for the action's conformity or irregularity. Such relation, which he called *anomy*, was the *form* of sin. Bramhall had previously stated: "to speak properly, the free will of man is not the efficient cause of sin, sin having no true entity or being in it; but rather the *deficient* cause."[71] Bramhall drew support for his claim in the crucial passage from 1 John 3:4.

> Sin is nothing but the irregularity of the act. So St. John defineth it in express terms, *hē hamartia estin hē anomia* – "sin is anomy," or "an irregularity," or "a transgression of the Law." For "sin is nothing else but a declination from the rule," that is, an irregularity ... An irregular action is sin materially; irregularity is sin formally.[72]

Bramhall wanted to rebuke Hobbes's determinism because of its consequences at the ethical level; yet, Bramhall's *Animadversions* can also be understood as a rebuttal of the Puritan doctrines. Hobbes's position in relation to the basic issues of human nature, reason, and freedom of the will was in fact very close to the position of Puritans and Calvinists.[73] For them as for Hobbes, the individual had an essentially corrupt nature; human reason was nothing more than reasoning about words, a nominalism which had little to do with reality; and the human will was powerless since every human action was predetermined by God. In addition, Hobbes, like the Puritans and the Calvinists, expressed a deep distrust of classical philosophy: "And I believe that scarce anything can be more absurdly said in natural philosophy, than that which now is called *Aristotle's Metaphysics*; nor more repugnant to government, than much of that he hath said in his *Politics*; nor more ignorantly, than a great part of his *Ethics*."[74] For Hobbes, as for Calvin and their common forerunner William of Ockham, God was above and beyond human reason: He did not command actions that were good; instead, He made them good by commanding them. This amounted to saying that not reason, but the power of the sovereign compelled human action. Of course Hobbes was not deaf to Bramhall's arguments and their internal consistency. In his 1668 Latin version of the *Leviathan* Hobbes recalls the terms of the controversy:

They admit that God is the first cause of things and actions, and then they try to make their argument consistent by referring to Aristotle who calls sin *anomian*, that is, the very incongruity with the law, a pure privation, not a deed fact or action.[75] Therefore, while they recognize that God is the cause of every deed and of the law, they deny that he is the cause of their incongruency.[76]

The controversy between John Bramhall and Thomas Hobbes gained enormous popularity, and anomy acquired a legitimate place in the English language. In his 1755 *Dictionary*, Samuel Johnson could list the word "anomy" as meaning "breach of law." He quoted Bramhall: "If sin be good, and just, and lawful, it is no more evil, it is no sin, no *anomy*."[77]

The rediscovery of *anomia* in Renaissance England was essentially the result of a confrontation between religious and philosophical factions as they dealt with crucial ethical issues: law, transgression, free will, and the role of human reason in the moral sphere. The temptation to attribute such a rediscovery to a reaction of Renaissance humanists against the dangerous ethical doctrines of the Reformation is great; however, it would be inappropriate to characterize all the humanists as anti-Reformation or all the Puritans as anti-humanist. Even in the face of widely divergent positions about the character of human nature and the role of reason, the different religious groups drew their ideological waters at the same well of classical culture and philosophy. Quentin Skinner, for one, has pointed at "the almost paradoxical extent to which the Lutherans as well as radical Calvinists relied on a scheme of concepts derived from the study of Roman law and the scholastic moral philosophy."[78] The notion of *adiaphora*, the *res mediae* or things indifferent, is one of the instances in which a concept was adopted by different religious and political factions both in England and on the Continent to justify their own position.[79] Describing its vicissitudes, Skinner argues that although it would be erroneous to see the notion of *adiaphora* as shifting from a Lutheran concept with Melanchton to a strong point of Anglican doctrine with Starkey and later with Hooker, "There is no doubt, however, that Starkey was able to make a fruitful use of the concept at a crucial moment, as a means of steering a *via media* between the position of the radical Lutherans and the traditional Catholics."[80]

The discussions about anomy offered an exemplary albeit secondary instance of how classical ideas were used to justify opposite religious and moral views. We saw three distinct interpretations of anomy that were functional to the ideological claims of three different religious factions. For the Rhemists, anomy was a *condition* of disorder, or "swerving" from the law, which justified their doctrine of a venial and mortal sin; for the Puritans, anomy was equal to *sin* as such, supporting their view of a hopelessly sinful human nature. Between these two extremes, and attempting to mediate between them, were the Anglicans, who upheld a more sophisticated view of anomy which encompassed both the *formal* condition and the *substantive* act of transgression. They sought to overcome the impasse of an uncompromising confrontation between Roman Catholics and Puritans. Peculiar to the Anglican approach, on this account, was the effort made to harmonize conflicting doctrinal claims through the use of reason. The Anglicans' position reiterated the main goal of Renaissance humanists, to integrate classical moral philosophy and Christian ethics.[81]

During the tumultuous years of the Civil War and of Cromwell's Protectorate, the ideological thrust of Anglican thought persists in England with the writing of the Cambridge neo-Platonists. They are much less vociferous than their predecessors for obvious reasons, for "The waves of political, philosophical and theological controversy swirling around them break in upon them from all sides, and threaten finally to engulf the very existence of the ideas they represent."[82] Still, the neo-Platonists stand by the classical learning and represent a continuation of the humanistic tradition found in the Oxford Reformers (Colet, Erasmus, and Thomas More), and in the Anglican Aquinas, Richard Hooker. Cassirer writes: "Here again, in the midst of the serious religious and sectarian disputes of the seventeenth century, of the political and spiritual crises of English puritanism, the old humanistic ideal of religion reappears in all its purity and power."[83]

Nathaniel Culverwell's *An Elegant and Learned Discourse of the Light of Nature* is an exemplary instance of the neo-Platonists' sophisticated and comprehensive discussion of the relations between law, reason, and freedom of the will; it also offers, in the context of these issues, a valuable discussion of anomy. The *Discourse*, from which I quoted at the beginning of this chapter, was "conceived at a time when a flood of popular literature was stridently arguing the traditional Antinomian position that Gospel liberty had overcome the law."[84] In his *Discourse* Culverwell expounded the Biblical verse, "The understanding of man is the Candle of the Lord,"[85] presenting a detailed argument in defense of human reason as the basis of law and morality. The debate on whether the law was based on reason or will was an old one, dating back to Ockham's criticism of Thomistic realism. Culverwell espoused, in his *Discourse*, the position outlined in Suarez's *De Legibus*: law was "founded in reason and formalized by will."[86] The neo-Platonists of Cambridge were firmly opposed to a voluntaristic ethics because it led "on the one hand to the 'atheism' of Hobbes, and on the other to an anti-humanistic, anti-rational fideism rooted in the firm ground of Calvinism."[87] For the neo-Platonist Culverwell, human reason was, together with the will, a *sine qua non* of law. His definition of *anomia*, then, was a corollary of this main axiom, as Culverwell argued.

> A Law 'tis founded in intellectuals, in reason not in sense, it supposes a Noble and free-borne creature, for where there is no Liberty, there's no Law, a Law being nothing else but a Rational restraint and limitation of absolute Liberty ... By all this you see that among all irrational beings there is no *anomia* [lawlessness], and therefore no *hamartia* [guilt], and therefore no *timória* [punishment]: from whence it flows that the Law of *Nature* is built upon Reason.[88]

A few pages later, distinguishing between positive and natural law, Culverwell points out that in the former actions are evil because they are forbidden by the law, whereas in the latter they are forbidden because they are evil in themselves (*mala per se*).[89] Therefore, if these latter are "so intolerably bad, as that they cannot but be forbidden," there has to be a law, a natural law that sanctions them. "For, *Ubi nulla Lex, ibi nulla praevaricatio*: Where there's no Law, there's no *Anomia*; where there's no Rule, there's no Anomaly; if there were no prohibition of this, 'twould not be sin to do it."[90]

Culverwell's view, that the law of nature is built upon reason, and that *anomia* is but a corollary to the existence of a Law of Nature, reaffirms the classical tradition and echoes the ideas of Renaissance humanists and Anglicans. Yet Culverwell considered himself a Calvinist, and his acknowledgment of God's will in Natural Law was chastised by another neo-Platonist, the "Anglican Apologist," Joseph Glanvill, who argued: "If there be no settled Good and Evil, Immutable and Independent on any Will or Understanding, then God may have made his reasonable Creatures on purpose to damn them for ever."[91] He was perhaps reading beyond Culverwell's intentions – Glanvill was chiefly a "theological apologist for the Anglican establishment."[92] Overly concerned with upholding the *via media*, Glanvill wrote: "Every truth is near an Errour ... so that the best way to avoid the danger is to steer the middle course; in which we may be sure is Charity and Peace, and, very probably, Truth in their company."[93]

In his *Lux Orientalis*, written in 1662, Glanvill defended the theory of pre-existence of the soul; his project "Being a Key to unlock the grand mysteries of Providence in relation to mans Sin and Misery."[94] Here Glanvill argued that the original sin was at the root of human misery; one had to look there for the origins of anomy.

> Thus is Eve brought forth, while Adam sleepeth. The lower life, that of the body is now considerably awakened, and the operations of the higher, proportionally abated. However, there is yet no *anomy* or *disobedience*, for all this is but an innocent exercise of those faculties which God hath given us to imploy, and as far as it is consistent with the divine law to gratify ... But at length, unhappily, the delights of the body betray us, through our overindulgence to them, and lead us captive to anomy and disobedience. The sense of what is grateful and pleasant by insensible degrees gets head over the apprehension of what is just and good.[95]

In all previous writings anomy was simply contrasted with righteousness; Glanvill offered an additional element by focusing on the *process* through which anomy takes hold of the individual. As long as the exercise of human faculties is *consistent* with the divine Law, anomy is absent; however, it is through "overindulgence" to the senses that a condition of lawlessness ensues. In an earlier book, *The Vanity of Dogmatizing*, published in 1661, Glanvill had discussed the causes of the original sin with these words: "Whether our purer intellectuals or only our impetuous affections, were the prime authors of the *anomie*, I dispute not: sin is as latent in its first cause, as visible in its effects."[96]

Locke and the Beginnings of Modern Social Theory

After the sophisticated arguments of Bishop Bramhall and the writings of Culverwell and Glanvill, the literature on anomy quickly rarefied; the few additional instances in the use of the word in the 1680s added little or nothing to the discussion of the concept.[97] English dictionaries document no further instances of its use after 1700.[98] The previous disputations had, still, brought to the fore a number of important points; what seemed to be a querulous debate about problems of semantics or Biblical exegesis was, in fact, a discussion about the nature of reason, morality, and anomy. The Anglican thinkers, and the neo-Platonists after them had made it clear that reason was at the source of moral activity and that it was the foundation of the law of nature; they also claimed that the freedom of the will was a *sine qua non* of morality; in relation to anomy *per se*, then, they made it clear that it was to be described as a *relation* between the action and the rule and that its roots were to be sought in the human intellect's being overcome by the senses with the original sin.

The specific discussion about anomy had subsided, but the discussion about morality and reason was far from over. The influence of Anglican and neo-Platonist doctrines, as well as the one of scholastic philosophy and humanistic scholarship, continued to be felt in the writings of John Locke, who at the turn of the seventeenth century admirably synthesized Renaissance learning and utilized it as a springboard to produce a rational moral philosophy.[99]

Locke's moral philosophy and social theory are much indebted to the writings of Anglicans and neo-Platonists. The *Essays on the Law of Nature*, written by Locke between 1654 and 1663, are compelling evidence of his knowledge of English humanism. On the one hand, Locke expressly acknowledged the ideas of Richard Hooker and "was fond of quoting his words, usually adopting the current designation of him as 'the judicious Hooker'."[100] On the other, he was far more indebted in his *Essays* to Culverwell's *Discourse*.[101] Locke and Culverwell shared a Calvinistic background which made them entertain a voluntaristic notion of law; they both needed, however, to bring together the volitional and the rational elements. To accomplish such a task Locke follows Culverwell as a voluntarist, "yet, his position shifts and inclines toward the 'intellectualist' theory of the Realists, according to which law has its foundation in a dictate of Right Reason, in the essential nature of things, and is thus independent of will."[102] Locke states, with Culverwell, that the law of nature is discovered by reason: "If a man makes use properly of his reason and of the inborn faculties with which nature has equipped him, he can attain to the knowledge of this law."[103] Locke argues for the existence of such law by resorting to the familiar passage from Romans, "*Ubi nulla Lex, Ibi nulla Praevaricatio*," which we saw cited in Culverwell's *Discourse*. Locke writes: "Without natural law there would be neither virtue nor vice, neither the reward of goodness nor the punishment of evil: there is no fault, no guilt, where there is no law."[104]

Locke was clearly influenced by natural-law theorists, but one would be mistaken to consider him as falling squarely in the social realists' camp. In Locke's social thought there was a strong empiricist and individualist emphasis which coexisted, side by side, with his philosophical realism. Locke was obviously a follower of Hooker and Culverwell, but Locke's interpretation of natural law was quite different from the interpretation of Renaissance Anglicans and neo-Platonists. As George H. Sabine points out, Locke "interpreted natural law as a claim to innate, indefeasible rights inherent in each individual ... Consequently, his theory was by implication as egoistic as that of Hobbes."[105] Whereas Hooker, Culverwell, and others saw their work as a justification of social institutions, Locke saw his effort as a defense of both individual rights and social norms. Accordingly, Locke's theory moved back and forth between individualistic nominalism and social realism. For Locke, Sabine writes, "Both government and society exist to preserve the individual's rights, and the indefeasibility of such rights is a limitation on the authority of both. In one part of Locke's theory, therefore, the individual and his rights figure as ultimate principles; in another society itself plays this part."[106]

The oscillation between voluntarism and realism is apparent in Locke's discussion of free will. Locke modified his position on this topic when rewriting his *Essays*, as he "suspected a lurking fallacy in his reasoning."[107] In his final stance, however, Locke was convinced that human liberty was "a power to act or not to act, according as the mind directs."[108] Earlier on, Locke had explained that, "To deny that a man's will, in every determination, follows his own judgment, is to say, that a man wills and acts for an end that he would not have, at the time that he wills and acts for it."[109]

Locke's combination of empiricism and rationalism made his theory highly ambiguous. On the one hand he claimed that ideas come from the senses and are grounded in experience, and on the other he proposed a view of natural law as a self-evident truth. Hobbes had professed a radical empiricism and had therefore attracted criticism from all sides; Locke, instead, was able to offer a palatable version of individualism by joining it with elements of social realism. Describing Locke's theory, Sabine comments:

> He left standing the old theory of natural law with all its emotional connotations and almost religious compulsions, but he completely changed, without knowing it, the meaning which the term had in writers like Hooker. Instead of a law enjoining the common good of a society, Locke set up a body of innate, indefeasible, individual rights which limit the competence of the

community and stand as bars to prevent interference with the liberty and property of private persons.[110]

Locke provided an intellectual bridge over which the ideas of Renaissance England could be carried, albeit greatly modified, to the Enlightenment; he was a transition figure between seventeenth-century deism and the eighteenth-century age of reason. The concept of anomy, associated with theological controversies and doctrinal diatribes, was doomed to oblivion; yet, the notions developed in discussing anomy, reason, and human freedom continued to be at the center of discussion for years ahead.

With the writings of seventeenth-century Anglicans and neo-Platonists, the concept of anomy had exhausted its course as a religious concept. The moral dimension of anomy, however, was recovered after almost two centuries of silence, when nineteenth-century French social philosophers appropriated the concept of *anomie*, divested of all apparent religious connotations, as a purely ethical term. Needless to add, the elimination of religious overtones did not do away with the debates and opposing ethical viewpoints documented in the English Renaissance. The diatribes simply moved to a different theoretical level. Realism and nominalism, transcendentalism and immanentism, continued to confront each other in the secular debates of the social philosophers of nineteenth-century France.

Notes

1 The *Discourse* was written in 1646 and published posthumously in 1652. Nathaniel Culverwell died in 1651, at the age of 32.

2 Nathaniel Culverwell, *An Elegant and Learned Discourse of the Light of Nature*, ed. Robert A. Greene and Hugh MacCallum (Toronto: University of Toronto Press, 1971), 28.

3 In seventeenth-century English literature the word appeared in English as either anomy or anomie (see note 35 below); I use the -y ending because it was the more common spelling; however, instances of *anomie* are found in Robert Shelford, *Five Pious and Learned Discourses* (Cambridge: The Printers to the University, 1635), 269; Joseph Glanvill, *The Vanity of Dogmatizing* (London: printed by E. C. for H. Eversden, 1661), 11; Edward Hooker, "Praefatory Epistle," to John Pordage, *Theologia Mystica* (London, 1683), 23.

4 See Otto Prinz, ed., *Mittel-Lateinisches Wörterbuch* (Munich: Verlag C. H. Becker, 1967), 34, 683–4; J. H. Baxter and Charles Johnson, *Medieval Latin Word-List from British and Irish Sources* (Oxford: Oxford University Press, 1934), 21; Charles du Fresne du Cange

(ed.), *Glossarium Mediae et Infimae Latinitatis* (Niort [France?]: L. Favre imprimeur-éditeur, 1883), 26, 292.

5   *Oxford English Dictionary*, s.v. "abnormal" and "anormal."

6   The root word of *anomalos* is *homos* which means one and the same; the root of *anomos* is *nomos*, which is anything distributed or apportioned; it can be argued that the notions of distribution and evenness go hand in hand, since evenness requires an equal distribution just as equal distribution requires evenness. With the Latin words equality and equity (and their opposites, inequality and iniquity) the similarity is even more apparent.

7   Already in Ambrogio Calepino's groundbreaking *Dictionarium*, published in 1502, we find the word *abnormis* derived from the Greek *anomos*, whereas the word *anormis* is derived from *anomalos*. See Calepino, *Dictionarium* (Antwerp: apud haeredes A. Birckmanni, 1572), 7, 82.

8   Balbi, a Dominican priest from Genoa, wrote the *Catholicon* in 1286; there, he "treats the etymology of the Latin terms in vogue during the Middle Ages." Cf. Margaret Bingham Stillwell, *Gutenberg and the Catholicon of 1460* (New York: Hackett, 1936), 12. For an assessment of the *Catholicon*'s influence on English Renaissance Dictionaries, see Dewitt T. Starnes, *Renaissance Dictionaries* (Austin: University of Texas Press, 1954).

9   *Ortus Vocabulorum* (1500; reprinted Menston: Scolar, 1968); for a description of the dictionary and its sources, see Starnes, *Renaissance Dictionaries*, 28–37.

10   John Rider, *Bibliotheca Scholastica* (1589; reprinted Menston: Scolar, 1970), Directions for the Reader; cf. also Starnes, *Renaissance Dictionaries*, 218–36.

11   Although the *Oxford English Dictionary* gives 1591 as the year when anomy first appeared with William Lambarde's *Archeion*, a section of it, the manuscript on the Star Chamber, was actually completed by 1589 (Folger MS. 511121.1, Washington, DC). Cf. Lambarde, *Archeion*, ed. Charles H. McIlwain and Paul L. Ward, (Cambridge, Mass.: Harvard University Press, 1957), 151.

12   Instances are found in the Medieval Latin dictionaries cited in note 4 above.

13   Quentin Skinner, *The Foundations of Modern Political Thought*, Vol. 1 (Cambridge: Cambridge University Press, 1978), 198. Of course these time boundaries are purely instrumental; I do not deny the influence of a solid medieval tradition on the later Renaissance. Cf. Walter Ullmann, *Medieval Foundations of Renaissance Humanism* (London: Elek, 1977).

14   Leo Spitzer, *Linguistics and Literary History* (Princeton: Princeton University Press, 1948), 21.

15   On Valla's legal humanism see Donald R. Kelley, *Foundations of Modern Historical Scholarship* (New York: Columbia University Press, 1970), 39–43.

16 Erasmus, "Preface," in Heiko A. Oberman, *Forerunners of the Reformation* (New York: Holt, Rinehart & Winston, 1966), 314.

17 Although the so called "Complutensian Edition" of the Greek New Testament was printed in 1514 by the Spaniards, it was not until 1520 that it became available to the public. Cf. Samuel Prideaux Tregelles, *An Account of the Printed Text of the Greek New Testament* (London: Bagster, 1854).

18 Albert Rabil, Jr, *Erasmus and the New Testament* (San Antonio: Trinity University Press, 1972), 101–2.

19 Desiderii Erasmi Roterdami, *Opera Omnia*, Vol. 6 (1705; reprinted London: Gregg, 1962), 571; my translation.

20 Luther, *Commentary on the Epistle to the Romans*, trans. J. Theodore Mueller (Grand Rapids: Zondervan, 1960), 42.

21 Luther, *Works*, ed. Jaroslav Pelikan, Vol. 30 (Saint Louis: Concordia, 1959), 269.

22 Skinner, *Foundations*, Vol. 2, 4.

23 Erasmus gave the first impulse to the humanistic jurisprudence of northern Europe. See Guido Kisch, *Erasmus und die Jurisprudenz seiner Zeit* (Basle: Helbing & Lichtenhahn, 1960).

24 John E. Sandys, *A History of Classical Scholarship*, Vol. 2 (New York: Hafner, 1958), 175–6. Such a claim would today be considered an overstatement. On the overall influence of Latin and Greek on the English language during the Elizabethan period, see Henry E. Shepherd, *The History of the English Language* (New York: Hale, 1974), 155–72.

25 Lambarde died in 1601, at the age of 65; two editions of the *Archeion* appeared in 1635. For a comparison of the two, see Paul L. Ward, "Appendix," in Lambarde, *Archeion*, 145–76.

26 Skinner, *Foundations*, Vol. 1, 208.

27 See Retha M. Warnicke, *William Lambarde* (London: Phillimore, 1973), ch 9; Wilbur Dunkel, *William Lambarde* (New Brunswick: Rutgers University Press, 1965). On the movement of historical research in Elizabethan England, see Catherine Drinker Bowen, "Historians Courageous," *Proceedings of the American Philosophical Society* 101 (June 1957).

28 Cf. Dunkel, *William Lambarde*, 130–2.

29 On the reception of Roman law in England during the Renaissance see Frederic W. Maitland, *English Law and the Renaissance* (Cambridge: Cambridge University Press, 1901), 7–11; Maitland's estimate of the problem is today regarded as exaggerated: cf. William S. Holdsworth, *A History of English Law*, Vol. 4 (1924; reprinted London: Methuen, 1966), 252–62.

30 On Lambarde's handling of this issue, see Faith Thompson, *Magna Carta* (Minneapolis: University of Minnesota Press, 1948), 186–90.

31 Lambarde, *Archeion*, 44. On the notion of "positive law" and its origins in classical and medieval thought, see Stephan Kuttner, "Sur les origines du term 'droit positif'," in *The History of Ideas and*

Doctrines of Canon Law in the Middle Ages (London: Variorum, 1980), 728–40.

32 Aristotle *Nichomachean Ethics* 1137B25; trans. Hippocrates G. Apostle.

33 Lambarde, *Archeion*, 67.

34 ibid., 66.

35 The evidence drawn from seventeenth-century English writings contradicts the widespread belief that anomy was the only English form and anomie was its French counterpart. Such a notion is upheld, for instance, in Robert M. MacIver, *The Ramparts We Guard* (1950; reprinted New York: Macmillan, 1956), 76–7; Robert K. Merton, "Continuities in the theory of social structure and ano-mie," in *Social Theory and Social Structure* (revised ed. New York: Free Press, 1957), 161; Herbert McClosky and John H. Schaar, "Psychological Dimensions of Anomy," *American Sociological Review* 30 (February 1965):14n; Peter L. Berger, *The Sacred Canopy* (New York: Doubleday, 1969), 190n. As early as 1827, Henry J. Todd's revision of Samuel Johnson's *Dictionary* misled the readers by adding under the voice "anomy" a quotation from Robert Shelford, where the word appeared with the -y instead of the correct -ie ending used by Shelford. Moreover, Todd mentioned in the "anomy" entry a French "anomie," without specifying that this term had been coined much later than its English counterpart (around 1760), and that it had a quite different meaning. In fact, the *Dictionnaire de l'academie française*, published in 1762, listed "ano-mie or anomiee," but its only definition was that of a mollusk, a shellfish, so named because of its irregular or "lawless" form.

36 In "The Preface to the Reader," the Rhemists write of the Protest-ants' work: "They have in steede of Gods Law and Testament, & for Christes written will and word, given them their owne wicked writing and phantasies, most shamefully in all their versions Latin, English, and other tonges, corrupting both the letter and sense by false translation, adding, detracting, altering, transposing, pointing, and all other guileful meanes: specially where it serveth for the advantage of their private opinions." *The New Testament* (1582), reprinted in *English Recusant Literature*, Vol. 267 (Menston: Scolar, 1975).

37 ibid., 682.

38 Fulke, *The Text of the New Testament* (London: Impensis G. B., 1601), 831. The author had died twelve years earlier, in 1589.

39 *Rhemists' New Testament*, 682.

40 Cartwright, *Confutation of the Rhemists' Translation* (1618; reprinted Amsterdam: Theatrum Orbis Terrarum, 1971), 693–4.

41 Henry Offley Wakeman, *The Church and the Puritans* (London: Longmans, Green & Co., 1892), 78. For an overall view of the Anglicans' mediating position in philosophical and political thought, see the two-volume work by W. K. Jordan, *The Development of Religious Tolerance in England* (London: Allen & Unwin,

1932 and 1936). On the Anglicans' notion of human nature and reason, and how it differed from the Puritans' notion, see John F. H. New, *Anglican and Puritan* (Stanford: Stanford University Press, 1964); Horton Davies, *Worship and Theology in England*, Vol. 1 (Princeton: Princeton University Press, 1970), 40–75.

42 Robert Hoopes, *Right Reason in the English Renaissance* (Cambridge, Mass.: Harvard University Press, 1962), 123. For an overview of Hooker's *Laws*, see A. S. McGrade, introduction to Hooker, *Of the Laws of Ecclesiastical Polity*, ed. A. S. McGrade and Brian Vickers, (London: Sidgwick & Jackson, 1975), 11–40.

43 *The Folger Library Edition of the Works of Richard Hooker*, ed. W. Speed Hill, Vol. 1, *Of the Laws of Ecclesiastical Polity* (Cambridge, Mass.: Belknap Press of Harvard University Press, 1977), 139.

44 ibid., 134–42.

45 ibid., 145.

46 ibid., 147.

47 Quoted ibid., 151.

48 ibid., 94–5.

49 ibid.

50 Cf. Peter Munz, *The Place of Hooker in the History of Thought* (London: Routledge & Kegan Paul, 1952).

51 Perhaps the Anglicans were indebted to Hooker also in their linguistic innovations; Shepherd writes: "In the 'Ecclesiastical Polity' of Hooker, the language of theology attained its loftiest excellence. His style is Latinized, complicated, and sometimes obscure, but he is considered the first prose writer, 'that exhibits philosophical precision and uniformity in the use of words, and this is the peculiarity of his style which gives it its greatest philological value'." Shepherd, *History of the English Language*, 177–8.

52 *Dictionary of National Biography*, s.v. "Hall, Joseph."

53 Hall, *No Peace with Rome* in *Works*, ed. Josiah Pratt, Vol. 9 (London: Whittingham, 1808), 57–8.

54 ibid.

55 ibid.

56 Jordan writes: "The Puritans were in no sense Separatists"; yet they "maintained steadily that they were the Church of England and declined either to recognize or to tolerate any other religious organization within the realm." Jordan, *Development of Religious Tolerance*, Vol. 2, 201.

57 ibid., 130.

58 Shelford, an MA of Peterhouse, died in 1627 at the age of 64. His book, *Five Pious and Learned Discourses*, was published in 1635 by the University of Cambridge. In a prefatory section we find a poem by Richard Crashaw summarizing the content of Shelford's *Discourses*, entitled "On a treatise of charity." There, Crashaw closes with these verses: 'On sum, no longer shall our people hope,/ To be a true Protestant's but to hate the Pope."

59 Quoted in Christopher Hill, *Antichrist in Seventeenth-Century England* (Oxford: Oxford University Press, 1971), 36–7.

60 Shelford, *Five Pious*, 269. Shelford's rendering of *anomia* is indebted to the definition given in H. Stephanus, *Thesaurus Linguae Graecae*, Vol. 5 (1572; reprinted London: In Aedibus Valpianis, 1823), 6333. There we read: "*Anomia, he, Vita exlex* a life without law, Iniquitas, Injustitia." Samuel Johnson's *Dictionary*, in Henry Todd's 1827 revision, spells Shelford's passage as "anomy" instead of the correct "anomie."

61 Shelford, *Five Pious*, 272–4.

62 Austin Warren, *Richard Crashaw* (Baton Rouge: Louisiana State University, 1939), 4–5.

63 Quoted in L. C. Martin, ed., *The Poems English, Latin, and Greek of Richard Crashaw* (Oxford: Clarendon, 1957), 438.

64 Cf. Jordan, *Development of Religious Tolerance*, Vol. 2, 137–42; see also Wakeman, *Church and Puritans*, 119–70.

65 A pamphlet of the period written by S. P. (Simon Patrick?) in 1662, was entitled "A brief account of the new sect of latitude-men." There, S. P. wrote in defense of the Latitudinarians: "Nor is there any point in Divinity, where that which is most ancient doth not prove the most rational, and the most rational the ancientest; for there is an eternal consanguinity between all verity; and nothing is true in Divinity, which is false in Philosophy, or on the contrary." (London, 1662), 11. For a description of the ideas and aims of the Latitudinarians, see Jordan, *Development of Religious Tolerance*, Vol. 2, 349–421; G. R. Cragg, *From Puritanism to the Age of Reason* (Cambridge: Cambridge University Press, 1950), 61–86.

66 On the circumstances surrounding the controversy and its later publication, see Samuel I. Mintz, *The Hunting of the Leviathan* (Cambridge: Cambridge University Press, 1962), 11–12.

67 John Laird, *Hobbes* (London: Benn, 1934), 189.

68 John Bramhall, *The Discourses against Mr Hobbes*, in *Works*, Vol. 4 (reprinted Oxford: Parker, 1844), 63.

69 ibid., 72.

70 ibid., 319–20.

71 ibid., 74. This notion of *causa deficiens* seems to have been a standard view during the Middle Ages.

72 ibid., 319.

73 I do not claim that Hobbes was a Puritan; on the contrary, it has been argued that his political theory grew out of a rejection of the Puritan indoctrination he received during his Oxford education; see Winfried Foerster, *Thomas Hobbes und der Puritanismus* (Berlin: Dunker & Humblot, 1969). I claim, instead, that Hobbes' notions of human nature, reason, and freedom were, essentially, the ones of a godless Puritan: in being diametrically opposite to the Puritans' religious views, he was closer to them than all other writers who stood in between the two extremes.

74 Thomas Hobbes, *Leviathan*, in *The English Works of Hobbes*, ed.

William Molesworth, Vol. 3 (1655; reprinted London: Bohn, 1839), 669.

75 Hobbes probably had in mind Aristotle's *Rhetorica ad Alexandrum* 1430a31–5 and 1443a15–24.

76 Hobbes, *Leviathan*, in *Thomae Hobbes Malmeburiensis Opera Philosophica Quae Latine Scripsit Omnia*, ed. William Molesworth, Vol. 3 (London: Bohn, 1841), 501; my translation.

77 Samuel Johnson, *A Dictionary of the English Language* (1755; reprinted London: Times Books, 1979). Johnson gives there the correct Greek etymology of "anomy," but he offers only a narrow interpretation of its meaning. He identifies the quote as "Bramham (!) against Hobbes."

78 Skinner, *Foundations*, Vol. 1, xv. See also Ullmann, *Medieval Foundations*, 149–202.

79 In discussing the concept of *adiaphora*, Skinner fails to mention its origins in classical stoic philosophy; cf. I. G. Kidd, "Stoic intermediates and the end for man," in *Problems in Stoicism*, ed. A. A. Long (London: Athlone, 1971), 150–72. This is a curious oversight, given that Skinner wanted "to emphasize the remarkable extent to which the vocabulary of Renaissance moral and political thought was derived from Roman stoic sources." *Foundations*, Vol 1, xiv.

80 Skinner, *Foundations*, Vol. 2, 104.

81 Such a programme had its first northern Renaissance impulse in Erasmus's *Enchiridion Mulitis Christiani*, published in 1503.

82 Ernst Cassirer, *The Platonic Renaissance in England*, trans. James P. Pettegrove (London: Nelson, 1953), 42.

83 ibid., 34. For a discussion of the main exponents of Cambridge neo-Platonism, and an overview of its minor figures, see John Tulloch, *Rational Theology and Christian Philosophy*, Vol. 2 (1874; reprinted Hildesheim: Olms, 1966).

84 Greene, Introduction to Culverwell's *Discourse*, xv.

85 Culverwell, *Discourse*, 13. The King James version reads: "The spirit of man is the Candle of the Lord." The Latin verse, from Proverbs 20:27, is "Mens hominis lucerna Domini."

86 Greene, Introduction to Culverwell, *Discourse*, xxv.

87 ibid., xxix.

88 Culverwell, *Discourse*, 42, 45.

89 On the dichotomy of natural and positive law, see Kuttner, "Sur les origines," 736–9.

90 Culverwell, *Discourse*, 51. The Latin phrase is from Romans 4:15, but it is also found in Suarez's *De Legibus* (bk 2, ch. 5, para. 2 and bk 2, ch. 6, para. 7), and in Hobbes's *Leviathan* (pt 1, ch. 13).

91 Glanvill, *Two Choice and Useful Treatises*, 17; quoted in Jackson I. Cope, *Joseph Glanvill Anglican Apologist* (St Louis: Washington University Press, 1956), 49.

92 Cope, *Joseph Glanvill*, 42.

93 Glanvill, *Catholick Charity Recommended*, 54–5; quoted in Cope, *Joseph Glanvill*, 54.

94 Glanvill, *Lux Orientalis* (London: J. Collins and S. Lowndes, 1682), subtitle.

95 ibid., 115–17.

96 Glanvill, *The Vanity of Dogmatizing*, 11. In this earlier work Glanvill spelled the word with the -ie ending. This shows that the two spellings were used interchangeably by English writers.

97 See John Howe, *The Blessedness of the Righteous* (1668), in *Works of John Howe* (reprinted London: F. Westley and A. H. Davis, 1832), 194; Edward Hooker's "Praefatori Epistle" to John Pordage's *Theologia Mystica* (1683), 23; and an anonymous 27-page pamphlet entitled "An Apology for the failures charged on the Reverend Mr George Walker's printed account of the Siege of Derry," (1689), 15. This last example, for instance, rehashes Bramhall's distinction with these words: "You Presbyterians distinguish between the Action and the Anomy, or Irregularity of it, which later you say in the Original makes the sin." Edward Hooker's discussion, instead, echoes Glanvill's: "Lusts now are become Laws ... Hence we see Praecepts wil do no good against Sins ... against men's Lusts, animosities, enormities, Anomies."

98 My statement is based on the survey of four English Dictionaries (Johnson, 1755; Richardson, 1863; *Oxford English Dictionary*, 1888; Stanford, 1892). Still the word continued to be used, even if very sparsely. For instance, Benjamin Rush, the eighteenth-century American physician, coined in 1786 the term *anomia* to describe the total absence of moral faculties in the individual. Benjamin Rush, *Medical Inquiries and Observations upon the Diseases of the Mind*, Vol. 1 (1815; reprinted New York: Arno, 1972), 106.

99 Cf. Cragg, *From Puritanism*, 114–35.

100 Sterling Power Lamprecht, *The Moral and Political Philosophy of John Locke* (New York: Russell & Russell, 1962), 9.

101 This point is strongly argued by W. von Leyden in his Introduction of *John Locke's Essays on the Law of Nature* (Oxford: Clarendon, 1954), 40–3.

102 ibid., 51. On this matter, see also John Dunn, *The Political Thought of John Locke* (Cambridge: Cambridge University Press, 1969), 187–99.

103 Locke, *Essays on the Law of Nature*, 127.

104 ibid., 119–21.

105 George H. Sabine, *A History of Political Theory* (1937; reprinted New York: Holt, Rinehart & Winston, 1961), 525.

106 ibid., 525–6.

107 Lamprecht, *The Moral and Political Philosophy*, 98.

108 Locke, *An Essay Concerning Human Understanding* (1690), bk 2, ch. 21, para. 56.

109 ibid., para. 48.

110 Sabine, *A History*, 529.

CHAPTER 4

The Ethics of Anomie in Nineteenth-Century France

The notion of studying anomie is valuable and interesting, clearly, because of the fortune of the word in modern sociology. As one gets closer to the contemporary debates on anomie, the increase of available literature and the intellectual affinity for the issues discussed seem to make one's research much easier – but this is only apparently so. If it is true that primary and secondary sources on Durkheim's notion of anomie abound, it is also true that, to paraphrase Francis Bacon's remark, the idols of our "sociological cave" prevent us from studying the recent past in a sufficiently detached, objective manner. It is easy to accept uncritically the secondary literature on anomie theory, but knowing the pre-sociological history of the concept can alert us against such a temptation.

The evidence on the history and meanings of anomie has been, so far, one of contrasting views concerning social order, human nature, laws, reason, and morality. Anomie, we have learned, never had a single, univocal meaning; instead, anomie acquired different nuances depending on the socio-historical context in which it was employed, and on the ideological claims it was to support. It would be unlikely that the variation in meanings should have come to an abrupt end in nineteenth-century France, and the historical evidence supports this assumption.

Most sociologists credit Emile Durkheim as the first modern author to write about anomie in *The Division of Labor in Society*, in 1893.[1] It was six years earlier, however, that Durkheim first used the term anomie, in his review of a book, *L'Irréligion de l'avenir* (*The Non-Religion of the Future*), written by the French philosopher and sociologist, Jean Marie Guyau.[2] There Durkheim described Guyau's use of the term, not only in the book under review but also in Guyau's earlier book, the *Esquisse d'une morale sans*

94

obligation ni sanction (Sketch of a Morality without Obligation or Sanction). Moreover, in the 1893 Introduction to *The Division of Labor in Society*, which he later modified, Durkheim specifically quarrels with Guyau's notion of anomie and underlying ethics,[3] and alters the concept by placing it within his own interpretive framework. The fact remains, however, that Durkheim discovers the concept in Guyau's writings. The confrontation that Durkheim began in his review of Guyau's book did not take place; Guyau died, in 1888, at the age of 33.

The supposition that Durkheim was the first sociologist to use the term would be a minor error in the discussion of anomie, suitable perhaps for a footnote in the history of sociology, were it not for the relevance of Guyau's concept of anomie for both ethical and sociological theory. Guyau builds his concept of anomie on the immanentistic tradition, which argues that the moral codes governing human behavior are not transcendental, but are situational and embedded in individual relationships. Durkheim on the contrary claims that moral codes constrain individual relationships and are external to them.[4] In both cases the concept of anomie is linked to the authors' philosophical interpretation of morality. Guyau is straightforward in this regard, but Durkheim, pulling the cover of science over his work, is less open about the historical antecedents and philosophical implications of his ethical theory.

In this chapter I will clarify the genesis of the concept of anomie in sociology by reconstructing Guyau's treatment of the concept and his approach to ethical and sociological theory. I will then show how Durkheim's concept of anomie relates to his own very different moral philosophy. My argument proceeds in four steps. First, I describe the historical and intellectual milieu in which Guyau and Durkheim elaborated their different theories about morality and anomie. Second, I relate Guyau's sociological and ethical perspectives to his concept of anomie. Third, I show that Durkheim learned of the term anomie from Guyau, and reconceptualized it to fit his own positivistic approach toward ethics. Fourth, I compare Guyau's and Durkheim's concept of anomie in relation to their moral philosophy and to their approach to social phenomena. I also suggest that Guyau's concept of anomie should be revived, because it is a theoretically and historically sound alternative to Durkheim's concept.

The contemporary sociology of anomie has acknowledged Durkheim's work, ignoring Guyau's contribution altogether. The primary and secondary accounts of Durkheim's social theory and of his concept of anomie are so numerous that to add one more account would be redundant to say the least. A study of the genesis of the concept of anomie in modern sociology and a description of an alternative view to Durkheimian anomie will prove more useful and interesting. Guyau's notion of anomie is not simply a piece of "sociological trivia"; far from that, it is the needed alternative to Durkheim's concept. Twentieth-century theories of anomie are not univocally Durkheimian; on the contrary, as I will show in the next chapter, contemporary theories of anomie often echo Guyau's notion of anomie more than Durkheim's, upholding an immanentist, individualistic notion of morality against the transcendental social ethics so dear to Durkheim.

Nineteenth-Century France: *Guyau and Durkheim*

In his book on Durkheim, Robert A. Nisbet wrote:

> The history of moral philosophy, from Socrates and Plato to the modern existentialists, reveals the centrality of this truth: that ideas do not, in Sir Isaiah Berlin's vivid phrasing, beget ideas as butterflies beget butterflies. Ideas are dialectical responses, caught up in the logic and circumstances of antithesis.[5]

Nisbet's claim holds true not only in relation to the concept of anomie as it was developed in nineteenth-century France, but also in relation to the broader social theories of Guyau and Durkheim. Both men grew up during a period of political instability in French history; both witnessed when only teenagers the defeat of the Second Empire by the Prussians in 1870, the startling events of the Paris Commune, and the slow beginnings of the Third Republic in 1871. Of Durkheim, Steven Lukes writes that "His experience of the French defeat may have contributed to a strong (though in no way militant) patriotism, a defensive sense of national decadence and a consequent desire to contribute to the regeneration of France."[6] Indeed, Durkheim devoted much of his intellectual efforts to a consolidation of the liberal Third Republic against the monarchists and the influence of the Catholic Church. The high point of political confrontation was the celebrated Dreyfus affair, at the turn of the century. But Guyau did not live long enough to have an equal impact on French intellectual and political life.

Broadly speaking, the intellectual climate of the second half of the nineteenth century was characterized, in France, by a critical appraisal of Comte's positivistic metaphysics which had dominated French intellectual life in the first half of the century. Three main currents of thought developed from this appraisal. A first current produced a revised version of positivism; its major exponents were philosophers like Vacherot, Taine, and Renan. A second was the one of neo-Kantianism or neo-criticism, espoused by men like Curnot and Renouvier. A third was strongly critical of positivism; its exponents, known as "spiritualists" were, among others, Boutroux, Fouillée, Guyau, Bergson, and Blondel.[7]

Durkheim was influenced by all three currents of thought: he subscribed to the basic tenets of positivism and was an admirer of Taine's integration of rationalism and empiricism; he was a disciple of Renouvier and always described himself as a "rationalist"; he was also influenced by his teacher, Emile Boutroux, to whom he dedicated his thesis on *The Division of Labor*. Spiritualism, of the three, had the least effect on Durkheim's thought. Lukes writes:

> Bouglé has aptly characterized Durkheim's perspective as "rationalism impregnated with positivism." Durkheim, however, always spoke of himself as a rationalist, never as a positivist. He also always objected to being labelled as either a "materialist" or a "spiritualist."[8]

If Durkheim emphasized rationalism as the fulcrum of his social theory, Guyau stressed the role of individual will. The spiritualist current descended from Maine de Biran's philosophy of activism and voluntarism. Spiritualism acquired new vitality in the 1860s with the work of Ravaisson who, in 1867, wrote a famous philosophical manifesto, "a call to free spirits to assert themselves in favour of a valid idealism."[9] The most direct influence on Guyau's thought was, however, the one of his own stepfather, Alfred Fouillée. Ideas, Fouillée thought, had an independent effect on human action. "The love of freedom arising from the idea of freedom creates in the long run this freedom ... To conceive and to desire the ideal is already to begin its realisation."[10]

Durkheim and Guyau stood from the onset on the shoulders of two quite different traditions. Durkheim was the heir of Comte's positivism and of Renouvier's rationalism; Guyau was the descendant to a line of thought critical of both crude positivism and dogmatic rationalism. While Durkheim's emphasis on social facts and on the social nature of reason led him to claim the superiority of a social opposed to an individual morality, the spiritualists' awareness of the limitations of positive science and their emphasis on voluntarism led Guyau to claim the superiority of an individually-based morality. Accordingly, the two authors fashioned two distinct concepts of anomie. The dialectical development of Durkheim's notion of anomie becomes evident once it is compared to the earlier, antithetical formulation of his compatriot, Guyau. Let us look at each notion in some detail.

Guyau's Concept of Anomie

The concept of anomie was apparently absent from Western culture during the eighteenth and most of the nineteenth century. There were, to be sure, a few scattered examples where the Greek word appeared, as in a nineteenth-century English religious publication, where we read: "In the household of faith the pestilential influence of that lawlessness – that *anomia* – which is a chief spiritual disease of this era of the world's history, is not altogether unfelt."[11] But the word had been mostly out of use since the late seventeenth century.

In nineteenth-century France anomie showed renewed vitality in the writings of the philosopher and sociologist Jean Marie Guyau. Although he died at the age of 33, Guyau produced an extraordinary wealth of literature during his short career, and quickly obtained an international reputation.[12]

Born in Laval Mayenne (France) in 1854, he was raised in a stimulating cultural environment. His mother was a writer in the field of education, and his stepfather, Alfred Fouillée, was a well known philosopher. Under Fouillée's supervision, Guyau became acquainted in his youth with the works of Plato and Kant, the history of religions, philosophy, aesthetics, and ethics. At the age of 19 Guyau wrote his *Mémoire sur la morale utilitaire depuis Epicure jusqu' à l'école anglaise* (*History of Utilitarian Ethics from Epicurus to the English School*), a 1,300-page work that won a prize from the French Academy of Moral and Political Sciences in 1874. He was appointed as lecturer in philosophy at the Lycée Condorcet in Paris, but soon discontinued teaching because of a pulmonary disease. By 1888, the year of his untimely death, Guyau had already published six books, and three more manuscripts were posthumously published by his stepfather. Guyau's book *Education et hérédité* (first published in 1889 and translated into English, as *Education and Heredity*, in 1891), was especially popular in early American sociology.[13]

The American philosopher, Josiah Royce, considered Guyau "one of the most prominent of recent French philosophical critics."[14] As Royce described him,

Guyau was interested in ethics and metaphysics, in aesthetics and in educational theory. He shared and expressed the modern

98

interest in sociological problems ... He speculated with equal interest upon anthropological problems, such as the origin of religions, and upon confessedly transcendent problems, such as immortality.[15]

Guyau devoted most of his work to a critical analysis of modern philosophical and ethical theories. An enthusiastic admirer of English utilitarianism, he did not, however, spare his criticism of Bentham's and Mill's approach to morality. Viewing the work of Bentham and his successors as an update of Epicurean moral philosophy, Guyau stated that a valid theory of ethics needed to consider the moral sphere as consisting not merely of *moral facts*, as the utilitarians do, but more importantly of *moral ideas*: 'Utilitarians might object that here we are dealing with 'metaphysics' rather than with practical morality: this would be a mistake. In this instance, metaphysics and ethics are one and the same.'[16] Utilitarians based their ethics on the principle of material pleasure alone, disregarding the fact that intellectual and aesthetic pleasures have a moral value as well.

The lack of an holistic perspective on ethics, however, was not a peculiarity of the utilitarian doctrine. Guyau's criticism applied in equal measure to Kantian ethics, where one finds the conception of moral ideas without a practical foundation in society. Through his concept of autonomy of the ethical sphere, Kant had abandoned a theological world-view where human will was morally bound to obey the divine law. But according to Guyau, Kant did not adequately ground ethics in an alternative world-view. Kant placed his theory of ethics in a philosophical vacuum by claiming at the same time the autonomy of the individual and the universality of the moral law. Guyau argues that Kant failed to recognize the social basis of individual morality and of individual choice.

Guyau thought that utilitarian and Kantian ethics needed to be brought together and set himself the task of producing an original synthesis that would faithfully describe the characteristics of modern morality. His third book, the *Esquisse d'une morale sans obligation ni sanction* was the outcome of this work. In the *Esquisse* Guyau claims that while intuitionists and idealists set their moral theory on a hypothetical basis, concerning themselves with the ideal morality, naturalists and utilitarians instead followed the inductive model of positive science, producing a practical morality that was concerned with moral facts alone. Guyau argues that the moral freedom of the individual derives from limiting scientific determinism to moral facts, leaving the sphere of moral ideas to metaphysical speculation. Guyau demonstrates how the distinction between moral facts and moral ideas generates the historical disappearance of obligation and sanction:

> On the one hand, naturalist and positivist morality cannot produce *invariable* principles, in relation to either obligation or sanction; on the other hand, if the idealistic morality can perform this task, it is only on a *hypothetical* basis, with no assertive quality. In other words, what is in the order of facts is not universal, and what is universal is only a speculative hypothesis.[17]

On the one hand, Guyau reasoned, the social obligations and sanctions addressed by the positivists are only factual and contingent (that is, they are based on moral facts and cannot go beyond their specific instance); therefore a science of ethics cannot be universal. On the other hand, Guyau considered the idealistic ethics, based on moral ideas, as able to produce a universal law, but only in a purely speculative fashion (that is, having a hypothetical quality which is not binding in any compelling way). In other words, Guyau eliminated obligation and sanction from modern ethics because of the contingency of moral facts on one hand, and the speculative quality of moral ideas on the other.

It is here, in the introduction to the *Esquisse*, that Guyau introduces his concept of anomie. He writes the term first in Greek script, hinting at the likelihood that he learned the term directly from the Greek, and not from any western-language transliteration. Guyau was, in fact, a Greek scholar and his work on Epicureanism was punctuated by literal quotations in Greek. Moreover, he was familiar with the works of Plato and Plutarch where we saw *anomia* and its grammatical variations frequently used. Guyau states, in the introduction, that the variability of moral rules caused by the elimination of obligation and sanction should be considered the characteristic of the morality of the future. Then, he adds, "This one [the morality of the future] will be, under different points, not only *autonomos* [autonomous] but also *anomos* [anomic]."[18] Taking as a starting point the fact that moral values are characterized not only by their autonomy from the sphere of reason but also by the absence of any fixed law, Guyau uses the concept of anomie to elaborate a theory of ethics. He sees the progressive individualization of morality and moral rules as a necessary outcome of the positivistic revolution and of the decline of traditional religion in modern society. The history of ethics shows a gradual shift from collective and external criteria for ethical conduct towards individual and internal criteria. For

Guyau anomie is not to be considered an evil or an illness of modern time, but its distinguishing quality. While many social thinkers were concerned about how to restore the social order eroded by the industrial revolution and the advent of positivism, Guyau presented the intellectual risk of moral anomie as the challenge of the new era. Modern people could no longer rely on religious faith or transcendental truth. Rather, they had to find a standard of conduct within themselves, in their impulse toward life. Instead of the old aphorism "I must, therefore I can," Guyau proposes the reverse: "I can, therefore I must." The essence of human life is its impulse for action which not only creates physical fecundity but moral fecundity as well.[19]

Guyau's main goal in the *Esquisse* was to provide a satisfactory holistic approach to modern ethics. Positivists and idealists had considered only one aspect, either the factual or the ideal, at the expense of the other. Regarding the invasion of ethics by positivism, Guyau thought it a main project of his *Esquisse* "to assess the importance, the extent, but also the *limits* of an *exclusively scientific* morality."[20] In this regard, it is important to point out that Guyau was not concerned with founding his own science of morality, as some critics, like G. Aslan,[21] implied. Rather, he strived to specify the limits of a science of ethics that is based only on empirical observations. Not only are moral facts to be confronted with moral ideas, but the latter are the logical cause of the former. Guyau explains:

> Reason shows us two different worlds: the real world where we live, and a type of ideal world where we also live ... only when we refer to the ideal world does the general consensus disappear: each individual perceives it in his own way; some deny its existence altogether. However, it is the way we think about the ideal world that determines the way we will feel bound to act ... it is therefore impossible to ignore this productive source of activity.[22]

The world of moral ideas is no less important in ethics than the acts themselves; a proper understanding of the dynamics of the moral life must account for both elements. "We must rely on metaphysical thought in ethics as we rely on economic thought in politics and sociology."[23]

Once Guyau outlines the relevance of speculation about moral ideas, he defines anomie as a feature that distinguishes a metaphysical from a positivistic orientation towards ethics. First, he argues that metaphysical thought concerns moral ideas that are *unproductive* in any practical sense; that is, metaphysical thought is not motivated by interests or utilitarian considerations. Second, the metaphysics of ethics is eminently *hypothetical* because it is based on individual assumptions, not on empirical facts themselves. Third, such hypothetical speculations are characterized by *variation* among individuals. This variation, Guyau adds, "is the absence of a fixed law, that can be described as *anomie*, in contrast with the Kantian autonomy."[24] The complementarity of anomie and autonomy is, here, only apparently abandoned.

Guyau illustrates the concept of anomie throughout the *Esquisse*, but the concept retains the same essential features that appear in the introduction. Anomie is the distinguishing quality of Guyau's idea of modern ethics. The contrast of anomie with autonomy only seems to depart from Guyau's earlier definition; it is apparent from the context that Guyau did not intend to contrast anomie with Kant's autonomy, but rather to add to it. He considered Kant's combination of autonomy and universality of the moral sphere as logically contradictory:

> He thought that individual freedom of the moral subject could coexist with the universality of the moral law ... but, in the sphere of freedom, the good order is exactly the absence of preconceived order ... the real "autonomy" must produce individual originality, not general conformity.[25]

Guyau developed his concept of anomie with historical and logical consistency. To him the history of ethics clearly shows an increasing role of individual speculation throughout the centuries; he expands on this fact and finds it to be consistent with a modern ethic that is autonomously produced by the individual, and is, by logical consequence, free from external rules, i.e., anomic.

After its original formulation in the *Esquisse*, Guyau further develops the concept of anomie in his fourth book, *L'Irréligion de l'avenir* published in 1887, and reviewed by Durkheim in the *Revue philosophique* in the same year. This work, which Guyau started in 1884, was an attempt to study the history of religions from a sociological perspective. In the introduction, Guyau emphasizes that a sociological approach offers the best way to understand the origins of religious phenomena. Human sociability produces religious feelings because of the dependence we experience on other human beings, and because of our social need for affection, tenderness, and love.[26] Guyau also comments that researchers in the field of religion often fail to distinguish between the specific character of religious phenomena and the collateral issues of ethics and metaphysics. Positive religion is characterized by three observable features: mythic explanations, a system of dogmatic beliefs, and a cult and system of rites. Whenever these features are missing we do not have a natural religion, but only a metaphysical hypothesis that lacks positivity.[27] The absence, in modern times, of the positive elements found in old religions indicates that we are not heading toward a new religious form; rather we are witnessing the disappearance of religion. Guyau entitles his book "The *Non-Religion* of the Future" because he considers modern beliefs to be qualitatively different from former religious beliefs.

In *L'Irréligion* Guyau proposes his concept of *religious anomie* as the defining characteristic of modern religiosity. The concept parallels the moral anomie proposed by Guyau in his *Esquisse*. The myths and cults of natural religion are replaced in modern times by scientific investigation. Reality is now interpreted by empirical observation rather than by mythical explanation; the dogmatic religion of ancient times has given way to the religion of doubt, skepticism, and positive knowledge. Natural religion is divested of its moral function; individuals are nowadays left to their metaphysical speculation, to their religious individualism, to their religious anomie.[28]

Religious anomie and moral anomie are directly related, and Guyau connected the two as follows:

> We have elsewhere proposed as the ideal morality what we called moral *anomie*, the absence of apodictic, fixed, and universal rules.[29] We even more strongly believe that the ideal of any religion should tend towards *religious anomie* – towards the enfranchisement of the individual, whose freedom of thought is more important than his own life, and towards the elimination of dogmatic faith under whatever type of camouflage.[30]

In the ethical sphere moral anomie is the element that eliminates the imperative uniformity of moral codes. In the religious sphere religious anomie performs a similar function by substituting the faith of a transcendental approach with the doubt and skepticism of the individual. Religious anomie strives toward the elimination of all imperative external rules of conduct.

The practical side of religious phenomena, the one Guyau considered eminently sociological, survives in the idea of association. The associations of human beings found during the era of natural religions will persist in the future, but their character will be quite different. New associations lessen constraints upon members. Individuals freely choose to become members on the basis of their different interests and moral or religious hypotheses. Hence, the associations of individuals become more spontaneous and are subject to variations, following an increasing differentiation which Guyau calls the "law of progress." There will be associations for intellectual, moral, and aesthetic purposes.

In the *Esquisse* as well as in *L'Irréligion*, Guyau's concern is to approach the issues of morality and religion in an exhaustive way without ignoring the practical or theoretical implications of the themes studied. In Guyau's writings, observation and metaphysical speculation go hand in hand; both are equally needed. Positive science furnishes scientific statements about an observed reality; metaphysical thought allows for the study of processes, like the production of knowledge or morality, that escape empirical observation. The one-sided approach of both positivists and idealists was, in Guyau's view, detrimental to a proper understanding of ethical issues. Idealists made the mistake of identifying their speculations with the real world; positivists made the mistake of identifying what they see with what should be.

In his studies, Guyau compared the historical development of religions and ethical theories with the claims made by positivists; he showed that scientific generalizations about ethics are unwarranted and trespass on the area of scientific inquiry. The distinguishing features of modern ethics and religions can be defined only in a properly historical perspective: Guyau's concepts of moral and religious anomie are historically grounded, and have their justification in the development of ethics and religions in human societies.

Guyau died young, before he could elaborate his ethical theory in more detail, but the principles and method were already clearly stated in his first works. It was from these that Durkheim took and then developed his own concept of anomie; a concept that is integral to Durkheim's proposed "science of ethics."

Durkheim's "Pathological Anomie"

Durkheim became familiar with the concept of anomie some time before he produced his own version in *De la division du travail social* in 1893. In his review of Guyau's book, *L'Irréligion de l'avenir*, which appeared in the *Revue philosophique* in 1887,[31] Durkheim expressed satisfaction with the new sociological approach attempted by Guyau in his analysis of religious phenomena. The book included three sections: the genesis of religions, the dissolution of religions, and the non-religion of the future. Describing the third part, Durkheim reports:

Since the old religions are leaving us, and the growing progress of science with the vulgarization of the scientific spirit prevent the rise of a new religion, the religious ideal can only consist of a *religious anomie*, that is, the enfranchisement of the individual, and the abolition of all dogmatic faith. The author had already shown elsewhere how the ideal morality consists in the moral anomie.[32]

In his book review Durkheim did not discuss the specifics of Guyau's concept of anomie, but he did make some critical comments in relation to Guyau's underlying theory of social sentiments. There Durkheim advocated two distinct types of social sentiments. On the one hand, there are the sentiments generated by the interaction of the individual with fellow citizens; on the other, there are the feelings of belonging to the social organism in its entirety: "The first ones do not interfere with my autonomy and personality ... on the contrary, when I act under the influence of the others, I am nothing but a part of the whole ... it is for this reason that only the second ones can generate the idea of obligation."[33]

In Durkheim's opinion, Guyau correctly advocated a sociological approach to the study of religions, and showed how the development of religions parallels the development of society. However, Durkheim argues, Guyau wrongly emphasized the role of metaphysical speculation, and of the individual within it, in accounting for the religious and moral change in history. Durkheim's revision of Guyau's work was to shift Guyau's emphasis on the individual and the speculative to his own social and positivistic approach. If not specifically dealing with anomie, Durkheim still offered, *in nuce*, what later became his theory of moral sentiments and obligation as developed in *The Division of Labor*.[34]

The literature on Durkheim's concept of anomie is extensive. It is not my goal, here, to analyze this literature or to describe the evolution of anomie in Durkheim's writings. Both have been done by others.[35] I will instead limit myself to an examination of Durkheim's first formulation of anomie in *The Division of Labor*, showing that anomie appears from the onset to have been borrowed from Guyau, and to be closely related with Durkheim's stand on ethical theory.

Most sociologists consider the first chapter of the third book of *The Division of Labor* ("The anomic division of labor") as Durkheim's first statement about anomie.[36] However, if we read the introduction to the 1893 edition of *The Division of Labor* closely, we will find the concept of anomie discussed there. In a

105

large section of the introduction which was removed from later editions[37] Durkheim discussed at length the foundations of his "science of ethics." There Durkheim stated the following:

> The sentiment of obligation, that is, the existence of duty, is in danger of being weakened in admitting there is a morality, and perhaps a higher, which rests on the independent creations of the individual, which no rule determines, which is essentially *anomic* [*anomique*]. We believe, on the contrary, that *anomy* [*anomie*] is the contradiction of all morality.[38]

Even if apparently confined to a footnote, this statement indicates that Guyau's notion of anomie had continued to hold Durkheim's attention. Now he openly rejected Guyau's interpretation by taking an opposite point of view. Guyau had shown, through his historical analysis, that moral and religious anomie were distinguishing features of modern societies; the elimination of obligation and sanction in the ethical sphere was dictated by the development of human knowledge and the dissolution of transcendental rules of conduct. Durkheim claimed, instead, that obligation and sanction are a *sine qua non* of morality, whose features are given once and for all. Anomie is here axiomatically characterized as "the contradiction of *all* morality." From the above quotation it seems evident that Durkheim *first* proposed his concept of anomie in contradiction to Guyau's concept.

To show how Durkheim's anomie serves his notion of morality we need to examine in more detail his science of ethics. Durkheim considered *The Division of Labor* to be "an attempt to treat the facts of the moral life according to the method of the positive science."[39] To accomplish this task, he says, one must abandon the approach of traditional moralists who confront moral facts with a "pre-established general formula of morality." To found a science of ethics one needs to start with the analysis of moral facts, of "those duties generally admitted."[40] To recognize a moral fact one must rely on its externality and constraint, which Durkheim identifies as the *obligation* of its accomplishment and the *sanction* attached to its violation. Therefore, Durkheim argues, all rules of conduct whose transgressions are sanctioned are moral rules. Moreover, an act which is not obligatory cannot be a moral act.[41] In this context, any act left to the discretion of the individual would be, by definition, totally outside the realm of morality.

Durkheim's concept of anomie is an outcome of his moral philosophy rather than of his scientific empiricism. Durkheim claimed that society is the source of morality, and that the individual has no choice but to obey the rules of conduct pre-established by society. The history of ethics showed a change in social location from which morals were produced (from the ancient gods to the modern state) but no change in the compelling quality of moral rules. Morality remained societal, external to individuals, and coercive upon human behavior. Durkheim represents, in this context, the transcendental tradition that considers the relationships between man and society as pre-given. John Horton gives a clear account of Durkheim's transcendentalism:

> Preoccupied with the nature of order rather than change, Durkheim emphasized the passive side of the man–society relationship, how society makes and constrains men. His definition of anomie with its focus on the problems of social control and morality presupposes an absolute and eternal distinction between man and society and a dualistic conception of human nature ... Durkheim's man is *homo duplex*, part egoistic, anarchistic and self seeking, part moral in so far as he is regulated and constrained by society, which is the source of all logic and morality.[42]

Durkheim proposed as a scientific method and a scientific fact what was, in reality, a propositional statement about human nature, society, and morality.[43]

In 1902, when Durkheim dropped the 30-page section of the Introduction devoted to his science of ethics, he also added a second preface in which the concept of anomie had clear prominence. The preface to this new edition shows the development of Durkheim's thought on anomie. In 1902 Durkheim writes:

> If anomie is an evil, it is above all because society suffers from it, being unable to live without cohesion and regularity. A moral or juridical regulation essentially expresses, then, the social needs that society alone can feel.[44]

Once Durkheim had set forth his equation that morality equals social order, he made it inevitable that the concept of anomie should follow the same path. From being a simple negation of true morality, as Durkheim had claimed in 1893, anomie becomes any form of *deregulation* or lack of cohesion from which society may suffer. Moreover, Durkheim adds a juridical meaning to the originally moral connotation of anomie.[45] This development is still consistent with the premises of Durkheim's science of ethics. Society is the mainspring of moral rules; anomie is the negation of society and hence the negation of all morality; any loosening of societal rules, whether moral or juridical, can be labeled as anomie. Durkheim's conclusion to *The Division of Labor* states this quite clearly: "Man is a moral being only because he lives in society, since morality consists in being solidary with a group and varying with this solidarity."[46]

Despite the variety of themes covered by Durkheim in later works, his moral philosophy and the derived concept of anomie remained essentially unchanged. The technical use of anomie in parts of *The Division of Labor* and in *Suicide* can be considered a variation on the moral concern that produced Durkheim's original formulation. In later works, like *Moral Education* and *The Elementary Forms of the Religious Life*, the word anomie disappears, but the concern with moral order and the search for a solution to the pathological absence of moral norms in modern society is more explicit than in Durkheim's previous works.[47]

Anomie, Ethics, and Social Theory

Despite the wide divergence between the work of Guyau and that of Durkheim which I have outlined, there are also some similarities. Both authors are concerned with moral issues and with the development of new forms of morality. Their critique of both utilitarian doctrines and Kant's imperative morality is also a common feature; although their conclusions were quite different.[48] Both authors looked at the historical development of moral and religious ideas in relation to individuals and society, and both felt that the complete identification of the individual with the social group, a classical feature of the past, was giving way to the increasing freedom of individual speculation. Both agreed that this freedom caused a definite strain between society and its members. A reconciliation of the dualism was needed, and both authors saw this as their main task. They differed, however, in how they accomplished the task.

Guyau considered the rapid increase in knowledge of modern times as the main element reconciling the individual with society. Sociability itself arises from human speculation, in that human speculation reveals the illusory nature of egoistic pleasures. The more we become knowledgeable, the more our human pleasures assume a social and sociable character,[49] he argued. Guyau envisioned that the growth of knowledge and science would result in increasingly sociable moral sentiments, autonomously produced by individual speculation. The individual is at the center of history in modern times, being the primary source of knowledge and of moral ideas formerly held by religions. The new morality and the future religion are produced in a situation of individual autonomy and moral anomie. Their increasing differentiation means an advancement in the moral sphere, since evolution is characterized by going from the more homogeneous to the more heterogeneous.

Anomie, with autonomy, is historically grounded, being the logical outcome of the increasing relevance of individual speculation in society. Anomie is a recognition of the place that history has given to the individual in our society rather than a metaphysical escape from modern times. Modern individuals must not be afraid of a diversity of beliefs, Guyau warns: "If two men think in a different way, all the better; they are closer to the truth than if they would both think the same way." Moreover, he adds, the further we progress in our speculative ability, the more we will converge towards a shared intellectual ground.[50]

Individual speculation is not born in a vacuum, but is the outcome of human development throughout the centuries. It is also a skill in which individuals need to be trained. When morality is left to individual speculation, ignorance becomes synonymous with immorality: "Intellectual elevation," Guyau argues, "is always accompanied by moral elevation." If we educate the new generations in the spirit of free thought in which we believe, we are giving our pupils the speculative ability that will produce the sociability of moral and religious anomie.[51] Guyau devotes an entire book, *Education et hérédité*, to explaining the paramount role that education plays in modern society. Rather than providing a method of producing universal conformity, education should be pursued as an end in itself, as being an indispensable element for the attainment of total autonomy and anomie in the thought of the individual. Historically, education moved from the dogmatic ground of religious beliefs, to the speculative ground of free inquiry. The modern individual receives, through education, a training for the production of moral anomie.

While Guyau favors anomie and sees education as a means of promoting it, Durkheim opposes anomie and sees education as a means of overcoming it.

The major lines of Durkheim's opposition to anomie, which run through all his works, first appeared in his 1887 criticism of Guyau's *L'Irréligion de l'avenir*. The review contains five major points of concern. First, Durkheim criticizes Guyau for emphasizing the role of pure speculation in the genesis of religions at the expense of sound scientific explanations. Second, whereas Guyau considered religious phenomena as an outcome of human need for knowledge and sociability, Durkheim proposes that sociability, not knowledge, is the determining cause of religious sentiments. Third, Durkheim specifies the existence of two types of social sentiments: those between individuals, and those between individuals and representations of society as a whole. While Guyau considers inter-individual sentiments as more relevant in the origins of religions, Durkheim stresses the role of societal sentiments, since these are the only ones he believes capable of generating obligation in the individual. Fourth, Guyau identifies the progress of knowledge and scientific advancement as the cause of dissolution of traditional religions. Durkheim, on the contrary, argues that since religion is a social phenomenon one must find what it is that has changed in the nature of societies to cause the decline of traditional religions. Fifth, and last, Durkheim contests Guyau's claim that metaphysical speculation will survive the decline of traditional religion. Durkheim argues:

> What, moreover, guarantees that metaphysics must be eternal? The great service which it rendered to science was to remind it constantly that it had limits, and that is why it has endured. But why should it not happen one day that this feeling of the limits of our science, confirmed by long experience, should not penetrate science itself, and become an integral element of the scientific spirit?[52]

Durkheim's objections to Guyau are both methodological and substantive; two issues are at stake here. First, does positive science adequately explain the genesis of religions? Durkheim's criticism of Guyau (first and fifth points) argues that it does. Second, does the separation of individual and society enhance our understanding of religious phenomena? Durkheim says yes, and he reiterates this point in his second, third, and fourth criticism of Guyau's work. Guyau emphasizes the separation of science and values through the combined use of positive and speculative methods. Also he preserves the unity of the individual and society in his attempt to explain religious phenomena. Durkheim, instead, advocates the use of a positive method alone and considers the social phenomena as altogether separate and distinct from the individual. With these premises, Durkheim sets himself to the task of explaining through scientific observation all aspects of social life, beginning with the most relevant one, morality.

In *The Division of Labor* Durkheim claims that moral facts are eminently social, and he attempts to build a science of ethics that relies solely on their empirical observation. Durkheim denies the separation of moral facts from their value: "What reconciles science and ethics is the science of ethics, for at the time that it teaches us to respect the moral reality, it furnishes us with the means to improve it."[53] The identification of moral actions with their desirability caused all phenomena that departed from the normal moral order to be considered anomic, a negation of all morality. Because of its disruptive effect on the normal status anomie was, for Durkheim, an undesirable phenomenon in the social organism.

In later stages of his career, i.e. in *Moral Education*, Durkheim recognizes the factor of knowledge, underestimated in earlier works, as an important element of modern morality. His approach to it is still antithetical to Guyau's. Guyau sees education and knowledge as active producers of religious individuality and moral anomie; Durkheim, rather, considers education as a passive method of achieving social consensus, a constraining factor to the moral anomie of his time.

Durkheim describes, in *Moral Education*, three main elements of morality: a spirit of discipline, attachment to social groups, and autonomy or self-determination. With regard to autonomy Durkheim argues:

> To act morally, it is not enough – above all, it is no longer enough – to respect discipline and to be committed to a group. Beyond this, and whether out of deference to a rule or devotion to a collective ideal, we must have knowledge, as clear and complete an awareness as possible of the reason for our conduct. This consciousness confers on our behavior the autonomy that the public conscience from now on requires of every genuinely and completely moral being.[54]

Autonomy, Durkheim adds, is what distinguishes the secular morality of our days from the religious morality of former times. But the autonomy that Durkheim advocates is only a fictitious one. Since moral understanding comes from science, science is certainly a source of autonomy. Such autonomy, however, does not imply a freedom of moral choice:

> To the extent that we see that it is everything it ought to be – that it is as the nature of things implies – we can conform, not simply because we are physically restrained and unable to do otherwise without danger, but because we deem it good and have no better alternative.[55]

The educational process, then, is not a step forward in the emancipation of individual freedom, but a more sophisticated way of obtaining a general consensus. The social changes that Guyau had outlined – the new religion, the new morality – do not appear in Durkheim's theory. Durkheim favors, rather, the reconstruction of traditional values on a new social platform, as he acknowledges himself:

> Now it is apparent that we have succeeded in expressing all these moral realities in rational terms. All that we needed was to substitute for the conception of a supernatural being the empirical idea of a directly observable being, which is society.[56]

Guyau saw a dynamic and changing society with the individual as the active agent of such change. Durkheim, instead, stressed that despite apparent changes in society, the externality and constraint of moral codes remained unchanged. Clearly, Durkheim's and Guyau's concepts of anomie are embedded in divergent methodological and substantive claims; their assumptions about the nature of society and the way society should be studied are, in the end, what make the two concepts so different.

Now, in conclusion, I briefly want to argue that Guyau's concept of anomie is historically and theoretically grounded, and presents itself as a valid alternative to Durkheim's. Guyau identifies, in the history of ethics, an evolution of moral forms that is worth investigating in its own right. Morality is not, for Guyau, a mere representation of social solidarity. Instead, morality has an autonomous life of its own. The relationship between individual and collectivity is shaped equally by different moral forms. Durkheim equates morality with solidarity, thereby preventing the possibility of historical variation of forms of morality.[57] Guyau believes that different moral forms have developed historically, and that moral anomie, the absence of fixed moral rules, is characteristic of the ethics of modern time. In contrast, by proposing his interpretation of morality, Durkheim falls victim to his concern for social order and therefore disregards the historical forms of morality, and their changing relation to social solidarity.

Guyau's concept of anomie is a valid alternative to Durkheim's, not only because it is historically well grounded, but also because it is theoretically sound. Durkheim creates an unbridgeable gap between individual and society, by claiming that social phenomena can only be explained in terms of the social. His view of society as different and qualitatively superior to the individual, and his concept of morality as a prerogative of society alone, cause Durkheim to build a theoretical system that is teleologically closed, that comes full circle. Durkheim's conclusions are implicit in the assumptions he initially made about the nature of society. Guyau, instead, argues that "there is a profound harmony underlying the antinomies between individual existence and collective existence."[58] According to Guyau, the individual and the social find their unifying element in the human impulse for action, a source, itself, of moral fecundity. Durkheim's idea is that society is transcendental, external to the individual; Guyau's idea is that society is immanent, that it is within the individual who is an active maker and remaker of the social environment.

Durkheim's and Guyau's concepts of anomie are intimately linked with their theories at large. Durkheim's theory is axiomatic in nature. Anomie can be identified only as a negation of morality, not as an alternative to a prevailing system of morality; this means that anomie does not have an autonomous identity, but exists only as a *lack* of moral status, a *deformation* of the ideal standard. Guyau instead proposes moral anomie as a form of morality independently created by the increase in human knowledge and rationality, a morality in its own right, not a mere negation, as Durkheim argues. Durkheim's equation of social facts with moral facts, and of these with the ideal morality, seems unwarranted because it overlooks the *formal* aspect of ethics under the pretense of empirically observing the *moral substance* in society. Such an approach covers with a pseudo-scientific method what, in the end, is an apology for immutable social order. Guyau's approach is well deserving of attention because it does not subsume the moral form under any social substance but analyzes it as it is, as an historical form. The blurring of formal morality and solidarity causes Durkheim to establish value hierarchies in his research. On the positive side, morality equals solidarity, which equals good. On the negative side, anomie equals lack of cohesion, which in turn equals evil. Guyau's crucial distinction between moral facts and moral forms allows for an historically sound and insightful description of ethics.

Durkheim's concept of anomie and his social theory in general have had a long-lasting effect on contemporary sociology; Guyau's concept of anomie is, in this respect, faced with an almost impossible task. But here the issue is not so much one of an either/or between the two concepts; instead, it is a matter of putting Durkheim's concept in the proper perspective, and of utilizing Guyau's notion of anomie as a salutary counterbalance to Durkheim's "oversocialized notion of man."[59] Moreover, we do not need to go too far in order to find modern discussions of anomie which, to some extent, subscribe to Guyau's views on anomie and morality. To make a point which might seem paradoxical, American sociology and its discussions of anomie have, in good measure, moved away from Durkheim's social realism, toward an individualism and a voluntarism which shows a striking intellectual affinity to Guyau's thought. It is then realistic to surmise that Guyau's theories of anomie and ethics are after all, much closer to the modern intellectual climate than the ones of Emile Durkheim. I will attempt to show their affinity in the next chapter.

Notes

1 Some state explicitly that Durkheim first resurrected anomie in sociology, while others assume it implicitly. See, for instance, Sebastian de Grazia, *The Political Community* (Chicago: University of Chicago Press, 1948), xii, 195; Robert K. Merton, *Social Theory and Social Structure* (New York: Free Press, 1957), 135n; Robert Bierstedt, "Anomy (anomie)," in *A Dictionary of the Social Sciences*, ed. Julius Gould and William Kolb (New York: Free Press, 1964), 29–30; Elton Mayo, *The Human Problems of an Industrial Civilization* (1933; reprinted New York: Viking, 1960), 124; Robert M. MacIver, *The Ramparts We Guard* (New York: Macmillan, 1956), 139; R. H. Brookes, "The anatomy of anomie (I)," *Political Science* (New Zealand) 3 (1951):44; Marshall B. Clinard, ed., *Anomie and Deviant Behavior* (New York: Free Press, 1964), 3.

2 As of 1983, when this chapter first appeared as a journal article, only Anthony Giddens had mentioned Durkheim's indebtedness to Guyau for the anomie concept. Cf. Anthony Giddens, *Capitalism and Modern Social Theory* (Cambridge: Cambridge University Press, 1971), 80n. Philippe Besnard informed me, in a personal communication, that Durkheim's borrowing of the term from Guyau is common knowledge, at least in France. See, for instance, J. C. Filloux, *Durkheim et le socialisme* (Geneva: Droz, 1977). Donald N. Levine has commented recently on the Guyau–Durkheim issue in his *The Flight from Ambiguity* (Chicago: University of Chicago Press, 1985), 61.

3 Emile Durkheim, *The Division of Labor in Society*, trans. George Simpson (1933; reprinted New York: Free Press, 1964), 431n.

4 In his *Critique des systèmes de morale contemporaine*, Alfred Fouillée distinguishes between transcendental and immanent moral theories (1883; reprinted Paris: Felix Alcan, 1912), 389–408. John Horton, describing Durkheim's concept of anomie, relates it to a transcendental interpretation of society. John Horton, "The Dehumanization of Anomie and Alienation," *British Journal of Sociology* 15 (December 1964):288–91.

5 Robert A. Nisbet, *Emile Durkheim* (Englewood Cliffs: Prentice-Hall, 1965), 9.

6   Steven Lukes, *Emile Durkheim: His Life and Work* (Harmondsworth: Penguin, 1973), 41.

7   For a detailed account of these three philosophical currents, see J. Alexander Gunn, *Modern French Philosophy* (London: T. Fisher Unwin, 1922).

8   Lukes, *Emile Durkheim*, 72.

9   Gunn, *Modern French Philosophy*, 74.

10 ibid., 81.

11 Quoted in *The Stanford Dictionary* (1892) s.v. "*anomia.*"

12 The international fame of Guyau is testified by the translation of his major works, shortly after his death, into English, German, Spanish, and Italian. Guyau's critique of religion and morality was compared to Nietzsche's, his philosophy of life to Bergson's, his aesthetics to Croce's.

13 See, for instance, E. A. Ross, "Social Control," *American Journal of Sociology* 2 (1897):255–63; Charles Horton Cooley, *Human Nature and the Social Order* (New York: Scribner, 1902).

14 Josiah Royce, *Studies on Good and Evil* (1898; reprinted New York: Appleton, 1910), 349.

15 ibid., 362.

16 Jean Marie Guyau, *La Morale anglaise contemporaine* (1879; reprinted Paris: Felix Alcan, 1885), 379. I have translated all original quotations.

17 Jean Marie Guyau, *Esquisse d'une morale sans obligation ni sanction* (1885; reprinted Paris: Felix Alcan, 1896), 5–6.

18 ibid., 6. Guyau uses, in this passage, the adjective anomic (*anomos*) rather than the noun anomie (*anomia*). A comparison between autonomy and anomie similar to Guyau's is found in Plutarch, *Moralia* 755B, a text probably familiar to Guyau.

19 Cf. Guyau, *Esquisse*, bk 1, ch. 1.

20 ibid., 7.

21 G. Aslan, *La Morale selon Guyau* (Paris: Felix Alcan, 1906). Aslan's work is a doctoral dissertation that advocated the superiority of the positive approach to morality, and was presented at the Sorbonne in Paris, where Durkheim was a member of the examination jury. The proceedings, with Durkheim's comments, appeared in the *Revue de metaphysique et de morale* 14 (July 1906): 12–14.

22 Guyau, *Esquisse*, 163–4.

23 ibid., 164.

24 ibid., 165.

25 ibid., 165–6.

26 Jean Marie Guyau, *L'Irréligion de l'avenir: étude de sociologie* (1887; reprinted Paris: Felix Alcan, 1921), vii.

27 ibid., xiii.

28 ibid., xv.

29 Guyau mentions in a footnote, at this point, his *Esquisse*.

30 Guyau, *L'Irréligion*, 323.

31 Emile Durkheim, "Guyau. L'Irréligion de l'avenir: étude de sociologie," *Revue philosophique* 23 (1887): 299–311.

32 ibid., 304.

33 ibid., 309.

34 Ernest Wallwork noted the importance of the remarks: "Durkheim himself provides the most succinct summary of the foregoing aspects of his early theory of moral sentiments and obligation in his review (1887) of Guyau's *L'Irréligion de l'avenir: étude de sociologie*." Ernest Wallwork, *Durkheim: Morality and Milieu* (Cambridge, Mass.: Harvard University Press, 1972), 40.

35 The evolution of Durkheim's concept of anomie is discussed, among others, by Marvin E. Olsen, "Durkheim's Two Concepts of Anomie," *Sociological Quarterly* 6 (Winter 1965):37–44; Stephen R. Marks, "Durkheim's Theory of Anomie," *American Journal of Sociology* 80 (September 1974):329–63; Talcott Parsons, *The Structure of Social Action* (1937; reprinted New York: Free Press, 1968), 334–8; Bernard Lacroix, "Regulation et anomie selon Durkheim," *Cahiers Internationaux de Sociologie* Vol. 55 (new series, 20th year), (July–December 1973):265–92; Philippe Besnard, "L'anomie dans la biographie intellectuelle de Durkheim," *Sociologie et Sociétés* 14 (1982):45–53. For an exhaustive list see the bibliographical appendix to this monograph. Some of the literature will be discussed in detail in the next chapter.

36 We can safely assume that all the authors who defined Durkheim's first concept as one of "economic anomie" had in mind the third book and not the introduction to *The Division of Labor*. Marks, "Durkheim's theory of anomie," 330, and Olsen, "Durkheim's two concepts," 39, explicitly state this.

37 In later editions Durkheim explained: "We feel justified in suppressing about thirty pages of the old introduction, which appear useless to us today." *Division*, 1n.

38 Durkheim, *Division*, 431n. While Durkheim does not explicitly mention Guyau in the passage, the context would support my hypothesis. Durkheim's object of discussion was the claim made by some (read Guyau), that the aesthetico-moral activity had a certain superiority. Guyau had extensively made such a point in his *L'Art au point de vue sociologique* (1889; reprinted Paris: Felix Alcan, 1930). Maurice Blondel, a French philosopher, echoed Durkheim's remark: "The estheticism marks, no doubt, a further step in the development of the intellectual and moral anomie." Maurice Blondel, *L'Action* (1893; reprinted Paris: Presses universitaires de France, 1950), 18.

39 Durkheim, *Division*, 32.

40 ibid., 411.

41 ibid., 431.

42 Horton, "The Dehumanization of Anomie," 289–90.

43 This point has also been made by Niklas Luhmann in his introduction to the German translation of *The Division of Labor*. Cf. Niklas

Luhmann, *The Differentiation of Society*, trans. Stephen Holmes and Charles Larmore (New York: Columbia University Press, 1982), 3–19.

44 Durkheim, *Division*, 5.
45 Previous historical examples of a concept of juridical anomie are found, as we have seen, in the writings of the English jurist William Lambarde, not to mention the works of Plato and Aristotle in ancient Greece. See Chapters 1 and 3 above.
46 Durkheim, *Division*, 399.
47 Cf. Marks, "Durkheim's Theory of Anomie."
48 Durkheim shared Guyau's criticism of the utilitarian doctrine to the point of citing Guyau's *Morale Anglaise* in the introduction to *The Division of Labor* (415n).
49 Guyau, *Esquisse*, 113.
50 ibid., 166–7.
51 Guyau, *L'Irréligion*, 232.
52 Emile Durkheim, *Selected Writings*, edited, translated, and with an introduction by Anthony Giddens (Cambridge: Cambridge University Press, 1972), 221.
53 Durkheim, *Division*, 36.
54 Emile Durkheim, *Moral Education*, trans. Everett K. Wilson and Herman Schnurer (New York: Free Press, 1960), 120.
55 ibid., 115.
56 ibid., 104.
57 Cf. Alessandro Pizzorno, "Lecture actuelle de Durkheim," *Archives Européennes de Sociologie* 4 (1963):1–36.
58 Jean Marie Guyau, *Education and Heredity: A Study in Sociology*, trans. W. J. Greenstreet (London: W. Scott, 1891), xix.
59 Cf. Dennis H. Wrong, "The Oversocialized Conception of Man in Modern Sociology," *American Sociological Review* 26 (April 1961):183–93.

CHAPTER 5

Contemporary Anomie Literature

The history of the concept of anomie takes us, in this chapter, away from the intellectual world of Western Europe, to the American context. This transition has major and far-reaching consequences for the development of anomie theory. The change of intellectual climate is so drastic that the apparently fragmentary outlook of the new field of sociology on one side of the Atlantic acquires a unitary character, when compared with the sociological outlook on the other side. It is in relation to American sociology that European sociology acquires a distinctive identity, just as it is in comparison with the European outlook that American sociology can be characterized as having certain specific qualities.

European writers obviously influenced the American intellectual world, but the socio-historical conditions of the "New Continent" were so different that the same ideas could hardly mean the same thing on both continents. The chief role of European intellectuals was to be critical of the existing social arrangements, but most American intellectuals were more concerned with the consolidation of a liberal society.[1] The difference is not a minor one, for it can be detected not only in the cultural climate at large, but also in the specific contributions of American sociological theories and related concepts of anomie. Geoffrey Hawthorn summarizes the issue:

> In Europe, as Durkheim, for instance, and his opponents saw ... to be an intellectual was to criticise, to criticise not merely the ways in which various groups sought to achieve their ends but also, and much more importantly, to criticise the ends themselves. In America, the ends have been given, given both in the ideological sense and also, and much more forcefully, in the very constitution of the society itself. To mount an argument against them has been to mount an argument against America

and thus, to mount an argument that immediately disqualifies itself from serious consideration as a relevant argument at all.[2]

Durkheim's concept of anomie and the one found in contemporary American sociology differ exactly in this crucial way: for Durkheim anomie refers to the ill-conceived cultural goals of industrial societies, whereas for American sociologists anomie refers to the inadequacy of means for the fulfillment of society's culturally sanctioned goals. These goals, by and large, have been implicitly adhered to in American sociology. This shift of focus implies an abandonment of the European sociological tradition of a "Grand Theory" which sketches the blueprint of a utopian society in favor of a piecemeal social engineering which looks for technical improvements in an otherwise sound social structure.

My basic claim concerning contemporary anomie theory is that it has departed significantly (even if unconsciously) from Durkheim's theory. Hardly anyone today subscribes to Durkheim's original notion of anomie; this is not surprising, since the cultural context and the metatheoretical assumptions of Durkheimian nineteenth-century sociology and of American twentieth-century sociology are just as divergent as are their respective notions of anomie. That Durkheim's and contemporary concepts of anomie differ is not altogether a new insight – it has been pointed out by several commentators (mostly European sociologists) who often criticized such divergence.[3] What has been missing so far, however, is the attempt to clarify the crucial moral implications of contemporary anomie theories, and their relation to the socio-cultural context of contemporary America.

The contemporary anomie literature can be classified under three headings: (1) American theories of sociological and psychological anomie; (2) commentaries on classical and contemporary theories of anomie; (3) literature which focuses directly on the value implications of modern anomie. In this chapter I will address in turn each of these three themes in order to show the underlying trend in contemporary writings away from a transcendental, hypostatized concept, toward an empirically grounded, instrumental use of anomie. Moreover, I will show that the shift in the anomie literature parallels the changing moral assumptions of modern societies.

American Theories of Anomie

The two main theories of anomie in American literature are those of Robert Merton (on the social–structural aspects of anomie) and of Leo Srole (on the psychological characteristics of anomie).[4] Chronologically, Merton's theory goes back to the late 1930s, while Srole's work appeared in the early 1950s; yet, the two elaborations share common theoretical bases and have been integrated in much anomie research.[5] For the purpose of this study it is unnecessary to review every article or book devoted to anomie;[6] what is necessary, instead, is to clarify as much as possible the position of the main theories in relation to the moral issues that have emerged from the history of the concept up to this point. For this purpose, I will gloss over details in the literature and focus selectively on some key moral assumptions. This will often require a simplification of the original arguments, but such simplification will not distort, I hope, the basic meaning of the theory analyzed.

MERTON ON ANOMIE

The most significant contribution to an American theory of anomie is the one initiated by Robert Merton in his classical essay, "Social Structure and Anomie," first published in 1938. The restoration of the anomie concept in the sociological literature began sometime before Merton's essay appeared; already in the late 1920s American sociologists had revisited Durkheim's thought and modified their previous negative assessment of Durkheim's social realism in favor of a more selective and positive interpretation of his writings.[7]

The concept of anomie resurfaced with the re-evaluation of Durkheim's thought. Two assessments of Durkheim's theory of anomie before 1938 are particularly relevant: Elton Mayo's description and utilization of the concept of anomie in his 1933 book, *The Human Problems of an Industrial Civilization*, and Talcott Parsons' extensive analysis of Durkheim's theory of anomie in his 1937 book, *The Structure of Social Action*.[8] Both assessments are relevant to Merton's own formulation of a theory of anomie. In Mayo's work, anomie is for the first time adopted in American social science as a valid research concept. By taking the concept of anomie and applying it to the practical problems addressed by Chicago sociologists, Mayo turns Durkheim's ideological anomie into a term that will better define the problems of social disorganization.[9] Parsons' contribution is even more relevant for the formulation of Merton's theory. In his attempt to bring

120

together into a theoretical synthesis the works of Marshall, Pareto, Durkheim, and Weber, Talcott Parsons recasts Durkheim's theory of anomie into his own theory of social action. The interpretation Parsons offers is that anomie is explained, by Durkheim, on two grounds: by the lack of equilibrium between means and ends of action, and by the unclear definition of the ends themselves.[10] For Parsons, Durkheim's theory of anomie had developed from *The Division of Labor* to *Suicide*: in the earlier work anomie simply described a deregulation of means in relation to set goals; in the latter it included the lack of specified social ends of action as determinants of anomie.[11]

In the framework of a general theory of action, Parsons sees Durkheim's concept of anomie as illustrating the problems created by what Pareto calls "interests" – the generalized means of wealth and power in the economic and political spheres.[12] Force and fraud are the means often used for the acquisition of wealth and power; "The appearance of either or both on a considerable scale may be considered a symptom of lack of social integration."[13] Especially the use of fraud, Parsons points out, "is a symptom of a kind of individualization, the dissolution of community ties ... approaching as a polar type the state Durkheim called *anomie*."[14]

By reworking Durkheim's sociology theoretically, Parsons brought him within the voluntaristic perspective of American social theory. The relevance of Durkheim's theory to the means–ends scheme of social action was located in its usefulness for explaining conditions of social disorganization. The next obvious step was to tease out the practical usefulness of Parsons' operation, a task accomplished by Robert Merton in his highly influential paper, "Social Structure and Anomie."

Merton's theory of anomie is most significant because there we find not another commentary on Durkheim, but an altogether *new* theory. Merton was obviously familiar with Durkheim's sociology, he knew Pareto's works, and he had been a critical reader of Parsons; but the three authors are hardly mentioned in his paper.[15] From the context of Merton's theory, however, it is clear that he is concerned not with the anomie generated by the unclear definition of cultural goals, but with the anomie deriving from the lack of equilibrium between means and ends of action. This corresponded to Parsons's description of Durkheim's first explanation of anomie.[16] However, Merton goes beyond this point; his theory takes a relevance of its own by articulating the logical possibilities that an imbalance between culture goals and institutional means entails. He also provides in his theory a crucial distinction between the imbalance as it relates to the "culture patterning" and as it relates to the "modes of adjustment or adaption *by individuals*".[17]

The basic argument of Merton's paper is that the coupling of culture goals and institutional means can be characterized either by a disproportionate emphasis on culture goals at the expense of institutionalized means (as we find in American culture), or by an opposite emphasis on means at the expense of goals (when ritualistic conformity dominates). Between the two opposites Merton locates the (theoretical) instance of "groups where the balance between culture goals and institutionalized means is maintained."[18] Taken together these describe, in Merton's words, "three ideal types of social orders constituted by distinctive patterns of relations between culture ends and means."[19]

Merton states clearly that "We shall be primarily concerned with ... a disproportionate accent on goals."[20] However, it seems that anomie would apply to any kind of imbalance between culture goals and institutionalized means. Merton's relevant statements about anomie clarify this ambiguity: anomie refers to a *specific imbalance* where cultural goals are overemphasized at the expense of institutionalized means. Merton writes that in this condition of imbalance, "the technically most feasible procedure, whether legitimate or not, is preferred to institutionally prescribed conduct. As this process continues, the integration of society becomes tenuous and *anomie ensues*."[21] In the same section Merton remarks in a footnote that "We are considering the unintegrated monetary-success goal as an element in producing anomie."[22] It seems clear, then, that anomie only pertains to this type of imbalance between the culture goals and institutional means – where the goals are overemphasized. Merton reinforces this argument when he writes, "In groups where the primary emphasis shifts to institutional means, i.e., when the range of alternatives is very limited, the outcome is a type of *ritualism rather than anomie*."[23]

Merton then moves from the "types of *culture patterning*" to individual modes of adaptation. Here we find the well-known five categories of conformity, innovation, ritualism, retreatism, and rebellion, generated by different emphases between goals and means at the level of modes of individual adaptation. The first three modes parallel Merton's three types of culture patterning; retreatism and rebellion, instead, describe two new logical possibilities regarding the means–ends distinction.

In Merton's "Social Structure and Anomie," the major concern in relation to both culture patternings and to individual adaptations is clearly with the anomic type – exemplified by American society's emphasis on the goal of success and by the "illegitimacy

adjustment" as a "normal" response to such cultural malintegration.[24] Regarding culture patterning Merton remarks that "we
shall be primarily concerned with the ... disproportionate accent
on goals"; concerning modes of adaptation, he declares: "Our
major concern is with the illegitimacy adjustment."[25] Merton's
theory is, in the end, a straightforward functional theory of
deviance.[26] In a society where wealth and power (Pareto's
"interests") have been overemphasized as desirable ends of action,
the danger is always present that illegitimate means will be used for
the acquisition of these socially upheld ends. Merton points out:
"Fraud, corruption, vice, crime, in short, the entire catalogue of
proscribed behavior, becomes increasingly common when the
emphasis on the *culturally induced* success-goal becomes divorced
from a coordinated institutional emphasis."[27]

My reading of Merton's theory reduces the significance of an
important intervening element: the "differential access to the
approved opportunities for legitimate, prestige-bearing pursuit of
the culture goals".[28] For the purpose of clarifying the basic ethical
assumptions of Merton's theory of anomie, this aspect of his
argument seems of secondary import. It is not the structurally
limited opportunity for success that originally causes anomie;
rather, it is the *culturally induced pressure* to be successful that
accounts for the ensuing anomie. Merton points out: "Only
insofar as poverty ... is linked with the assimilation of a cultural
emphasis on monetary accumulation as a symbol of success is
antisocial conduct a 'normal' outcome."[29] This fact is clarified in
the expanded version of Merton's paper, where he points out that
"in the American Dream there is no final stopping point."[30] The
pressure toward non-conforming behavior is at work throughout
American society at large, because of its unending pursuit of
success; the variation in access to the socially sanctioned goals,
then, accounts for the likelihood that certain social groups, more
than others, will engage in rule-breaking behavior.[31]

Merton's theory of anomie departs significantly from Durkheim's classical formulation. Merton clearly moves away from
Durkheim's attempt to criticize social ends, and focuses instead on
the consequences of a certain kind of social pressure on the
behavior of individuals. For Merton, the great emphasis on the
monetary (or other) success-goal is problematic insofar as it leads
to aberrant conduct; it is not, as Durkheim would have it, an
undesirable social end *by definition*. Merton's approach to the
study of American cultural values is significant in that he limits his
analysis to the causal efficacy of these values, leaving aside the issue
of their desirability. More to the point, Merton is able to show that

anomie is fostered by the American egalitarian ideology, and that therefore anomie is, paradoxically, an unintended consequence of democracy; accordingly, anomie can be seen as a *normal response* to a specific kind of structurally generated social pressure.[32] This is a far cry from Durkheim's notion that anomie is inevitably an abnormal form, and that it is, as such, the "contradiction of all morality."[33] In the same vein, Merton argues that monetary success is a likely candidate as the culturally approved goal in a democratic society, because money is "highly abstract and impersonal."[34] In contrast to other standards of social prestige and success, money as such is, so to speak, status-blind; it is more likely to undermine social arrangements based on tradition and caste systems.

Seen from this angle, Merton's theory leans clearly toward an empirically grounded, instrumental notion of anomie; it moves away from the transcendental moral philosophy of Durkheim and situates itself in the mainstream of a scientifically-oriented, value-free kind of inquiry. Here, the concept of anomie is used to clarify the contradictory consequences of an overwhelming emphasis on the monetary success-goal coupled with the inadequacy of the existing opportunity structure. The problem, accordingly, is seen in terms of the imbalance between cultural goals and institutional means, not in terms of appropriate or inappropriate cultural goals.

The empirical research which developed following Merton's classical work explored various aspects of his anomie theory. The overwhelming majority focused on the "illegitimacy adjustment" as a structural explanation for criminal activity in general and juvenile delinquency in particular.[35] Other researchers focused on the full or partial typology of modes of adaptation in relation to various situations where an emphasis on achievement of set goals is particularly strong.[36] Whether such literature applied Merton's theory straightforwardly or whether it sought to modify or integrate it with other existing theories of deviant behavior, the implicit consensus was that the explanation of anomic phenomena had to be carried out scientifically by withholding judgment about the desirability of observed culture goals in contemporary society. In this sense, Merton's basic theoretical insight was fully endorsed.[37] We will later analyze some of the literature criticizing Merton's theory and show the varying presuppositions of such critiques.

SROLE'S THEORY OF ANOMIA

Although it highlighted individual modes of adaptation, Merton's theory was proposed as a social-structural explanation of individual malintegration. In the words of Benjamin Nelson, "Aiming at a distinctively *sociological* approach to *anomie* and 'deviant' behavior, Merton pitted Durkheim against Freud and appeared to succeed in bracketing psychological factors as 'residual categories'."[38]

Merton's "Social Structure and Anomie" provided a theory of anomie indigenous to American sociology and stimulated much empirical research on the topic; it also favored, somewhat paradoxically, the reappraisal of Durkheim's original insights about anomie. A rereading of Durkheim's texts resulted in either a restoration of Durkheim's concern with the desirability of certain social ends in modern society, or it focused on the psychological aspects of anomie which surfaced regularly, if surreptitiously, in Durkheim's work.

Sebastian de Grazia's monograph, *The Political Community*, was the result of a reappraisal in the first direction.[39] As it might be expected, de Grazia's attempt was to have little impact on the later literature, since it resurrected the value judgments which had made Durkheim's theory unappealing to American theorists. If Merton had attempted to free Durkheim's theory of its ethical overtones, de Grazia moved in the opposite direction by totally ideologizing the concept.

For several reasons the literature on the psychological aspects of anomie was more stimulating to American sociologists than de Grazia's traditionalist plea. First, the accounting of anomie on a psychological level was appealing to the voluntaristic individualism of many American social scientists. Second, the emphasis on psychological components was not sought in opposition to Merton's structural emphasis, but rather was seen as a complement to it. Third, the formulation of a psychological concept of anomie favored empirical systematization through the construction of a scale which measured anomie in individuals.

To clarify the moral assumptions of the psychological theory of anomie it will be useful to look at two most relevant works: R. M. MacIver's *The Ramparts We Guard* and Leo Srole's "Social Integration and Certain Corollaries."[40] In his book, published in 1950, MacIver defines psychological anomie (or anomy, as he calls it) as "the breakdown of the individual's sense of attachment to society."[41] He relates such a breakdown to three problematic characteristics of modern democratic society: (1) culture clash, (2) capitalistic competitiveness, and (3) violence of [social] change.[42] For MacIver, Merton was wrong in associating anomie *exclusively* with capitalistic competitiveness;[43] two additional aspects needed to be assessed as well. MacIver distinguishes, accordingly, three types of anomic individuals who mirror, at the psychological level, the three social dimensions of anomie. Culture clash is epitomized by "those who, having lost ... any system of values ... having lost the compass that points their course into the future, abandon themselves to the present"; capitalistic competitiveness is characteristic of "those who, having lost their ethical goals ... transfer this drive into extrinsic values to the pursuit of means instead of ... ends, and particularly to the pursuit of power"; rapid social change is exemplified by those who "have lost the ground on which they stood, the ground of their former values."[44]

Widening the range of structural conditions related to psychological anomie MacIver saw modern democracy as instrumental to the rise of anomie: "The association of democracy with anomy is then a special one."[45] This fact, however, did not lead him to seek a forced type of solidarity, but a strengthening of democracy's positive qualities. It is through the substantive application of the principles of equality and freedom that a democratic society can command the voluntary allegiance of its members.[46] Srole draws clearly on MacIver's psychological theory, but compared to MacIver's, Srole's theory is less concerned with the cultural determinants of anomie than with the identification of its specific traits at the individual level. To distinguish between the social and the psychological dimensions, Leo Srole coined the term *anomia* to describe, at the general level, a psychological condition of "self-to-other alienation."[48] Srole distinguishes five dimensions of anomia which he operationalized into five interview questions constituting the anomia scale. The five items refer to: (1) "The individual's sense that community leaders are detached from and indifferent to his needs"; (2) "The individual's perception of the social order as essentially fickle and unpredictable"; (3) "The individual's view ... that he and the people like him are retrogressing from the goals they have already reached"; (4) "The individual's sense of the meaninglessness of life itself"; and (5) "The individual's perception that his framework of immediate personal relationships ... was no longer predictable or supportive."[48]

The background assumption of Srole's scale is that the desirable condition of social systems is characterized at the macrosocial (*molar*) level by the "integratedness" of different social systems or subsystems, and at the microsocial (*molecular*) level by the functional integration of individuals in relation to the social normative situation. Anomia expresses the malintegration or dysfunctional relation of individuals to their social worlds; more specifically, the anomic individual will appear to be alienated from the political system (item 1), the cultural system (item 2), the economic system (item 3), "internalized social norms and values" (item 4), and the primary socialization group (item 5). Srole acknowledges that individual anomia can be explained by the presence of social anomie, but he points out that the opposite causal link is also significant, as psychological anomia feeds back to social anomie. (On this ground he argues that "considerations of operational efficiency" point to the development of a scale measuring anomia as a psychological state.)[49]

Srole's anomia items are in good measure related to MacIver's earlier formulation of psychological traits of anomie: Srole's third and fifth anomia items resemble MacIver's third "type of anomy" which is characteristic of those who "have lost their former connections [Srole's item 5], their social place, their economic support [item 3]." Similarly, the second item ("Nowadays a person has to live pretty much for today and let tomorrow take care of itself") echoes MacIver's anomics who "abandon themselves to the present, but a present emptied of significance."[50]

Still, the relevance of Srole's anomia scale goes beyond its re-elaboration of MacIver's insights. The articulation of an empirically useful scale which measured anomia made it possible to shift the focus of attention away from the structural determinants of anomia toward the effect of such a psychological condition on other individual attitudes and conditions. No longer a phenomenon to be explained, anomie had been turned into an explanatory variable. Srole's approach shifted the burden of identifying the presence and the extent of anomie away from the theorists and put it into the hands of individual respondents. This shift provided the concept of anomie with an objective, standard measurement. The concept itself was now amenable to "objective" assessment – the scale had provided the empirical grounding of anomie.

We still need to clarify the theoretical and ethical meanings of Srole's scale. At both the *molar* and the *molecular* level, the underlying notion is that the anomic condition is problematic because of the *dysfunctional relation* among social subsystems or of individuals to these subsystems. Capitalistic competitiveness, culture clash, and rapid social change are not deemed problematic or undesirable *per se*; rather, it is the *inability* of the social-system components and of individuals to re-equilibrate themselves functionally which characterizes (social) anomie and (psychological) anomia. Srole's work parallels Merton's in that both theories deem it appropriate to bypass the evaluation of culture goals in American society (because they implicitly regard such evaluation as scientifically inappropriate) and focus instead on the undesirable (not normatively but empirically undesirable) consequences of a lack of co-ordination between social subsystems and individual psychological states. The problem is one of instrumental adequacy, not of normative adequacy.

In Srole's development of an anomia scale, as in Merton's theory of anomie, the key concern is to *detect* the presence or absence of functional balance. Merton's theory of socio-cultural malintegration interprets anomie as the unintended (but inevitable) consequence of a generalized emphasis on the success-goal coupled with the democratic ideals of equal access to structured opportunities. Srole's scale is similarly instrumental in clarifying a set of anomic social-psychological dimensions which are related to cultural ambiguity, economic competitiveness, and rapid social change. Unstated but apparent in both authors' work is the notion that anomie and anomia are *structural conditions* of modern social life: that they "go with the territory."

The distinctive characteristic of American theories of anomie consisted in their elimination of the moral overtones which anomie carried in Durkheimian sociology. This was done by considering anomie as a contingent problem of modernity by reason of its dysfunctional effects on individuals and the social system. Both Merton and Srole refused to consider anomie evaluatively, from an ideological, transcendental viewpoint; instead, they promoted a structurally embedded concept of anomie. This development had two consequences which are normatively at odds with each other. On the one hand, a structurally embedded theory of anomie endorses, implicitly, a relativism of ultimate ends.[51] By refusing to evaluate anomie as a moral concept, Merton and Srole are open to the possibility that value anomie *might* be morally desirable. The only scientific criterion for evaluating the desirability of anomie is, for them to assess the *consequences* of anomie at the individual or social level. On the other hand, the value-free stance endorses, by default, the existing value system – that is, it promotes (social) conformism, or the absoluteness of contingent values. To focus exclusively on the functional integration of social systems and of individuals to these social systems implies the unquestioned acceptance of the culture goals provided in a given society. The culturally contingent values become "the only values," since they are the only ones that can be empirically observed and evaluated. To be sure, a detection of the dysfunctional effects of anomie is, implicitly, a critique of existing social arrangements, but such a critique is *from within* the system. It is a critique which does not undermine a society's core values.

Later I will argue that Merton's and Srole's theories of anomie provide the background to the notion that value relativism is a "moral requirement" of modernity. Before turning to this argument, however, it will be useful to review the key characteristics of the contemporary literature on Durkheim's, Merton's, and Srole's theories of anomie. Such a review will help to define more clearly the key characteristics of contemporary anomie theory.

Commentaries on Durkheim, Merton and Srole

A large share of contemporary anomie literature has been devoted to analyzing the main classical and contemporary theories of anomie. Especially since the late 1950s, both European and American sociologists have increasingly sought to evaluate the adequacy of Durkheim's , Merton's, and Srole's work at the theoretical and empirical level. This secondary literature comprises a variety of assessments and evaluations which are useful for detecting the main patterns of sociological perspectives as they relate to anomie theory. As in the previous section, my overview of this literature will be selective and analytical, rather than descriptively exhaustive.

CONFRONTING DURKHEIM'S ANOMIE

As one of the founding fathers of sociology and the purported originator of the anomie concept, Durkheim has been an inevitable point of reference for all contemporary literature on the topic. Especially since the early 1960s, a sizable share of anomie literature has been devoted to analyzing Durkheim's theory of anomie. Such close study has yielded results which, at first sight, could be described as mixed or altogether inconclusive and contradictory. But if this body of literature cannot tell us the real meaning of Durkheim's anomie theory, it can perhaps show us the reason for failing to come up with a univocal answer.

Commentaries on Durkheim's theory of anomie usually set out to answer one or more of the following questions: Is the concept scientific? Is it historically grounded? Is it theoretically sound? Is it clear and distinct? On each of these issues, contrasting answers have been offered, and some of these will be discussed in detail. But first I should point out that the questions themselves say something about the characteristics of modern sociology. In fact, the questions express the key concerns of modern sociological research at various analytical levels. At the general level we find the problems of scientific validity; at the more specific level the problems of conceptual distinctiveness; and in between the issues of historical grounding and theoretical validity.

The answers offered by commentators on each of these issues are also sociologically significant. On each topic investigated, in fact, the commentators have offered contrasting interpretations depending on their frame of reference. More specifically, commentators can be classified as either theoretically or empirically inclined, and it can be shown that their inclination affects the position they take on the issues at hand.

Given the above distinction, the literature confronting Durkheim's theory of anomie can be arranged taxonomically as shown in Table 1. As a guideline, I entered in each column some representative examples of the literature which falls into that category, but the list of authors is not exhaustive. I will discuss briefly each theme and offer some relevant illustrations.

Table 1 Confronting Durkheim's Theory of Anomie

Approach Issue	Empirically oriented		Theoretically oriented	
	Interpretation	Literature examples	Interpretation	Literature examples
Scientific standing	Elimination of normative elements	Mayo 1933 Merton 1934 Parsons 1937	Incorporation of normative elements	de Grazia 1948 Berger 1969 Mestrovic
Historical grounding	Empirical verification of normative claims Historical distortion	Lukes 1967 Pizzorno 1963	Claim to historical grounding Radically situated view	Giddens 1971 Horton 1964
Theoretical validity	Empirically disproven Empirically untestable	Krohn 1978 Abrahamson 1980 Pope & Johnson 1983	Formally valid Self-consistent	Lacroix 1973 Cherkaoui 1981
Anomie's internal validity	Division of Labor's anomie differs from Suicide's anomie	Parsons 1937 Olsen 1965	Division of Labor's anomie equals Suicide's anomie	McCloskey 1976 Willis 1982
Anomie's external validity	Anomie equals Egoism	Johnson 1965 Pope 1976	Anomie differs from Egoism	Mawson 1970 LaCapra 1972

Scientific Grounding

Upholding a value-free social science has undoubtedly been the modal tendency in twentieth-century anomie theory. Sometimes avowedly, at other times by default, contemporary sociologists have eliminated the political and moral implications of the original anomie concept. The most successful strategy, obviously, has been to come up with a new theory of anomie altogether, but here I want to point out that a criticism of the normative assumptions of Durkheim's anomie theory paved the way to the new theoretical formulations. Regarding its scientific grounding, the most common criticism of Durkheim's theory has been that it is an ideological construction, that it exaggerates the problem at hand, that it is at odds with Durkheim's own methodological assumptions, that it leans towards a *normative* science of ethics, and that it is a by-product of Durkheim's extreme social realism.

Some American sociologists realized that Durkheim's notion of anomie as a pathology of modern societies was at odds with Durkheim's own definition of what is normal and what is pathological in a society. As early as 1915, Gehlke identified this discrepancy between Durkheim's positivistic method and his idealistic ethics.[52] Merton's 1934 review of Durkheim's *Division of Labor* brought the discrepancy into sharper focus noting that Durkheim was "faced with a perturbing dilemma":

> As a positivist, to admit the irrelevance of ends to a scientific study of society; as an anti-individualist, to indicate the effectiveness of social aims in conditioning social action, and thus in effect to abandon radical positivism.[53]

As Merton saw it, Durkheim's notion of anomie was an "ideal construction" which Durkheim mistook for the real phenomenon. Merton proposed, alternatively, that anomie might simply be interpreted as a reaction to the increasing division of labor, instead of an abnormal form of it.[54]

Another objection to Durkheim's notion of anomie is that it somehow implies a *normative* ethics. Parsons pointed out that Durkheim's concept is valuable, because it offers an insight into "the role and importance of moral conformity"; but he also realized that such an approach runs the risk of "elevating social conformity into the supreme moral virtue."[55] Parsons clarified his concern by arguing:

> A *science des moeurs* is perfectly reasonable and possible ... But this is to be thought of as an explanatory science, not a normative one, even though the phenomena it has to explain are

norms in their relation to human action. It is not concerned with explaining the moral validity of norms, but their causal efficacy.[56]

Overall, it is apparent that the common denominator in objecting to Durkheim's anomie theory is that it blurs the evaluative and descriptive elements. Durkheim's critique of the market morality is especialy seen as problematic from a scientific (i.e., value-free) point of view. Some critics retained the descriptive elements of Durkheim's concept of anomie; accordingly, they favored its use to describe the results of a discrepancy between means and ends of action, rather than as an evaluative instrument to criticize the utilitarian ethics of a market-like world. As Parsons argued, the fruitfulness of the concept of anomie after Durkheim was made possible because of the ability of American sociologists to borrow Durkheim's concept without being encumbered by "his version of positivistic philosophy":[57] the anti-individualistic, organismic approach which made Durkheim's work lean increasingly toward idealism in his career.

The detection of normative elements in Durkheim's work has often been a point of criticism, but in some instances it has prompted enthusiastic endorsement. Sebastian de Grazia's *The Political Community: A Study of Anomie* is the prototypical work espousing Durkheim's normative stance. Radicalizing Durkheim's theory, de Grazia claims that anomie, in its acute form, is characterized by the deterioration of belief systems: it is "the disappearance of order and rules."[58] Going beyond Durkheim's critique of the utilitarian market morality, de Grazia argues that "If the community is to be regenerated, the competitive directive must be the one to go."[59] Peter Berger espouses a similar position in arguing that anomie is "the nightmare *par excellence*, in which the individual is submerged in a world of disorder, senselessness and madness."[60] As Berger sees it, "alienation is powerful over men precisely because it shelters them from the terrors of anomy."[61] We can see, here, that Durkheim's view of anomie as expressing the lack of externally provided coherence in the moral sphere is accepted and utilized. However, this is clearly the less frequent case.

Theoretical Validity
In relation to the theoretical standing of Durkheim's anomie theory, scholars have also come up with divergent verdicts, depending on their attention to the specific empirical aspects or the general theory issues. French sociologists like Lacroix and

Cherkaoui have, in different ways, upheld Durkheim's notion of anomie as theoretically consistent. Cherkaoui, for instance, argues that Durkheim's methodological definition of the normal and the pathological is totally consistent with his theory of anomie. The normal and the pathological are, for Durkheim, parts of a same continuum – not conflict, but its violent manifestations being pathological. Lacroix, then, finds in *Suicide* a sound theory of anomie. To the argument that Durkheim's theory is ideological, Lacroix replies that although it might seem ideological to us today, "it is far from evident that it was so in Durkheim's epoch."[62] As Lacroix sees it, Durkheim was simply sharing the epistemological presuppositions of his own time.

The theoretical validity of Durkheim's anomie has been questioned on the ground that the empirical evidence contradicts it or that it is empirically unverifiable. For instance, Krohn showed that anomie does not predict crime rates, and Abrahamson maintained that he had disproved Durkheim's theory of an anomie of affluence.[63] The recent work of Pope and Johnson, then, showed that Durkheim's concept of organic solidarity is ambiguous and contradictory, and that as a consequence his theory of anomie is problematic because it cannot be tested empirically.[64] Pope and Johnson write:

> By Durkheim's own account the abnormal forms of the division of labor are widespread in the modern world. They are also so interwoven with the normal form that it is difficult to see how one might empirically separate the normal from the abnormal. Yet anyone who wishes to test Durkheim's model must make the distinction, since the former undermines solidarity, whereas the latter engenders it.[65]

Whereas Cherkaoui emphasized the continuity between normal and pathological to demonstrate the theoretical soundness of Durkheim's concept of anomie, Pope and Johnson found the same continuity to be a stumbling block in the acceptance of the same theory. Clearly, the divergence between the two assessments is not a matter of different readings of the available evidence, but a matter of different standards of assessment on the part of the commentators. For Cherkaoui, a theory is sound if it appears to be self-consistent; for Pope and Johnson a theory is sound if it is empirically verified or verifiable.

The overall assessment of the theoretical standing of Durkheim's theory of anomie seems to show that the empirically oriented authors tend to discard it. Durkheim's theory can only be justified and retained by presenting it in a formalized, abstract fashion, as the more theoretically inclined researchers have done.

Historical Grounding

The question of the historical grounding of Durkheim's anomie theory is also close to the core concerns of modern sociology, albeit in a way different from the question of theoretical validity. Whereas the question of theoretical validity is answered by considering the anomie theory outside its specific historical context and by assessing the theory's explanatory power, the question of historical grounding is answered by looking at the adequacy of the anomie theory in describing the historical phenomenon at hand.

Most authors who comment on Durkheim's theory of anomie in a historical perspective point out the coexistence of historical and ahistorical elements in Durkheim's theory. However, they differ in the emphasis they put on each element. While for some Durkheim's theory is pre-eminently a product of his historical analysis of modern industrial societies, for others it is Durkheim's metaphysical view of human nature that is crucial. Thus, Anthony Giddens argues that Durkheim's notion of anomie stresses "the historical dimension in the conditioning of human needs";[66] Steven Lukes, instead, points out that Durkheim's theory can only be understood in relation to his assumptions about "the 'natural' condition of the individual in society."[67] Both authors agree, however, that Durkheim's theory is, in its original form, an "inextricable fusion of fact and value."[68]

The majority of commentators who assessed the scientific standing of Durkheim's theory of anomie found it flawed because it failed to separate adequately facts and values. On the issue of historical grounding, however, the coexistence of facts and values is perceived to be less troublesome. The main concern, from a historical point of view, is whether the theory of anomie provides an insightful interpretation of the historical evidence – not whether the theory is or is not value-free.

From a historical perspective it is apparent that the modern idea of scientific inquiry is itself based on certain shared core values; this makes the historian more sensitive to the crucial role of values in sociological discourse. From this perspective John Horton shows how Durkheim's concept of anomie, by being anchored to the philosophical conservatism of his time, was historically grounded and ethically powerful. As Horton sees it, the concept of anomie is crucial *because* it contains "radical ethical and political directives."[69] Through his theory of anomie Durkheim attacks "the economic and political organization of the European industrial middle classes."[70]

Within the historical perspective, however, the excessive emphasis on the normative element has also been considered detrimental. This is the view of Alessandro Pizzorno, who claims that Durkheim's overwhelming concern with the problem of anomie and the need for integrative structures in society made him bypass the more relevant issue of how different levels of integration had historically come into being. As a consequence, says Pizzorno, Durkheim failed to "recognize the specific traits of contemporary society."[71] Durkheim misjudged the historical role of anomie by treating it as a pathological phenomenon of modern societies instead of treating it as their distinguishing feature.

It is apparent that Horton and Giddens give a favorable assessment of Durkheim's theory because they see the radical implications of the anomie concept. Both authors, in fact, find it to have an affinity with Marx's concept of alienation. Lukes and Pizzorno, on the other hand, have major reservations about Durkheim's theory because they see it as a by-product of Durkheim's meta-theoretical assumptions about human nature, or of his overwhelming concern with social integration. The divergence between the two assessments results from considering Durkheim's ideological commitment as either a positive asset to his theory, or as its detrimental feature.

Conceptual Evolution

The historical grounding of Durkheim's theory of anomie has been a typical concern of European sociologists who have sought to achieve a contextual understanding of Durkheim's work. In contrast to the historical dimension, the conceptual standing of Durkheim's theory of anomie has been investigated mostly by American sociologists who have engaged more than others in the analysis of Durkheim's texts in order to assess their adequacy for contemporary social research. Two issues have been addressed regarding the concept of anomie *per se*: (1) Does the concept have a univocal meaning throughout Durkheim's writings, and (2) does the concept have a distinct meaning in relation to other contiguous concepts?

Most authors claim that the *Division of Labor* and *Suicide* offer two different interpretations of anomie; as Olsen succinctly put it, in the former work anomie describes the problem of functional integration, in the latter it describes the problem of normative integration.[72] Parsons had already detected the shift in his *The Structure of Social Action*, in 1937. Other writers, however, have emphasized that both elements, the functional and the normative, are present throughout Durkheim's work. What brings one or the other aspect to the foreground is the context of their use. So, Willis states that Durkheim's anomie is always "concerned with how self-interest involves the pursuit of needs/desires *ad infinitum* in a modern industrial society."[73] In a similar vein, McCloskey argues that "the very essence of Durkheim's notion of anomie and egoisme concerned the 'infinity of dreams and desires' which underlies the 'moral anarchy' plaguing the modern world."[74]

The commentators who claim that Durkheim's concept of anomie has a univocal meaning throughout his writings justify their position by referring to Durkheim's basic notion of human nature's inherent egoism and insatiability. Durkheim's consistency is proclaimed by deduction from his moral philosophy. On the other hand, the commentators who identify a shift in Durkheim's notion of anomie rely on a contextual reading of the relevant passages. The incongruency is assessed inductively. The former approach is meta-theoretically oriented, while the latter is empirically informed.

Conceptual Distinctiveness
A last question addressed by commentators regards the unambiguous exclusiveness of the anomie concept in relation to other contiguous concepts. Discussing the distinction between the concepts of anomie and egoism in Durkheim's *Suicide*, some authors emphasized the commonalities, others the distinctive features of each concept. From an empirical point of view, Johnson noted that Durkheim never analyzed the separate effects of egoism and anomie – he only offered instances where both conditions occurred together. Moreover, he adds, Durkheim himself stated that egoism and anomie "are usually merely two different aspects of one social state."[75] In his book, *Durkheim's Suicide*, Pope reached a similar conclusion, stating that "the overlap between the theory of egoism and that of anomie is virtually complete."[76]

The conceptual distinction between anomie and egoism is emphasized from a theoretical point of view. La Capra, for instance, states that Durkheim's distinction between anomie and egoism is an outcome of his neo-Kantian assumptions. "In this sense, 'anomie' referred to a pathological practical reason and 'egoism' to a pathological theoretical reason."[77] Similarly, A. R. Mawson argues that "a weakening external control over the *passions* is the distinguishing feature of anomie, deregulation of the *intellect* ... [of] egoism."[78] In both instances, the distinction is justified not on the basis of observed differences, but of hypostatized notions of a dualistic human nature. The justification, that is, is theoretical not empirical.

Metaphysics and Empiricism

While it might be distressing to realize that the analysis of the various aspects of Durkheim's anomie theory yielded conflicting results, it is encouraging to notice that such seeming inconclusiveness has an explanation. For all the issues addressed, the commentators' opinion has been located at opposite ends of an empirico-theoretical continuum. At the theoretical end, Durkheim's theory is considered to be legitimately normative, theoretically sound (at the formal level), historically grounded, conceptually univocal and distinctive. At the empirical level, Durkheim's theory is seen as illegitimately value-laden, disproven or unverifiable, ahistorically grounded or historically limited, conceptually both equivocal and indistinct. The commentators located at the empirical end, it is apparent, are more critical of Durkheim's theory; they are mostly the ones who endorse the modern versions of anomie theory. The commentators located at the theoretical end, instead, provide elements for understanding Durkheim's theory in its own right, and accept it as sound; but their interpretation does not go beyond Durkheim's insight.

From my classification of the literature follow two consequences: Durkheim's concept of anomie is itself mostly a theoretical construct since it can be more easily understood and accounted for from such a viewpoint; the modern concept of anomie, which is empirically oriented, stands *in critical contrast* to Durkheim's concept. To call the modern approach empirical is not to claim that theoretical assumptions are extraneous to it; instead, it is to qualify it as espousing the relativistic values of "scientific" social research. As the dominant values of sociological discourse have changed, so has the meaning attributed to the concept of anomie. An analysis of the secondary literature on Merton's and Srole's theories of anomie will help clarify the nature of this change.

CONFRONTING MERTON'S AND SROLE'S THEORIES

Considering the distinction between the Durkheimian theory of anomie and the ones of contemporary sociologists, we would expect such a distinction to be reflected in the secondary literature on Merton's and Srole's theories of anomie. More precisely, since we saw the theoretically oriented commentators support Durkheim's theory, we would expect the same group to be strongly critical of Merton's and Srole's value-neutral stance. The empirically oriented researchers, on the other hand, are likely to provide a contingent assessment of one or another aspect of contemporary anomie theories.

The key topic of discussion, in regard to Merton's theory of anomie, has been his identification and handling of dominant cultural values. As we have seen earlier in this chapter, Merton's theory of anomie revolves around the notion of an overemphasis, in American culture, on success goals (especially monetary success) at the expense of legitimate institutionalized means for reaching such goals. Merton, the critics argue, ignores the issue of whether success (monetary or otherwise) is *in itself* desirable as a culture goal; Merton's value-free stance is the target of most theoretical critics. As their reasoning goes, Merton's anomie theory emasculates Durkheim's original insight,[79] leaves out critical elements of Durkheim's theory,[80] or is totally unrelated to the classical formulation.[81] The common thread running through these various claims is that by leaving aside the issue of whether monetary success is an appropriate societal goal Merton has left out the most crucial contribution of Durkheim's theory; furthermore, such an operation is interpreted by the commentators as an endorsement, by default, of the monetary success-goal in American society. So Horton writes: "Merton's value-free concept rests on acceptance of the success and self-interest ethic of the American middle class."[82] Ritsert comments along the same line that whereas Durkheim was concerned with the anomie of cultural patterns in modern society, Merton takes the same patterns as given and outside the realm of scientific investigation.[83]

Whereas the above commentators criticize Merton's theory for mishandling Durkheim's original formulation, others assess Merton's work by referring to other theoretical traditions. Scott and Turner, for instance, claim that "Merton's discussion of the value of pecuniary success is but a restatement of Weber's analysis of the spirit of capitalism."[84] Gouldner, instead argues that Merton's theory of anomie rests "on certain Marxian domain assumptions – especially those concerning the 'internal contradictions' of a system."[85] Both commentators chastise Merton for falling short of his purported theoretical mentor. For Scott and Turner, Merton follows Weber's general thesis but not his methodology.[86] For Gouldner, Merton's theory is inadequate because it emphasizes the acceptance or rejection of culturally prescribed means and ends while it disposes rather quickly of another crucial choice: rebellion.[87] From the ideological–theoretical point of view, both commentators find Merton's theory seriously defective because it disregards the sociological masters' legacy.

A different picture emerges from a more instrumental analysis of Merton's theory of anomie. Two main objections are voiced here. One points out that the success-goal orientation is specific to mainstream American culture and cannot be extended to other cultures or minority groups within American culture. This is shown in many pieces of empirical research.[88] At the theoretical level, such a case is made by Parsons when, in *The Social System*, he comments: "Merton's paradigm is most readily applicable to a social system where achievement values are prominent ... Where ascriptive values were institutionalized, especially in combination with particularism, this outlet would largely be closed."[89]

Another group of commentators, then, rejects the notion of a univocal clear perception of culture goals on the part of individuals. They point out that an analysis of sources of anomie should also consider situations of "conflicting norms and goals,"[90] structurally created ambivalence,[91] or variation in the internalization of success values across classes.[92] A more general critique of Merton's model was offered from a symbolic interactionist perspective which charged that Merton's depiction of contemporary American society as having "a common value hierarchy, either culturally transmitted or structurally induced, strains credulity."[93]

The instrumental evaluations of Merton's theory lament its rigidity or oversimplifications, but do not reject it in principle; instead, they propose specifications of variations within the theory in order to make it more applicable to specific empirical cases.

The approach of the two groups of commentators I have described seems to support my claim that value-free and value-committed analyses of Merton's theory lead to different conclusions about the validity of the theory as such. The value-committed, ideological interpretations of the theory see it running against the basic task of classical sociology of criticizing the dominant values in society. The instrumental assessments of the theory, instead, aim at articulating the conditions where the theory applies, or at specifying variations within it. Even if some of these assessments are quite critical, they never question the sociological legitimacy of Merton's theory.

Srole's five-item scale of anomia has been the most widely adopted in the social sciences,[94] and accordingly it is the one which has been scrutinized most closely. However, whereas Durkheim's and Merton's theories were often studied for their theoretical or normative implications, Srole's scale has been mostly the object of methodological considerations. This shift of concern can be related to the origins and purposes of the anomia scale which was not proposed as a theoretically articulate view about anomia, but simply as a viable, tentative device for measuring anomia.[95]

Commentators on Srole's anomia scale focused first on problems of internal validity of the scale and on the effect of social desirability on the respondents' answers.[96] In 1966, Miller and Butler argued that Srole's scale did not meet the generally accepted criterion of a pure Guttman scale, and Srole's measure should therefore be used as an anomia–eunomia dichotomy.[97] In a cross-cultural study of American and Italian respondents, Arnold Rose suggested that Srole's anomia scale might not be sufficiently culture-free to make it valid when used in a country like Italy.[98] Within the United States, Leslie Carr showed that Srole's interview questions produced acquiescence effects in respondents;[99] and in 1975, Eckart and Durand indicated that Srole's scale lacked equivalence for black and white subgroups in different contextual settings.[100]

The actual meaning of Srole's scale was also subjected to close scrutiny. In a 1975 article, James Teevan pointed out the conceptual confusion in the anomia scale: "Ideally there should be two separate measures of an individual's perception of his own anomia and his perception of the anomia of others. Unfortunately, the two have been confused."[101] In fact, Srole's scale, which "purports to measure the individual's perception of his own social psychological anomia," is actually measuring "the individual's perception of others' anomia."[102]

Going beyond the purely methodological aspects, other commentators sought to clarify the meaning of the anomia scale.[103] But again, their aim was not to discredit Srole's scale but to strengthen its standing. Although flawed in some respects, the anomia scale was and still is adopted extensively in many areas of social science research.[104] The theoretical and methodological problems of the scale have been generally considered acceptable because of the practical advantages the scale offers in empirical research.

From Durkheim to Merton and to Srole the trend has been towards a less theoretically encumbered, more empirical formulation of a concept of anomie. The elimination of evaluative dimensions in the modern formulations has favored the popularization of the anomie concept in the social sciences, even if at the expense of theoretical clarity about the modern meaning of the concept. But the withholding of value-judgment does not imply that values have disappeared. Nor does the lack of theoretical articulation mean that no theory is there to be found. Instead, I claim that the modern concept of anomie has far-reaching theoretical and normative significance. By restricting its legitimate field of analysis to the functional relations between means and ends of action, the American theories of sociological and psychological anomie left open the question of what implications their theory of an anomie of means would have for a theory of values in modern society. In the next section I will draw on some of the recent literature in order to tease out the modern meaning of anomie at this level.

Value-Freedom, Value-Relativism, and Anomie

I characterized Merton's theory of anomie as crucially concerned with the functional integration of institutional means and cultural goals, and Srole's scale as centering on the functional integration of individuals with their social worlds. In both contributions the focus was not on the social or individual value-orientations, but on the instrumental integration between means and ends of social or individual action. Still, as I pointed out earlier in this chapter, Merton's and Srole's value-free approach can be seen as implicitly endorsing value-relativism. To say that evaluation of the desirability of given cultural goals is scientifically inappropriate means, implicitly, that no particular cultural goal can be endorsed scientifically. Merton's and Srole's attention to the instrumental balance between means and ends of action can be complemented , at the level of cultural or individual ends, by the notion that value relativism is characteristic of modern societies and individuals. The support for this notion is found in recent anomie literature which assess the implications of an anomie of cultural goals and of individual value orientations, and their causal efficacy, from a sociological standpoint.

The claim that anomie is a positive characteristic of modernity is not altogether new. We have seen in the preceding chapter that the French social philosopher Jean Marie Guyau formulated a similar hypothesis about a century ago. Guyau argued emphatically that anomie was to be the morality of the future, but his theory was not sufficiently articulated. The more recent literature has been less emphatic in arguing in favor of value anomie in modern societies, but it is based on more solid empirical ground. Analytically, we can distinguish between the sociological aspects and implications of modern value anomie, and its psychological counterpart.

SOCIOLOGICAL VALUE-ANOMIE

At the sociological level, the point has often been made that anomie is typically a phenomenon of modern urban societies. Merton points out that in the urban context, more than anywhere else, we find both the greatest achievements and the worst problems of modern society. Merton comments that "these extremes can be regarded as responses to different aspects of the same underlying condition of urban life."[105] Elwin Powell's research provides the larger historical context of modern anomie. While it is today considered to be mostly an urban phenomenon, anomie is, for Powell, only the latest stage in the unfolding of the ethos of individualism. Anomie can be linked to the structural sources of modern individualism: Protestantism, capitalism, and democracy.[106] These comments make it clear that anomie is a substantive component of modernity, not an abnormal phenomenon, but a distinguishing trait of Western historical development. Durkheim made a similar remark when he argued: "The entire morality of progress and perfection is [thus] inseparable from a certain amount of anomy."[107]

The pertinence of anomie to modern social structure is demonstrated by a recent shift in the sociological literature regarding the functional relation between anomie and the relevant issues of social order and change. Whereas the assumption of classical formulations was that anomie inevitably disrupted the workings of society, recent literature pointed out that anomie performs positive functions as well. Milton Yinger, for instance, writes: "In the modern world, some anomie may be desirable, both for the society and for the individuals who experience it. It may create flexibility and help to create permeable boundaries that facilitate interaction with other societies."[108] In a later work Yinger observes that an increase in anomie should perhaps be seen as "an inevitable part of the process whereby old tyrannies are broken and new values given in a field for growth."[109] The basic sociological insight is that a society characterized by rapid social change *requires* normative flexibility or anomie.[110]

The positive approach to anomie is clarified in Jean Duvignaud's article, "Anomie et mutation sociale."[111] There, against Durkheim's conservative and restricted understanding of anomie, Duvignaud proposes a generalized theory of anomie and social change. For Duvignaud, the idea of anomie marks the transition from a passive culture dominated by the idea of destiny and fatalism to a Promethean culture in which human productivity is capable of dominating the determinism of nature.[112] To paraphrase it in John Dewey's words, anomie marks the transition from a religious or philosophical quest for theoretical certainty in the ideal world, to a scientific quest for security through planned changes in the environment.[113] Duvignaud writes: "It is quite evident that without these anomic individualities the human experience of historical and cumulative societies would never turn into a continuous overcoming or going beyond itself."[114] It is an historical fact that charismatic founders of new religions and moral innovators have been perceived as anomic personalities; their introduction of new social forms has scandalized society.[115]

Duvignaud characterizes anomie as the individual's ability to produce change in a static social system. Gouldner takes this view full circle when he argues that social anomie, in its turn, can trigger individual change which reflects back on society. Gouldner writes:

> When a social system has fruitlessly exhausted its routine solutions for its problems, then anomic randomness may be more useful to individuals and to the culture they bear, than the treadmill and orderly plying of the old structures ... Growing anomie may be useful for the human and cultural systems.[116]

These remarks reflect a common insight: that normative flexibility and anomie are *necessary* requirements of social change. The single-minded concern with social integration is incompatible with the modern notion of an ever-changing social environment. Richard Schacht comments that such unilateral views of anomie (as the omnipresent threat to social integration) "foster the misinterpretation of the emerging situation, imposing backward-looking categories upon it, and encouraging its misguided assimilation to cases of mere social disintegration."[117] Social scientists often perceive societies as inevitably sliding toward either anarchy or tyranny; such perception ignores, in Schacht's view, crucial alternative social forms. For instance, we can envision a *pluralistic* society in which "institutions largely replace the society (and culture) more generally as the locus of value and goal articulation."[118] Or we can envision an *autonomistic* society in which "the members of society are to be thought of as formulating and elaborating *their own* aims and related courses of action."[119] In both instances, we have social forms which depart substantially from the *Gemeinschaft* type without falling inexorably into total chaos or anarchy. Much of what has been labelled negatively as anomic in modern social phenomena can, in fact, be related to new forms of social integration.

PSYCHOLOGICAL VALUE-ANOMIE

The sociological arguments illustrating the positive effects of anomie are paralleled, in the contemporary literature, by a psychological counterpart. If the sociological point is that anomie is a required condition of modern societies, its psychological counterpart is that flexibility regarding social norms and values is also a desirable trait of individuals in modern society. In his book, *The Structure of Freedom*, Christian Bay argues that modern individuals should develop a psychological freedom which will give them "the ability to tolerate anomie and other kinds of environmental ambiguity."[120] Given the increasing complexity of the social world and the lack of a unified normative framework for individuals to follow, it is necessary that they develop the ability for autonomous judgment.

Empirical evidence supporting the notion that the development of autonomous judgment helps the individual to handle normative complexity is provided by Anton F. Deman. His research shows that children who are encouraged to develop autonomy show lower levels of anomie when compared with children who are more closely controlled by their parents.[121] In the area of social work, Donald Krill points out the advantage of developing normative flexibility in the psychotherapy of anomic patients: "The process of growth requires the ongoing assertion of freedom – the capacity to transcend what one has been before."[122] Similarly, Robert Young comments that the solution to psychological anomie requires that the individual "gain awareness of his inner conflicts and ... replace the disorder with a realistic hierarchical ordering that reflects the priorities with which he would prefer to identify."[123] The cited literature seems to suggest that the best solution to the negative psychological reactions to socio-cultural relativism is the development in the individual of a self-conscious ethical relativism.

Durkheim's classical formulation considered ethical relativism is the realm of ultimate values as the source of institutional anomie. For him, the ultimate values must come from society: "It alone has the power necessary to stipulate law and to set the point beyond which the passions must not go."[124] Durkheim claims that the individual cannot find moral guidance within the self; only society can provide moral rules. The literature we analyzed offers an alternative to Durkheim, by showing that autonomy, not dependency on social rules, characterizes the competent member of society. The notion that value-relativism is a source of anomie has been proven dubious in recent empirical research. In their article, "Ethical Relativism and Anomia," Putney and Middleton demonstrate that a belief in absolute ultimate values is not essential in order to avoid anomie. They write: "Relativists are not ... more anomic than absolutists ... Relativism is as effective a basis for normative behavior as absolutism ... the sanctification which absolutism bestows on a norm is functionally unnecessary."[125] Relativists and absolutists appear to differ significantly in the structure of their belief system, but such difference is not mirrored in their actual behavior. "Relativists are not ... more anomic than absolutists ... in evaluating actions, ... making too many exceptions to principles, failure to live up to norms which are verbally accepted, or general normlessness."[126]

The irrelevance of ethical absolutism in providing a solution to anomie is demonstrated by recent empirical studies which focused on the relationship between religiosity or religious affiliation and anomie. The classical view expressed by Durkheim was that religion provided a viable normative structure for the individual to live by; more recently, Peter Berger radicalized this view, claiming that "religion has been one of the most effective bulwarks against anomy throughout human history."[127] The empirical evidence shows, however, that religious individuals are not significantly less anomic than non-religious individuals;[128] nor is the level of religiosity related to levels of anomie.[129] Carr and Hauser's recent research on "Anomie and Religiosity" reached these conclusions: "No significant relationship was found between anomie and religiosity ... current empirical research does not support those who have interpreted Durkheim to say that religion reduces anomie in modern society."[130]

These empirical findings indicate that neither is ethical relativism a source of anomie, nor is ethical absolutism the solution to anomie. On the contrary, there is evidence that a more adequate solution to normative anomie is the development of ethical flexibility in the individual, that an anomic condition at the social-institutional level requires individuals who are able properly to adjust to varying situations. Paradoxically, the ethical anomie of individuals may be the most appropriate answer to socio-cultural anomie.

MEANS-ANOMIE AND VALUE-ANOMIE

At first glance it might seem that a positive assessment of value-anomie is irreconcilable with the anomie theories of Merton and Srole; after all, they viewed anomie as detrimental to socio-cultural integration. However, we must emphasize that Merton and Srole focused on the dysfunctional relation *between* institutional means and cultural goals – or between individuals and their social worlds. The positive assessment of value-anomie, instead, focuses on the possible configurations *within* the socio-cultural or individual value-orientations. That is, given the normative complexity and the wide variation in the rules characterizing different social worlds, an anomic value-orientation seems adequate for handling such a condition. The notion of value-anomie as sociologically adequate is not opposite, but complementary to Merton's and Srole's theories. They are two sides of the same coin.

Labelling value-anomie as sociologically adequate might seem an unwarranted value judgment, but I would claim otherwise. The adequacy of value anomie is not, in fact, assessed in terms of its adherence to some *a priori* moral axiom; but rather, it is assessed in terms of observable consequences at the socio-cultural and at the psychological level. The adequacy is claimed on sociological and psychological grounds – not on ethical ones.

The development of value-anomie is a key feature of modernity: it is an integral component in the development of democracy, of modern science, of modern individualism. Durkheim himself acknowledged that "among peoples where progress is and should be rapid, rules restraining individuals must be sufficiently pliable and malleable."[131] Merton makes the point more clearly:

> Some (unknown) degree of deviation from current norms is probably functional for the basic goals of all groups. A certain degree of 'innovation,' for example, may result in the foundation of new institutionalized patterns of behavior which are more adaptive than the old in making for realization of primary goals.[132]

The constitution of value-anomie can be perceived as one such attempt to highlight new "adaptive" patterns of behavior. Again, the assessment is sociological, not ethical; although it is inevitably relevant to ethical matters.

Not only is a theory of value-anomie consistent with Merton's theory, but it is also consistent with the more general presuppositions of an empirically grounded social science. Value-anomie parallels the ethical implications of the scientific method. Science cannot furnish us with absolute ultimate values; in the realm of substantive values, science is anomic. As Merton writes, "Most institutions demand unqualified faith; but the institution of science makes scepticism a virtue."[133] And G. H. Mead, "Scientific method is at war with dogmatism whether it appears in doctrine, or cult, or in social practice."[134]

Articulating more fully this line of reasoning, I would argue that if science cannot furnish us with absolute ultimate values, then we need to regard the values we choose as working hypotheses which are functionally adequate to our needs, but which are always amenable to modifications as life situations change. The efficacy of modern anomic morality is assessed according to its ability to provide the individual with effective guidelines for interaction, not in terms of external standards which have been set once and for all, but in terms of the usefulness of the solutions they offer to the immediate problems one faces. The test for the validity of these working solutions, then is their empirical efficacy, not their theoretical validity.

The thesis of an instrumental, value-relative approach to anomie is supported by the historical evidence of debates about anomie in Western culture. There, we have seen that the immanent, voluntaristically grounded discussions of anomie have typically favored the progressive development of new social forms, whereas the transcendental views about anomie have often helped to perpetuate a traditional overformalized social order. In the conclusion I will attempt to strengthen this argument by reviewing synoptically the available historical evidence.

Notes

1 Cf. Geoffrey Hawthorn, *Enlightenment and Despair* (Cambridge: Cambridge University Press, 1976), 191–6.
2 ibid.,195.
3 See, for instance, John Horton, "The Dehumanization of Anomie and Alienation," *British Journal of Sociology* 15 (December 1964):283–300; François Chazel, "Considerations sur la nature de l'anomie," *Revue française de sociologie* 8 (April–June 1967):151–68; Jurgen Ritsert (1969), "Die Antinomien des Anomie Konzepts," *Soziale Welt* 20 (2):145–62; Philippe Besnard, "Merton à la recherche de l'anomie," *Revue française de sociologie* 19 (January–March 1978):3–38.
4 Robert K. Merton, "Social Structure and Anomie," *American Sociological Review* 3 (June 1938):672–82; Leo Srole, "Social Integration and Certain Corollaries," *American Sociological Review* 21 (December 1956):709–16.
5 The best illustration of such a convergence is Ephraim H. Mizru-

chi's monograph, *Success and Opportunity: A Study of Anomie* (New York: Free Press, 1964).

6   For an exhaustive bibliography of modern anomie literature see Appendix, IV.

7   Cf. Roscoe C. Hinkle, Jr (1960), "Durkheim in American sociology," in Wolff, ed., *Emile Durkheim*, 267–95.

8   Elton Mayo, *The Human Problems of an Industrial Civilization* (1933; reprinted New York: Viking, 1960); Talcott Parsons, *The Structure of Social Action* (1937; reprinted New York: Free Press, 1968).

9   Mayo, *The Human Problems*, 136.

10 Parsons, *The Structure of Social Action*, 335.

11 ibid., 338.

12 ibid., 685–6.

13 ibid., 291.

14 ibid.

15 Durkheim and Parsons are mentioned once, while Pareto is not mentioned at all. Cf. Merton, "Social Structure and Anomie," 673n, 676n.

16 Cf. Parsons, *The Structure of Social Action*, 335.

17 Merton, "Social Structure and Anomie," 676.

18 ibid., 673–4.

19 ibid., 676.

20 ibid., 674.

21 ibid, my emphasis.

22 ibid., 674n.

23 ibid., 675n, my emphasis.

24 ibid., 674, 678–81.

25 ibid., 678.

26 Stephen Cole writes: "Until the late 1960s, SS&A was probably the dominant theory in the area of deviance." Stephen Cole, "The growth of scientific knowledge," in Lewis A. Coser, ed., *The Idea of Social Structure* (New York: Harcourt Brace Jovanovich, 1975), 175.

27 Merton, "Social Structure and Anomie," 675–6.

28 ibid., 679.

29 ibid., 681.

30 Robert K. Merton, "Social structure and anomie," in *Social Theory and Social Structure* (revised edn New York: Free Press, 1957), 136.

31 Professor Merton alerted me that my selective reading of his theory is "in direct opposition to the author's own reading of the paper and to that of most social scientists who have made use of it."

32 Cf. Merton, "Social Structure and Anomie" (1938), 672; see also Parsons, *The Structure of Social Action*, 338.

33 Emile Durkheim, *The Division of Labor in Society*, trans. George Simpson (1933; reprinted New York: Free Press, 1964), 431n.

34 Merton, "Social structure and anomie" (1957), 136.

35 See, for example, Milton L. Barron, "Juvenile Delinquency and American Values," *American Sociological Review* 16 (April

1951):208–14; Solomon Kobrin, "The Conflict of Values in Delinquency Areas," *American Sociological Review*, 16 (October 1951): 653–61; Vilhelm Aubert, "White Collar Crime and Social Structure," *American Journal of Sociology* 58 (November 1953):263–71.

36   E.g., Matilda White Riley and Samuel H. Flowerman, "Group Relations as a Variable in Communications Research," *American Sociological Review* 16 (April 1951):174–80; W. Baldamus and Noel Timms, "The Problem Family: A Sociological Approach," *British Journal of Sociology* 6 (December 1955):318–27; Warren G. Bennis, "Some Barriers to Teamwork in Social Research," *Social Problems* 3 (April 1956):223–34.

37   Cf. Cole, "The Growth of Scientific Knowledge," 175–220.

38   Benjamin Nelson, "Actors, Directors, Roles, Cues, Meanings, Identities: Further Thoughts on 'Anomie'," *Psychoanalytic Review* 51 (Spring 1964):137.

39   Sebastian de Grazia, *The Political Community: A Study of Anomie* (Chicago: University of Chicago Press, 1948).

40   Robert M. MacIver, *The Ramparts We Guard* (New York: Macmillan, 1950); Leo Srole, "Social Integration," 709–16.

41   MacIver, *The Ramparts*, 84.

42   Cf. ibid., 139.

43   ibid. MacIver seems to identify Merton's emphasis on the phenomenon of innovation of culture patterning and of individual adaptation as characteristics of the capitalistic ethos – I share MacIver's equation. However, it should be noted that capitalism is nowhere mentioned, directly, in Merton's relevant texts.

44   MacIver, *The Ramparts*, 85–7.

45   ibid., 142.

46   Cf. ibid., 90–2.

47   Srole, "Social Integration," 711.

48   ibid., 712–13.

49   ibid., 711.

50   MacIver, *The Ramparts*, 85.

51   This relativism of ultimate ends is theoretically limitless; in practice, in any culture at any given time there is only a limited set of ultimate ends.

52   Charles E. Gehlke, *Emile Durkheim's Contributions to Sociological Theory* (New York: Columbia University Press, 1915), 179–80.

53   Robert K. Merton, "Durkheim's Division of Labor in Society," *American Journal of Sociology* 40 (November 1934), 321.

54   ibid., 325.

55   Parsons, *The Structure of Social Action*, 390.

56   ibid., 325.

57   Talcott Parsons, "The point of view of the author," in Max Black, ed., *The Social Theories of Talcott Parsons* (Englewood Cliffs: Prentice-Hall, 1961), 315.

58   de Grazia, *The Political Community*, 74.

59 ibid., 188.

60 Peter Berger, *The Sacred Canopy* (New York: Doubleday, 1967), 22.

61 ibid., 90.

62 Bernard Lacroix, "Regulation et anomie selon Durkheim," *Cahiers internationaux de sociologie* 55 (July–September 1973):292.

63 Marvin D. Krohn, "A Durkheimian Analysis of International Crime Rates," *Social Forces* 57 (December 1978):654–70; Mark Abrahamson, "Sudden Wealth, Gratification and Attainment: Durkheim's Anomie of Affluence Reconsidered," *American Sociological Review* 45 (February 1980):49–57.

64 Whitney Pope and Barclay D. Johnson, "Inside Organic Solidarity," *American Sociological Review* 48 (October 1983):681–92.

65 ibid., 688.

66 Anthony Giddens, *Capitalism and Modern Social Theory* (Cambridge: Cambridge University Press, 1971), 228.

67 Steven Lukes, "Alienation and anomie," in Peter Laslett and W. G. Runciman, eds, *Philosophy, Politics and Society*, 3rd ser. (New York: Barnes & Noble, 1967), 142.

68 ibid.

69 Horton, "The dehumanization," 285.

70 ibid.

71 Alessandro Pizzorno, "Lecture actuelle de Durkheim," *Archives européennes de sociologie* 4 (1963):26.

72 Marvin E. Olsen, "Durkheim's Two Concepts of Anomie," *The Sociological Quarterly* 6 (Winter 1965):42.

73 Cecil L. Willis, "Durkheim's Concept of Anomie: Some Observations," *Sociological Inquiry* 52 (Spring 1982):111.

74 David D. McCloskey, "What Ever Happened to Anomie?" *Journal for the Scientific Study of Religion* 13 (December 1974):497.

75 Barclay D. Johnson, "Durkheim's One Cause of Suicide," *American Sociological Review* 30 (December 1965):882.

76 Whitney Pope, *Durkheim's Suicide: A Classic Analyzed* (Chicago: University of Chicago Press, 1976), 201.

77 Dominick LaCapra, *Emile Durkheim: Sociologist and Philosopher* (Ithaca: Cornell University Press, 1972), 165.

78 A. R. Mawson, "Durkheim and Contemporary Social Pathology," *British Journal of Sociology* 21 (September 1970):301.

79 Cf. Horton, "The Dehumanization of Anomie," and Ritsert, "Die Antinomien des Anomie Konzepts."

80 Cf. Nelson, "Further Thoughts on Anomie," and Chazel, "Considerations sur la nature de l'anomie."

81 Cf. Besnard, "Merton a la recherche de l'anomie."

82 Horton, "The Dehumanization of Anomie," 294.

83 Ritsert, "Die Antinomien des Anomie Konzepts," 145.

84 Marvin B. Scott and Roy Turner, "Weber and the Anomic Theory of Deviance," *Sociological Quarterly* 6 (Summer 1965):235.

85   Alvin W. Gouldner, *The Coming Crisis of Western Sociology* (New York: Basic, 1970), 426.

86   Scott and Turner, "Weber and the Anomic Theory of Deviance" 238–40.

87   Cf. Gouldner, *The Coming Crisis*, 427.

88   See, among others, Mizruchi, *Success and Opportunity*; Alex Thio, "A Critical Look at Merton's Anomie Theory," *Pacific Sociological Review* 18 (April 1975):139–58.

89   Talcott Parsons, *The Social System* (New York: Free Press, 1951), 258.

90   Cf. Robin Williams, *American Society* (New York: Knopf, 1951). 535.

91   Cf. Aubert, "White collar crime," and Albert K. Cohen, "The study of social disorganization and deviant behavior," in Robert K. Merton, Leonard Broom and Leonard S. Cottrell Jr, eds, *Sociology Today* (New York: Basic , 1959), 461–84.

92   Cf. Herbert H. Hyman, "The value system of different classes," in Reinhard Bendix and Seymour Martin Lipset, eds, *Class, Status, and Power* (New York: Free Press, 1953), 426–42; Elwin H. Powell, "Occupation, Status, and Suicide: Toward a Redefinition of Anomie," *American Sociological Review* 23 (April 1958): 131–9; Joel I. Nelson, "Anomie: Comparisons between the Old and the New Middle Class," *American Journal of Sociology* 74 (September 1968): 184–92.

93   Edwin M. Lemert, "Social Structure, Social Control, and Deviation," in Marshall B. Clinard, ed., *Anomie and Deviant Behavior* (New York: Free Press, 1964), 66.

94   Several alternative scales have been devised after Srole's. E.g., Dwight G. Dean, "Alienation: Its Meaning and Measurement," *American Sociological Review* 26 (October 1961):753–8; Herbert McClosky and John H. Schaar, "Psychological Dimensions of Anomy," *American Sociological Review* 30 (February 1965):14–40; T. M. Elmore and E. D. Chambers, "Anomie, Existential Neurosis, and Personality," *APA Convention Proceedings* 2 (1967):341–2. Srole's scale is the one used most frequently by far; its inclusion in the annual General Social Survey of the National Opinion Research Center probably contributed to its wide adoption (the scale appears in the surveys for 1973, 1974, 1976, 1977, 1980, 1982, 1984, and 1985).

95   Cf. Srole, "Social Integration," 713.

96   Elaine Cummings, Lois R. Dean, and David S. Newell, "What is 'Morale'? A Case History of a Validity Problem," *Human Organization* 17 (Summer 1958):3–8; Gerhard E. Lenski and John C. Leggett, "Caste, Class, and Deference in the Research Interview," *American Journal of Sociology* 65 (March 1960):463–7.

97   Curtis R. Miller and Edgar F. Butler, "Anomia and Eunomia: A Methodological Evaluation of Srole's Anomia Scale," *American Sociological Review* 31 (June 1966):400–5.

98   Arnold M. Rose, "Prejudice, Anomie, and the Authoritarian Personality," *Sociology and Social Research* 50 (January 1966):141–7.

99   Leslie G. Carr, "The Srole Items and Acquiescence," *American Sociological Review* 36 (April 1971):287–93.

100   Dennis R. Eckart and Roger Durand, "The Effect of Context in Measuring Anomie," *Public Opinion Quarterly* 39 (Summer 1975):199–206.

101   James J. Teevan, Jr, "On Measuring Anomia: Suggested Modifications of the Srole Scale," *Pacific Sociological Review* 18 (April 1975):162.

102   ibid.

103   Cf. Gary B. Thom, *The Human Nature of Social Discontent* (Totowa, NJ: Rowman & Allanheld, 1984), 11–12.

104   See, for some recent examples, Gunars Reimanis, "Anomie and Interest in Education," *Journal of Social Psychology* 119 (April 1983):243–8; Lawrence A. Troy Lovell, "Anomia among Employed Wives and Housewives: An Exploratory Analysis," *Journal of Marriage and the Family* 45 (May 1983):301–10; Jose Gutierrez, "Programme contre l'anomie de l'exil," *Information psychiatrique* 59 (January 1983):61–4; R. Thomas Dull, "An Empirical Analysis of the Anomie Theory of Drug Use," *Journal of Drug Education* 13 (1983):49–62; Frederick J. Deroches, "Anomie: Two Theories of Prison Riots," *Canadian Journal of Criminology* 25 (April 1983):173–90.

105   Robert K. Merton, "Anomie, anomia, and social interaction," in Marshall B. Clinard, ed., *Anomie and Deviant Behavior* (New York: Free Press, 1964), 222.

106   Elwin H. Powell, "Sources of Anomie in the Urban Community," *Indian Sociological Bulletin* 1 (January 1964):24–7.

107   Emile Durkheim, *Suicide*, trans. John A. Spaulding and George Simpson (New York: Free Press, 1951), 364.

108   Milton J. Yinger, "On Anomie," *Journal for the Scientific Study of Religion* 3 (April 1964):173.

109   Milton J. Yinger, *Toward a Field Theory of Behavior: Personality and Social Structure* (New York: McGraw-Hill 1965), 189–90.

110   One might object that normative flexibility and anomie are two very different things, the former leading to human progress, the latter to deviant behavior. I claim that the underlying condition of apparently opposite kinds of behavior is, in fact, one and the same. The freedom from traditional, institutionalized control opens the possibility for both legitimate human accomplishments and for illegitimate behavior. The lack of enforced regulation (anomie) is not, *per se*, a source of deviance.

111   Jean Duvignaud, "Anomie et mutation sociale," in Georges Balandier, ed., *Sociologie des mutations* (Paris: Editions anthropos, 1970), 63–81

112   ibid., 73.

Contemporary Anomie Literature

113 John Dewey, *The Quest for Certainty* (New York: Minton, Balch & Co., 1929).
114 Duvignaud, "Anomie et mutation sociale," 77.
115 ibid., 76–7.
116 Gouldner, *The Coming Crisis*, 224–5.
117 Richard Schacht, "Doubts about anomie and anomia," in S. Giora Shoham, ed., *Alienation and Anomie Revisited* (Tel-Aviv: Ramot, 1982), 75; see also Edward A. Tiryakian's article,"Sexual Anomie, Social Structure, Societal Change," *Social Forces* 59 (June 1981):1025–53.
118 Schacht, "Doubts about anomie," 86.
119 ibid., 87.
120 Christian Bay, *The Structure of Freedom* (Stanford: Stanford University Press, 1958), 114.
121 A. F. Deman, "Autonomy-Control Variation in Child-Rearing and Anomie in Young Adults," *Psychology Reports* 51 (August 1982):7–10.
122 Donald F. Krill, "Existential Psychotherapy and the Problem of Anomie," *Social Work* 14 (April 1969):41.
123 Robert Young, "Autonomy and the 'Inner Self'," *American Philosophical Quarterly* 17 (January 1980):40.
124 Durkheim, *Suicide*, 249.
125 Snell Putney and Russell Middleton, "Ethical Relativism and Anomie," *American Journal of Sociology* 67 (January 1962):437.
126 ibid.
127 Berger, *The Sacred Canopy*, 87.
128 E.g., Wendell Bell, "Anomie, Social Isolation, and the Class Structure," *Sociometry* 20 (June 1957):105–16.
129 E.g., Dwight G. Dean, "Anomie, Powerlessness, and Religious Participation," *Journal for the Scientific Study of Religion* 7 (Fall 1968):252–4.
130 Leslie G. Carr and William J. Hauser, "Anomie and Religiosity: An Empirical Re-Examination," *Journal for the Scientific Study of Religion* 15 (March 1976):73
131 Durkheim, *Suicide*, 364.
132 Robert K. Merton, "Continuities in the theory of social structure and anomie," in *Social Theory and Social Structure* (New York: Free Press, 1957), 182.
133 Robert K. Merton, "Science and the social order," in op. cit., 547.
134 George H. Mead, "Scientific Method and the Moral Sciences," *The International Journal of Ethics* 33 (April 1923):237.

CONCLUSION

This history of the concept of anomie has veered between two aims: the recovery of specific meanings of anomie in various socio-historical contexts in Western culture, and the drawing of diachronic similarities in the literature on anomie. In these final remarks I want to bring the two strands together and show their commonality.

The excursion through Greek philosophy, Biblical literature, seventeenth-century religious controversies, nineteenth-century French social thought, and contemporary American sociology demonstrates how past discussions of anomie covered a large number of topics; the diversity of meanings taken by anomie has often been greater than their similarity. The Greek diatribes on *nomos* and *physis* have little in common with the quarrels of Bishop Bramhall and Thomas Hobbes; the apocalyptic anomie of the New Testament, likewise, is quite different from the discussions about anomie in contemporary American sociology. One obvious conclusion of this study, then, is that there is not a timeless meaning of anomie, nor are there timeless problems which philosophers, theologians, and social theorists have addressed through the centuries. Instead, it is clear that, as the social circumstances and problems changed, the discussions about anomie shifted accordingly. It is only by relating the anomie literature of an historical period to the issues raised and discussed in that period, that we can obtain a somewhat accurate picture of the contextual meanings of anomie. As Quentin Skinner forcefully argues, "The classical texts, especially in social, ethical, and political thought, help to reveal – if we let them – not the essential sameness, but rather the essential variety of viable moral assumptions and political commitments."[1] If we take these words and the anomie literature seriously, we should hardly expect to find solutions to our contemporary problems in the philosophical discussions of fifth-century Athens. The problems we confront today are contingent on our socio-historical location and, as such, they can only be addressed by us today. And yet, recovering the history of the anomie concept is useful in other ways; in fact, our becoming aware of the historical variation in perspectives about the concept of anomie can, in turn, improve our understanding of the contemporary use of the concept, by seeing it as *historically relative*. Such relativization can help us to gain a better perspective on ourselves, and this is no minor achievement. If we accept the evidence that the concept of anomie does not trace a straightforward progression in a coherent line of thought, then we are in a position to understand better the contemporary meaning of anomie by comparing it with the pre-modern meanings of the concept.

Not only has this study shown the variability of problems addressed in the anomie literature and the variability of solutions offered, but it has also provided some broad generalizations on the characteristics of discussions about anomie and of social theory at large. Throughout the book I have characterized the debates about anomie in relation to the methodological and ethical positions espoused by the various factions. I have identified the methodological positions as tending either towards individualistic voluntarism or towards social realism, where the former favors an atomistic view of social phenomena, and the latter favors the social determinants of individual action. Next to the methodological, I identified an ethical position stressing either an immanentistic view of morality or a transcendentalistic view. The former locates the source of moral judgment in the individual actor, the latter locates it in the socio-cultural values (religious or otherwise) of the group.

The methodological and ethical dimensions are related to each other, but their relationship is not univocal. At first one might surmise that individualistic voluntarism at the methodological level goes with immanentism at the ethical level. In fact, if we look at the secular literature on anomie it is clear enough that an emphasis on the centrality of the individual actor in society signifies an emphasis on the existential, an emphasis on human life and activity; on the contrary, the stress on the reality of social forms translates into a stress on the extra-individual character of social life, on its externality and transcendence in relation to the individual actor. The former approach favors the role of the individual will, the latter approach favors the role of collective rationality. In this instance the relationship holds as we surmised.

But the relationship is reversed when we look at the religious literature on anomie. There, individualistic voluntarism is associated with ethical transcendentalism, whereas social realism is associated with ethical immanentism. Contrary to the secular trend, in religious thought individualistic voluntarism emphasizes the ethical absoluteness of divine will, beyond human reason and understanding; in contrast, social realism in religious thought stresses the relativity of divine will, since such will is bound by reasonableness.

The secular distinction between the transcendental society and the immanent individual becomes, in the religious realm, a distinction between the otherworldly God and the thisworldly society. The transcendental entity in secular thought is the collectivity; in religious thought, the individual. Conversely, the immanent entity in secular thought is the individual; in religious thought, the collectivity. Table 2 shows graphically the classification of anomie literature according to the methodological and ethical dichotomies.

Table 2   Classification of Traditions in the Anomie Literature

	Ethical Transcendentalism	Ethical Immanentism
Methodological Nominalism	Early Christianity Puritanism Calvinism	Sophists Jean Marie Guyau Contemporary Sociology
Methodological Realism	Platonism Durkheimianism	Judaism Catholicism Anglicanism

The tradition of voluntaristic nominalism which characterizes modern anomie literature finds its antecedents in sophistic philosophy, in early Christian thought, in Puritanism and Calvinism, and in the philosophy of Jean Marie Guyau. The collectivistic tradition of rationalistic social realism, instead, comprises Platonic thought, post-exile Judaism, Catholicism and Anglicanism, and Durkheim's social theory.

The two traditions are not altogether isolated from each other; rather, they are dialectically related as parts of a common discourse: a dialogue between sophists and Plato, late-Judaism and early Christianity, Puritanism and Anglicanism, Guyau and Durkheim. Indeed, the history of the anomie concept shows the constant tension between immanentism and transcendentalism, between nominalism and realism. In fifth-century Greece, the nominalism of the sophists was opposed by the realism of Plato. Their concept of anomie reflected such opposition: whereas the sophists thought of anomie as a contingent problem of human interaction to be solved in an *ad hoc* fashion, Plato thought of anomie as an inevitable malady of an all-too-human, less-than-ideal society.

In the Biblical literature the lines are not drawn quite so sharply; nevertheless, it is easy enough to detect strong elements of social realism in the post-exile Judaic thought, on the one hand, and a new emphasis on the one-to-one relation between the individual and God in the New Testament writings, on the other hand. Whereas Judaic thought stressed the externality of ethical rules and the primacy of the Torah, the New Testament shifted the emphasis from the constraint of external rules to the law of the Spirit which moves the individual internally.

The theological diatribes of the English Renaissance are also characterized by the dualism of reason and will, of realism and nominalism. The Anglican ideologists stress the role of reason and of natural law as compelling evidence of the desirability of existing social institutions and of a national church; the Puritans, instead, privilege the individual's direct relation with God and the voluntaristic quality of divine action. Their discussions of anomie reflect clearly the underlying difference of perspectives.

In nineteenth-century France, the opposition of the two sides, articulated by Jean Marie Guyau and Emile Durkheim, is even clearer than in previous epochs. There, the issue of anomie is addressed more directly and it is related in a straightforward way to the nominalism/realism antinomy. Durkheim is the social realist who espouses a transcendental view of morality, Guyau is the voluntarist who stands on the immanentistic side.

In contemporary American sociology, voluntarism is favored over social realism, and the theory of anomie of Robert Merton testifies to such inclination both as a theory in its own right and as a most representative piece of American social science. A comparison between Durkheim's and Merton's theories of anomie demonstrates clearly the divergence between the two perspectives, and testifies to the far-reaching consequences of a shift of emphasis from the social realism of the former to the individualistic voluntarism of the latter.

By comparison with the American scene, Western European sociologists have been much more comfortable with the social realism of the Durkheimian tradition, and the European literature on anomie reflects this inclination: it dwells on "the *nature* of anomie," on the illegitimacy and internal contradictions of Merton's theory, and on the "textual" interpretation of Durkheim's concept of anomie.[2]

It is clear that the tension between realism and nominalism, and between transcendentalism and immanentism, is a crucial feature in the history of anomie. Indeed, more than simply a feature of the anomie literature, it is a broad pattern in Western thought and culture in general. It is also clear that the two perspectives are not altogether distinct and separate; rather, they are parts of a same discourse, they are internally joined together – one view cannot be conceived without the other. The immanentist and the transcendentalist views coexist, and it is only by relating one view to the other that it is possible to make sense of the discussions about anomie throughout the centuries.

The anomie literature testifies to the steady confrontation of opposing views concerning individuals, societies, and their relation. At any given time in history, certain views have been dominant, but this should not detract from considering the existence, always, of alternative views present in the background. In Western culture, the concern with social order and with the deleterious effects of anomie have been favorite themes of sociological and pre-sociological social thought; we are still, by and large, under the spell of Plato.

The history of the anomie concept shows the dominant position in social thought of social realism and rationality (what I would call the "collectivistic axis") over individualistic nominalism and the will. This dominant position is exemplified not only by Plato's social theory, but also by the theories supporting the centuries of Church dominance in the Middle Ages, the alliance between the monarchy and the Anglican Church in Renaissance England, and the collectivistic bent of Durkheimian sociology in nineteenth-century France. But the literature on anomie shows that alternatives to the collectivistic axis have persisted despite their unorthodox reputation, and that they have contributed to socio-cultural change in crucial ways. In Durkheim, the concept of anomie reflected the dominant heritage of social realism, but in American sociology, such realism has undergone significant modifications. Anomie has acquired, in contemporary sociology, a new nominalistic quality which was absent in Durkheimian sociology. This shift, however, is not exempt from criticism. In the eyes of those who consider anomie to be a real phenomenon, not *a way of looking* at a phenomenon, there can only be *one* anomie, and only a careful study of Durkheim's texts can show *the real meaning* of anomie. Cary-Lundberg's critique of Powell, McCloskey's critique of Lee and Clyde, Besnard's critique of Merton and of Tiryakian, Mestrović's exegesis of Durkheim's concept, are but a few instances of an unwillingness to let go of the notion of anomie as a "thing."[3]

Contemporary literature on anomie is today little concerned

with Durkheim's views on anomie, but this turns out to be a mixed blessing. If, on the one hand, contemporary sociologists are able to move on beyond Durkheim's fixation with the problem of order, they also demonstrate, on the other, the lack of an explicit alternative framework in which to locate their anomie research. The concern with specific, contingent problems often becomes an apology for the "abstracted empiricism" criticized by C. Wright Mills.[4] But, as John Horton has pointed out, "Alienation and anomie, however dehumanized, contain values, and ... these values have changed rather than disappeared in the practice of objectivity."[5]

Contemporary studies of anomie have rejected nineteenth-century Durkheimian realism and its related system of values without proposing an alternative framework. Given the instrumental approach emphasized in contemporary social sciences, it is understandable that the anomie literature should itself appear to be anomic – that it should lack a meaningful, unifying framework. In fact, the background assumption of modern anomie research is that the only fruitful approach is one which addresses contingent, empirically observable problems – not one which dwells on broad, abstract theoretical issues.

The unifying trait of contemporary anomie literature is found in its relativistic stance *vis-à-vis* ultimate value orientations. Most anomie research today does not subscribe to a general theory of society and of its ideal status; instead, it tries to address contingent problems and issues as they emerge in the social environment. It is still a fact that often enough the background assumptions of such a position are not recognized by the very people who subscribe to them. For this reason, the history of anomie can be useful in providing the evidence of historical antecedents to the modern concept of anomie, and in some way clarify its theoretical implications. Previous historical discussions and treatments of anomie show in various ways similarities with the modern anomie literature.

Focusing on what I would call "the individualistic axis," the most striking parallel is the one between sophistic social theories of anomie and the ones of contemporary social scientists. The sophists' approach was crucially characterized by an interest in instrumental analysis and the solution of social problems; the sophists predated the modern approach by refusing to organize their discussions around a pre-set hierarchy of values. Instead, they would arrive at different conclusions (on the *nomos-physis* debate for instance), depending on the available evidence and on the goals of their investigation. More than that, they were very much aware of the conflicting claims made in different moral realms, but interpreted them as characteristic of social life, not as ethical aberrations. This view is not espoused explicitly by modern social scientists, but their research points definitely in the same direction. In the sophists' view, as in the one of modern social scientists, value relativism and empiricism go hand in hand. Moral requirements, in both cases, are expressed in terms of hypotheses and probabilities, not in terms of unchanging moral prescriptions. But whereas the sophists took straightforward positions on these matters, the modern social scientists have left them mostly in the background.

The literature of early Christianity is relevant to the modern approach to anomie in a different way from the sophistic literature. The relativization of norms and values is provided, in the context of early Christian writings, by *opposing* the changing worldly order to the unchanging otherworldly values. The result is, still, a relativized view of the social order which allows for a dynamic tension with this world while claiming a superior status for otherworldly values. This view is expressed by recognizing the contingency of socio-political and religious institutions while proclaiming the superiority of the law of the spirit over the written law (or, as the sophists would say, of *physis* over *nomos*). The results relevant to us are that the individual acquires, here, a privileged status, and the existing social institutions are, in this respect, relativized.

The radical religious thought of Puritanism and Calvinism is likewise related to the modern sociological approach to anomie because it rescues the individual from the hegemony of the institutional apparatus; in the Reformation, the one-to-one relation with God is resurrected. Accordingly, the sacrality of social institutions is again relativized by the radical religious message of Luther and Calvin. Protestantism promoted the development of modern thisworldly individualism by putting the authority of individual conscience above the objective authority of social institutions.

In the ethical theories of Jean Marie Guyau, then, we return full circle to the secular relativism inaugurated by the sophists, but at a higher level of complexity. Here, the implications of relativization are fully developed (at least theoretically) with the notion of a modern morality characterized by the absence of external obligations and sanctions, a morality which lacks pre-set rules, an anomic morality.

All these strands of thought contributed, in different ways, to the formation of the cultural backdrop against which we can situate contemporary anomie literature. This, as we have had occasion to point out, is characterized by an instrumental approach to the empirical normative aspects of social interaction, and by a relativistic approach to ultimate value-orientations. Such a view implies that the relationship between means and ends of human action is the subject of scientific inquiry, and that the relationship among ultimate ends is only a hypothetical one. The ethical framework of this approach was outlined by G.H. Mead in his description of the value system behind American contemporary "moral sciences."

> Society gets ahead, not by fastening its vision upon a clearly outlined distant goal, but by bringing about the immediate adjustment of itself to its surroundings, which the immediate problem demands. It is the only way in which it can proceed, for with every adjustment the environment has changed, and the society and its individuals have changed in like degree.[6]

In the context of a thisworldly moral science, the traditional tension between concrete existing conditions and abstract ideals is replaced by a tension between immediate problems and their potential solutions. Modern morality bridges the gap between "is" and "ought" by transforming the ought into a realistic possibility.

If this history of the concept of anomie is useful in making us aware of where we stand in relation to the past – in promoting a sociologist's self-awareness – it is also useful in clarifying some general issues about the place of ethics in the sociological discourse. Looking back on the sociological and pre-sociological literature on anomie one sees that the observation of social reality only accounts for some variation in the notions of anomie of different writers at different historical times. If only observation determined our view of the world, there would be total unanimity in our description of it. But this is not the case. On the contrary, the history of the anomie concept shows clearly that the variety of views is the only continuous feature in the anomie literature. The constant presence of alternative perspectives on a same social reality demonstrates that social theory is not simply a matter of observation but also, and more crucially, a matter of interpretation. If empirical reality provides the raw material for sociological analysis, the beliefs and values one holds provide the perspective through which social reality is interpreted. In this respect, social theory always shows a moral component and cannot do without an implicit or explicit *Weltanschauung*. The sociologist's view of what "ought to be" affects one's theory as much as the observation of what is actually out there. Views of the ideal world, notions of human nature, methodological assumptions, professed values and beliefs – they all contribute to one's selection of social phenomena and to one's theoretical formulation about these phenomena. The tension between facts and ideas about facts demonstrates, then, that the nominalism/realism dichotomy does not simply reflect the division of social theories in two camps, but it reflects the tension between facts and ideas *within* each given social theory. Whichever position a writer espouses, it is the result of such inner tension between what is and what could be.

The issues I have raised here are crucial topics of discussion in the social sciences, as their relevance goes beyond the narrow area of anomie literature to the core of social science discourse. While this monograph touches on many points which require further elaboration, such elaboration would change the nature of this work if it were to be carried out here. Suffice it to say that this study of anomie provides evidence of a strong link between social thought and ethics, and of a dialectical pattern in the construction of moral social discourse.

I would like to conclude by quoting from the sophistic fragment called *Dissoi Logoi (Twofold Arguments)*, which begins: "Twofold arguments on good and evil are made in Greece by those who philosophize. Some affirm that one thing is the good, another the evil; others, instead, affirm that they coincide, so that what for some is good, for others is evil, and for the same person, now good, now evil."[7] The history of the anomie concept reflects the moral relativism described by the sophists, and shows that theories of anomie are not and cannot be value-free.

I believe that a recognition of the moral dimension in social theory does not damage its credibility or usefulness. What should worry us is not that contrasting views exist on practically everything we discuss; instead, we should worry when the plurality of views is eliminated and anomie is brought firmly under control. This study of discussions about anomie should make us aware of the crucial role of moral diversity and variability in our cultural heritage. Far from being an obstacle, the variability of ethical views is, historically, a crucial element of social change and progress in Western culture.

Notes

1 Quentin Skinner, "Meaning and Understanding in the History of Ideas," *History and Theory* 8 (1969):52.
2 See, for instance, François Chazel, "Considerations sur la nature de

l'anomie," *Revue française de sociologie* 8 (April–June 1967):151–68; Philippe Besnard, "Merton à la recherche de l'anomie," *Revue française de sociologie* 19 (January–March 1978): 3–38; Bernard Lacroix, "Regulation et anomie selon Durkheim," *Cahiers internationaux de sociologie* 55 (July–December 1973):265–92; Mohamed Cherkaoui, "Changement social et anomie," *Archives européennes de sociologie* 22 (1981):3–39.

3   Cf. Isabel Cary-Lundberg, "On Durkheim, Suicide, and Anomie," *American Sociological Review* 24 (April 1959): 250–2; David D. McCloskey, "What Ever Happened to Anomie," *Journal for the Scientific Study of Religion* 13 (December 1974):497–502; Besnard, "Merton à la recherche de l'anomie," 23–35; Philippe Besnard, "Durkheim and Sexual Anomie," *Social Forces* 61 (September 1982):284–6; Stjepan G. Meštrović, "Anomia and Sin in Durkheim's Thought," *Journal for the Scientific Study of Religion* 24 (June 1985):119–36; Stjepan G. Meštrović and Hélène M. Brown, "Durkheim's concept of anomie as dérèglement," *Social Problems* 33 (December 1985):81–99.

4   C. Wright Mills, *The Sociological Imagination* (Oxford: Oxford University Press, 1959), 50–75.

5   John Horton, "The Dehumanization of Anomie and Alienation," *British Journal of Sociology* 15 (December 1964):298.

6   George H. Mead, "Scientific Method and the Moral Sciences," *The International Journal of Ethics* 33 (April 1923):247.

7   "*Dissoi Logoi*," in H. Diels and W. Kranz, *Die Fragmente der Vorsokratiker*, fr. 90.1.

BIBLIOGRAPHICAL APPENDIX

This bibliographical appendix lists the literary sources on the concept of anomie in Western culture. While I have attempted to provide an exhaustive list, some references will inevitably have escaped my attention. Lexicons and dictionaries of various sorts are not included, nor is the secondary literature on *anomia* for the classical Greek and the Biblical section. The endnotes to the monograph provide most of these titles. I have listed the classical Greek and the Biblical sources where the Greek word *anomia* or its grammatical variations appear. The bibliography is organized as follows:

I   Classical Greek Literature
II   Biblical Literature
      A   Old Testament
      B   Philo of Alexandria
      C   Pseudoepigrapha
      D   Qumran Manuscripts
      E   New Testament
      F   Early Christian Writings
III   Renaissance and Modern Literature, 1500–1884.
IV   Modern and Contemporary Literature, 1885–1986.
V   Alphabetical Index of Authors, 1885–1986.

I Classical Greek Literature

The sources are listed in alphabetical order. The sophistic fragments are found in H. Diels and W. Kranz, *Die Fragmente der Vorsokratiker*, 3 vols (10th edition; Berlin, 1960–1) and Mario Untersteiner, *Sofisti. Testimonianze e frammenti*, 4 vols (Florence: La Nuova Italia, 1961).

Aeschylus *Agamemnon* 151, 1142
Anonymus Iamblichi ffrr. 3.1, 6.1, 7.0, 7.6, 7.7, 7.9, 7.11, 7.12, 7.13, 7.17
Antiphon (orator) *The Third Tetralogy* 1.3, 1.7
Antiphon (sophist) ffrr. 4.1.2, 4.1.7
Aristophanes *Thesmophoriazusae* 1039
Aristotle *Rhetorica ad Alexandrum* 1430A, 1443A
Chrysippus in *Stoicorum Veterum Fragmenta* ch. 6, no. 335, and ch. 8, no. 502
Critias *Sisyphus* fr. 25.40
Demosthenes *Against Timocrates* 152

Diodorus Siculus bk 17, ch. 5, para. 4
Epictetus *Discourses* bk 3, ch. 26, para. 32
Euripides *Andromache* 491
       Bacchae 387, 995, 1015
       Hercules Furens 757, 779
       Ion 442–3
       Iphigenia in Aulis 399, 1095
       Iphigenia in Tauris 275
       Medea 1000
       Orestes 1455
       Phoenissae 380
Gorgias *Helen* fr. 11.7
       Palamedes fr. 11a. 36
Herodotus bk 1, 8:3–4, 96:2 to 97:3, 144, 162:1
Hesiod *Theogonia* 307
Isocrates *Archidamus* 64
       Busiris 38
       Concerning the Team of Horses 10
       Helen 27, 28
       On the Peace 96
       Panathenaicus 55, 259
       Panegyricus 39, 111, 113, 114, 168
       Plataicus 8, 52
Lysias *Against Simon* 17
       Against Theomnestus 22
Plato *Alcibiades II* 146B
       Epistle VII 336B
       Hippias Major 1.285A
       Laws 7.823E, 10. 885B
       Minos 314D1, 314D4, 317C2
       Politicus 291E, 302E
       Republic 6.496D, 9.572B, 9.575A
Plutarch *Life of Lycurgus* 40D
       Moralia 229D, 755B, 758D, 1051B
Sophocles *Oedipus at Colonus* 142
       Trachiniae 1095
Thucydides 2.53.1, 3.67.6, 4.92.7
Xenophon *Anabasis* 5.6.13, 5.7.33–4
       Cyropaedia 1.3.17
       Lacedaemonians 8.5
       Memorabilia 1.2.24, 1.2.44, 4.4.13

II Biblical Literature

The Old Testament sources are obtained from *A Handy Concordance of the Septuagint* (1887; reprinted London: Bagster & Sons, 1937). The number in parentheses indicates how often *anomia* and its variations appear in the same verse.

A Old Testament

Genesis 19:5
Exodus 32:7, 34:7 (2), 34:9
Leviticus 5:4, 16:21, 17:16, 18:30, 19:29, 20:14 (3), 22:16, 26:43.
Numbers 14:18, 32:15
Deuteronomy 4:16, 4:23, 4:25, 9:5, 9:12, 15:9, 31:29 (2)
Joshua 7:15, 24:19
1 *Samuel* 24:14, 25:28
2 *Samuel* 14:9, 19:19, 22:5, 22:24, 24:10
1 *Kings* 8:32 (2), 8:47
2 *Kings* 7:9
1 *Chronicles* 9:1, 10:13 (2)
2 *Chronicles* 6:23, 6:37, 20:35, 24:7
Ezra 9:6, 9:7, 9:13
Nehemiah 4:6, 9:2
Job 5:22, 7:21, 8:4, 10:6, 10:14, 10:15, 11:11, 11:14, 12:6, 13:23, 14:17, 19:29, 20:27, 27:4, 27:7, 31:3, 31:28, 33:9, 33:23, 34:8, 34:17, 34:20, 34:22, 34:37, 35:6, 35:14, 36:20
Psalms 5:5, 5:6, 6:9, 7:15, 13:4, 17:5, 17:24, 24:3, 25:10, 27:3, 30:19, 31:1, 31:5 (2), 35:3, 35:4, 35:5, 35:13, 36:1, 36:28, 37:5, 37:19, 38:9, 38:12, 39:13, 40:7, 44:8, 48:6, 49:21 (2), 50:3, 50:4, 50:5, 50:7, 50:11, 50:15, 51:3, 52:2, 52:5, 54:4, 54:10, 54:11, 56:2, 57:3, 58:3, 58:4, 58:5, 58:6, 63:7, 64:4, 68:28 (2), 72:3, 72:19, 73:20, 78:8, 84:3, 88:23, 88:33, 89:8, 91:8, 91:10, 93:4, 93:16, 93:20, 93:23, 100:8, 102:3, 102:10, 102:12, 103:35, 105:6, 105:43, 106:17 (2), 106:42, 108:14, 118:3, 118:78, 118:133, 118:150, 124:3, 124:5, 128:3, 129:3, 129:8, 138:24, 140:4, 140:9
Proverbs 1:19, 10:2, 12:3, 13:15, 14:16, 21:18, 27:21, 28:10, 29:8, 29:27
Isaiah 1:4, 1:5, 1:25, 1:28, 1:31, 3:8, 3:11, 5:7, 5:18, 6:7, 9:15, 9:17, 9:18, 10:6, 13:11, 21:2 (2), 21:4, 24:5, 24:20, 27:9, 29:20 (2), 31:6, 32:6, 32:7, 33:14, 33:15, 43:25, 43:26, 43:27, 44:22, 48:8, 50:1, 53:5, 53:8, 53:9, 53:12 (2), 55:7, 57:3, 57:4, 58:1 (2), 59:3, 59:4, 59:6, 59:12 (2), 64:6, 66:3
Jeremiah 2:29, 5:25, 6:13, 10:21, 16:18, 23:13, 36:23
Lamentations 4:6 (2), 4:22 (2), 5:7
Ezekiel 3:18 (3), 3:19 (3), 5:6, 7:11, 7:23, 8:6 (2), 8:9, 8:13, 8:15, 8:17 (2), 9:4, 11:18, 11:21, 12:16, 13:22, 16:2, 16:36, 16:43, 16:47, 16:49, 16:50 (2), 16:51 (2), 16:52, 16:58, 18:12, 18:13, 18:20 (2), 18:21 (2), 18:23, 18:24 (2), 18:27 (2), 20:4, 20:30, 21:3, 21:4, 21:25, 21:29, 22:2, 22:5, 22:11, 23:21, 23:36, 23:44, 28:16, 29:16, 32:27, 33:6, 33:8 (3), 33:9, 33:10, 33:12 (3), 33:13, 33:18, 33:19, 36:19, 36:31, 36:33, 37:23, 39:24, 43:8, 44:6, 44:7
Daniel 9:5, 9:15, 9:24, 11:32, 12:10 (3)
Hosea 6:9

Amos 4:4
Micah 6:10 (3), 6:11, 7:18
Habakkuk 3:13
Zephaniah 1:3, 1:9
Zechariah 3:4, 5:8
Malachi 1:4, 3:15, 3:18, 4:1, 4:3

B   *Philo of Alexandria*

Allegorical Interpretations 3.80
On the Change of Names 150
The Confusion of Tongues 108
On Drunkenness 143
The Embassy to Gaius 30
Every Good Man is Free 76
Moses 2.165
The Posterity and Exile of Cain 52
On Sobriety 25
The Special Laws 1.188, 1.279, 1.321
The Worse Attacks the Better 141
Who is the Heir 212

C   *Pseudoepigrapha*

1 *Enoch* 97:6, 98:1
Psalm of Salomon 1:8, 2:3, 2:13, 9:13, 15:9, 15:21
Testament of Dan 3:2, 5:4–6, 6:1–6, 9:24, 11:32, 12:10
Testament of Levi 2:3
Testament of Judah 20:1–5
Testament of Nephtali 4:1

D   *Qumran Manuscripts*

Book of Benedictions 3:7
Book of Mysteries 1:1, 1:5
Hymns 3:18, 5:8
Manual of Discipline 1:23–4, 3:18–21, 4:9, 4:17, 4:19–20, 4:23, 5:2,
    5:10, 9:8, 9:9, 9:20–2, 10:20

E   *New Testament*

Matthew 7:23, 13:41, 23:28, 24:12
Mark 15:28; also ending of Mark in the Freer Gospels (Washington)
Luke 22:37
Acts 2:23
Romans 2:12, 4:7, 6:19
1 *Corinthians* 9:21

2 *Corinthians* 6:14
2 *Thessalonians* 2:7, 2:8
1 *Timothy* 1:9
Titus 2:14
Hebrews 1:9, 8:12, 10:17
2 *Peter* 2:8
1 *John* 3:4

F Early Christian Writings

Didache 5:2, 16:4
Epistle of Barnabas 4:1, 4:9, 5:2, 5:9, 10:4, 10:8, 14:5, 15:5-7, 18:1-2, 20:2
Epistle to Diognetus 9:2-5
1 *Clement* 8:3, 15:5, 16:5, 16:9, 16:10, 16:13, 18:2, 18:3, 18:5, 18:9, 18:13, 35:5, 35:9, 45:4, 50:6, 53:2, 56:11, 60:1
2 *Clement* 4:5
Hermas Vision 1.3.1 (2), 2.2.2, 3.6.1, 3.6.4
　　　　Mandate 4.1.3, 8.3, 10.3.2
　　　　Similitude 5.5.3, 7.2, 8.10.3, 9.19.1
Martyrdom of Polycarp 3, 16.1

III Renaissance and Modern Literature, 1500–1884

The sources are listed in chronological order. The date in the column on the left refers to the year of first publication or, when marked with an asterisk, to the year of completion of the manuscript. In this list I have included works where anomie appears in either Greek, Latin, or English.

1504　Lorenzo Valla, *Novi Testamenti Interpretationem*, edited by Erasmus (Paris: Jean Petit).

1516　Erasmus Desiderius, *Novum Instrumentum* (Basileae).

1527*　Martin Luther, "Commentary on 1 John," in *Works*, Jaroslav Pelikan, ed., Vol. 30 (Saint Louis: Concordia Publishing House, 1959), 219–327.

1582　*The New Testament of Jesus Christ* (Rheims: Iohn Fogny).

1585*　? Thomas Cartwright, *Confutation of the Rhemists Translation* (Leyden: Brewster, 1618).

1589　William Fulke, *The Text of the New Testament of Jesus Christ* (London: imprinted by the Deputies of Christopher Barker).

1589*　William Lambarde, *Archeion; or A Discourse Upon the High Courts of Justice in England* (London: printed by E.P. for Henry Seile, 1635).

1614　Joseph Hall, *No Peace with Rome* (London: printed by Humphrey Lownes for Samuel Mucham).

1635　Robert Shelford, "A Treatise shewing the Antichrist not to be yet come," in *Five Pious and Learned Discourses* (posthumous publication; Cambridge: The Printers to the University).

1645* John Bramhall, *A Defence of True Liberty* (London: printed for J. Crook, 1655).

1646* Nathaniel Culverwell, *An Elegant and Learned Discourse of the Light of Nature* (London: printed by T.R. and E.M. for John Rothwell, 1652).

1657   John Bramhall, *Castigations of Mr Hobbes' Animadversions* (London: printed by E.T. for J. Crook).

1661   Joseph Glanvill, *The Vanity of Dogmatizing* (London: printed by E. C. for H. Eversden).

1662   Joseph Glanvill, *Lux Orientalis* (London).

1668   Thomas Hobbes, *Leviathan*, Latin version (London: C. Bee).

1668   John Howe, *The Blessedness of the Righteous* (London: Sarah Griffin for Samuel Thomson).

1683   Edward Hooker, "Praefatori Epistle," to John Pordage's *Theologia Mystica* (London).

1689   Anonymous, "An Apology for the failures charged on the Reverend Mr George Walker's printed account of the Siege of Derry," (27 pp. pamphlet, London?).

1786* Benjamin Rush, *An Inquiry into the Influence of Physical Causes upon the Moral Faculty* (Philadelphia: Haswell, Barrington, and Haswell, 1839).

1834–5 Edward Greswell, *An Exposition of the Parables and of other parts of the Gospel*, vol. 4 (London: J. C. & F. Rivington).

1884   *Tablet. A weekly newspaper and review.* London, p. 722.

IV Modern and Contemporary Literature, 1885–1986

This section only lists published works on anomie; papers presented at professional meetings, dissertations and working papers are excluded. An asterisk next to the date of publication indicates that the reference is also found in the 1964 "Inventory" by Stephen Cole and Harriet Zuckerman.

1885   Jean Marie Guyau, *Esquisse d'une morale sans obligation ni sanction* (Paris: Felix Alcan).

1887   Emile Durkheim, "Guyau. l'Irréligion de l'avenir: étude de sociologie," *Revue philosophique* 23 (January–June):299–311.

1887   Jean Marie Guyau, *L'Irréligion de l'avenir, étude de sociologie* (Paris: Felix Alcan).

1889   Jean Marie Guyau, *Education et hérédité* (Paris: Felix Alcan).

1893   Maurice Blondel, *L'Action: Essai d'une critique de la vie et d'une science de la pratique* (Paris: Felix Alcan).

1893* Emile Durkheim, *De la division du travail social* (Paris: Felix Alcan).

1897* Emile Durkheim, *Le Suicide* (Paris: Felix Alcan).

1898–1900   Emile Durkheim, *Leçons de sociologie. Physique des moeurs et du droit* (published in 1950; Paris: Presses universitaires de France).

1898   Gustavo Tosti, "Suicide in the Light of Recent Studies," *American Journal of Sociology* 3 (January):464–78.

1902   Emile Durkheim, "Quelques remarques sur les groupements professionels," *De la division du travail social* (second edition, Paris: Felix Alcan).

1906   G. Aslan, *La Morale selon Guyau* (Paris: Felix Alcan).

1906   Alfred Fouillée, "La doctrine de la vie chez Guyau," *Revue de metaphysique et de morale* 14 (July):514–44.

1915   Charles Elmer Gehlke, *Emile Durkheim's Contributions to Sociological Theory* (New York: Columbia University Press).

1923   G. Richard, "L'atheisme dogmatique en sociologie religieuse," *Revue d'histoire et de philosophie religieuse*, 125–37; 229–61.

1928*   Pitirim A. Sorokin, *Contemporary Sociological Theories* (New York: Harper & Bros).

1930   Maurice Halbwachs, *Les Causes du suicide* (Paris: Felix Alcan).

1933   Charles Blondel, *Le suicide* (Strasbourg: Librairie Universitaire d'Alsace).

1933   Louis I. Dublin and B. Bunzel, *To Be or Not To Be: A Study of Suicide* (New York: Harrison Smith & Robert Haas).

1933*   Elton Mayo, *The Human Problems of an Industrial Civilization* (New York: Macmillan).

1933   George Simpson, "Preface" to *Emile Durkheim on the Division of Labor in Society* (New York: Macmillan).

1934   Mabel A. Elliott and Francis E. Merrill, *Social Disorganization* (New York: Harper & Bros).

1934   Robert K. Merton, "Durkheim's Division of Labor in Society," *American Journal of Sociology* 40 (November):319–28.

1937*   Talcott Parsons, *The Structure of Social Action* (New York: McGraw-Hill).

1938*   Howard Becker and Harry E. Barnes, *Social Thought from Lore to Science*, 2 vols (New York: D. C. Heath & Co.).

1938*   Robert K. Merton, "Social Structure and Anomie," *American Sociological Review* 3 (June): 672–82.

1939   Harry Alpert, "Emile Durkheim and Sociologismic Psychology," *American Journal of Sociology* 45 (July):64–70.

1939*   Harry Alpert, *Emile Durkheim and his Sociology* (New York: Columbia University Press).

1940   Emory S. Bogardus, *The Development of Social Thought* (New York: Longmans, Green & Co.).

1942   Talcott Parsons, "Democracy and Social Structure in Pre-Nazi Germany," *Journal of Legal and Political Sociology* 1:96–114.

1942   Talcott Parsons, "Some Sociological Aspects of the Fascist Movement," *Social Forces* 21:138–47.

1946*   Robert K. Merton, with Marjorie Fiske and Alberta Curtis, *Mass*

Persuasion: Social Psychology of a War Bond Drive (New York: Harper & Bros).

1948* Sebastian de Grazia, *The Political Community: A Study of Anomie* (Chicago: University of Chicago Press).

1949 Ivan Belknap and Hiram Friedsam, "Age and Sex Categories as Sociological Variables in the Mental Disorder of Later Maturity," *American Sociological Review* 14 (June):367–76.

1949 Alan Gewirth, "The Psychological Approach to Politics," *Ethics* 59 (April):211–20.

1949 Robert K. Merton, "Social structure and anomie," (with revisions and extensions), in *Social Theory and Social Structure* (Glencoe: Free Press), 125–49, 378–82.

1950* Robert M. MacIver, *The Ramparts We Guard* (New York: Macmillan).

1950* David Riesman, with Nathan Glazer and Reuel Denney, *The Lonely Crowd* (New Haven: Yale University Press).

1951* Milton L. Barron, "Juvenile Delinquency and American Values," *American Sociological Review* 16 (April):208–14.

1951* R. H. Brookes, "The Anatomy of Anomie (I)," *Political Science* (New Zealand) 3:44–51.

1951* Solomon Kobrin, "The Conflict of Values in Delinquency Areas," *American Sociological Review*, 16 (October):653–61.

1951 Paul F. Lazarsfeld and Allen H. Barton, "Qualititive measurement in the Social Sciences", in Daniel Lerner and Harold H. Lasswell, eds, *The Policy Sciences* (Stanford: Stanford University Press), 155–92.

1951* Talcott Parsons, *The Social System* (New York: Free Press).

1951* Matilda White Riley and Samuel H. Flowerman, "Group Relations as a Variable in Communications Research," *American Sociological Review* 16 (April):174–80.

1951 George Simpson, "Editor's preface and introduction," to Emile Durkheim's *Suicide: A Study in Sociology*, trans. John A. Spaulding and George Simpson (New York: Free Press), 9–23.

1951* Robin Williams, *American Society* (New York: Knopf).

1952* R. H. Brookes, "The Anatomy of Anomie (II)," *Political Science* (New Zealand) 4:38–49.

1952 M. D. W. Jeffreys, "Samsonic Suicide or Suicide of Revenge among Africans," *African Studies* 11 (September):118–22.

1952 Harold D. Lasswell, "The threat to privacy," in Robert M. MacIver, ed., *Conflict of Loyalties* (New York: Harper & Bros), 121–40.

1952 Ralph Pieris, "Ideological Momentum and Social Equilibrium," *American Journal of Sociology* 57 (January):339–46.

1953* Vilhelm Aubert, "White Collar Crime and Social Structure," *American Journal of Sociology* 58 (November):263–71.

1953* Herbert H. Hyman, "The value system of different classes," in Reinhard Bendix and Seymour Martin Lipset, eds, *Class, Status, and Power* (New York: Free Press), 426–42.

1954   Gordon W. Allport, *The Nature of Prejudice* (Cambridge: Addison–Wesley).

1954*   Milton L. Barron, *The Juvenile in Delinquent Society* (New York: Knopf).

1954   Angus Campbell, G. Gurin and W. E. Miller, *The Voter Decides* (Evanston: Row, Peterson & Co.).

1954   Richard Christie and Marie Jahoda, eds, *Studies in the Scope and Method of "The Authoritarian Personality"* (Glencoe: Free Press).

1954   Andrew F. Henry and James F. Short, *Suicide and Homicide* (Glencoe: Free Press).

1954*   Bernard Lander, *Toward an Understanding of Juvenile Delinquency* (New York: Columbia University Press).

1954*   Celia Stopnicka Rosenthal, "Deviation and Social Change in the Jewish Community of a Small Polish Town," *American Journal of Sociology* 60 (September):177–81.

1954*   Walter John Herbert Sprott, *Science and Social Action* (New York: Free Press).

1954*   Ralph H. Turner, "Value Conflict in Social Disorganization," *Sociology and Social Research* 38 (May–June):301–8.

1955   W. Baldamus and Noel Timms, "The Problem Family: A Sociological Approach," *British Journal of Sociology* 6 (December):318–27.

1955*   Elinor G. Barber, *The Burgeoisie in Eighteenth Century France* (Princeton, NJ: Princeton University Press).

1955*   Albert K. Cohen, *Delinquent Boys* (New York: Free Press).

1955   P. Sainsbury, *Suicide in London. An Ecological Study* (London: Chapman & Hall).

1955   Helen L. Witmer, "Juvenile Delinquency and *Anomie*," *Children* 2 (September–October):188–91.

1956*   H. L. Ansbacher, "'Anomy,' the Sociologist's Conception of 'Lack of Social Interest,'" *Individual Psychology News Letter* (June–July):3–5.

1956*   Warren G. Bennis, "Some Barriers to Teamwork in Social Research," *Social Problems* 3 (April):223–34.

1956*   Richard A. Cloward, "Remarks," in Helen L. Witmer and R. Kotinsky, eds, *New Perspectives for Research in Juvenile Delinquency* (Washington, DC: US Government Printing Office), 80–91.

1956   Charles D. Farris, "'Authoritarianism' as a Political Variable," *Journal of Politics* 18 (February):61–82.

1956*   Ernest Greenwood, "New Directions in Delinquency Research: A Commentary on a Study by Bernard Lander," *The Social Service Review* 30 (June):147–57.

1956*   Arthur Kornhauser, Harold L. Sheppard and Albert J. Mayer, *When Labor Votes* (New York: University Publishers).

1956*   Robert K. Merton, "The social–cultural environment and *anomie*," in Helen L. Witmer and R. Kotinsky, eds, *New Perspectives for Research in Juvenile Delinquency* (Washington, DC: US Government Printing Office), 24–32.

1956* Alan H. Roberts and Milton Rokeach, "Anomie, Authoritarianism, and Prejudice: A Replication," *American Journal of Sociology* 61 (January):355–8.

1956* Milton Rokeach, "Rejoinder," *American Journal of Sociology* 62 (July):67.

1956* Leo Srole, "Anomie, Authoritarianism, and Prejudice," *American Journal of Sociology* 62 (July):63–7.

1956* Leo Srole, "Social Integration and Certain Corollaries: An Exploratory Study," *American Sociological Review* 21 (December):709–16.

1957* Wendell Bell, "Anomie, Social Isolation, and the Class Structure," *Sociometry* 20 (June):105–16.

1957* E. Gartley Jaco, "Social Factors in Mental Disorders in Texas," *Social Problems* 4 (April):322–8.

1957* Robert K. Merton, "Continuities in the Theory of Social Structure and Anomie," in *Social Theory and Social Structure* (revised ed. New York: Free Press), 161–94.

1957* Gwynn Nettler, "A Measure of Alienation," *American Sociological Review* 22 (December):670–7.

1957* Morris Rosenberg, *Occupations and Values* (New York: Free Press).

1957 Makoto Sanada, "Urban Society and Anomie," *Japanese Sociological Review* 7 (July):73–81.

1957 Tadashi Sanada, "Some Problems of Urban Community," *Japanese Sociological Review* 7 (February):72–6.

1958* Christian Bay, *The Structure of Freedom* (Stanford: Stanford University Press).

1958* David J. Bordua, "Juvenile Delinquency and 'Anomie': An Attempt at Replication," *Social Problems* 6 (Winter):230–8.

1958* Warren Breed, "Mass Communication and Socio-Cultural Integration," *Social Forces* 37 (December):109–16.

1958* Rose Laub Coser, "Authority and Decision Making in a Hospital: A Comparative Analysis," *American Sociological Review* 23 (February):56–63.

1958 Elaine Cummings, Lois R. Dean, and David S. Newell, "What is 'Morale'? A Case History of a Validity Problem," *Human Organization* 17 (Summer):3–8.

1958* Howard E. Freeman and Ozzie G. Simmons, "Wives, Mothers, and the Posthospital Performance of Mental Patients," *Social Forces* 37 (December):153–9.

1958* Martin Gold, "Suicide, Homicide, and the Socialization of Aggression," *American Journal of Sociology* 63 (May):651–61.

1958 Alvin W. Gouldner, "Introduction" to Emile Durkheim, *Socialism and Saint-Simon* (Yellow Springs: The Antioch Press), v–xxix.

1958* Charles Campbell Hughes, "Anomie, the Ammassalik, and the Standardization of Error," *Southwestern Journal of Anthropology* 14 (Winter):352–77.

1958* T. C. Keedy, Jr, "Anomie and Religious Orthodoxy," *Sociology and Social Research* 43 (September–October):34–7.

1958* René König, ed., "Anomie," in *Soziologie* (Frankfurt: Fischer Bucherei), 17–25.

1958 Walter A. Lunden, "Pioneers in Criminology, XVI–Emile Durkheim," *Journal of Criminal Law, Criminology, and Police Science* 49 (May–June):2–9.

1958* Elwin H. Powell, "Occupation, Status, and Suicide: Toward a Redefinition of Anomie," *American Sociological Review* 23 (April):131–9.

1958 Aubrey Wendling and Kenneth Polk, "Suicides and Social Areas," *Pacific Sociological Review*, 1 (Fall):50–3.

1959 Isabel Cary-Lundberg, "On Durkheim, Suicide and Anomie," *American Sociological Review* 24 (April):250–2.

1959 Marshall B. Clinard, "Criminological research," in Robert K. Merton, Leonard Broom and Leonard S. Cottrell Jr, eds, *Sociology Today* (New York: Basic Books), 509–36.

1959* Richard A. Cloward, "Illegitimate Means, Anomie, and Deviant Behavior," *American Sociological Review* 24 (April):164–76.

1959* Albert K. Cohen, "The study of social disorganization and deviant behavior," in Robert K. Merton, Leonard Broom and Leonard S. Cottrell Jr, eds, *Sociology Today* (New York: Basic Books), 461–84.

1959* Stephen H. Davol and Gunars Reimanis, "The Role of Anomie as a Psychological Concept," *Journal of Individual Psychology* 15:215–25.

1959* Bruce P. Dohrenwend, "Durkheim's Egoism, Altruism, Anomie and Fatalism: A Conceptual Analysis of Durkheim's Types," *American Sociological Review* 24 (August): 466–73. Also published in Spanish, *Revista mexicana de sociologia* 21 (September–December):1077–91.

1959* Robert Dubin, "Deviant Behavior and Social Structure," *American Sociological Review* 24 (April):147–64.

1959* Daniel Glaser and Kent Rice, "Crime, Age, and Employment," *American Sociological Review* 24 (October):679–86.

1959* Clarence Ray Jeffrey, "An Integrated Theory of Crime and Criminal Behavior," *Journal of Criminal Law, Criminology, and Police Science* 49 (March–April):533–52.

1959* Alan C. Kerckhoff, "Anomie and Achievement Motivation: A Study of Personality Development within Cultural Disorganization," *Social Forces* 37 (March):196–202.

1959* Dorothy L. Meier and Wendell Bell, "Anomia and Differential Access to the Achievement of Life Goals," *American Sociological Review* 24 (April):189–202.

1959* Robert K. Merton, "Social Conformity, Deviation, and Opportunity-Structures," *American Sociological Review* 24 (April):177–89.

1959   Ephraim H. Mizruchi, "Bohemianism and the Urban Community," *Journal of Human Relations* 8 (Autumn):114–20.

1959* Gwynn Nettler, "Antisocial Sentiment and Criminality," *American Sociological Review* 24 (April):202–8.

1959   Elwin H. Powell, "Rejoinder to Dr Cary-Lundberg," *American Sociological Review* 24 (April):252–3.

1959* Arnold M. Rose, "Attitudinal Correlates of Social Participation," *Social Forces* 37 (March):202–6.

1959   Melvin Seeman, "On the Meaning of Alienation," *American Sociological Review* 24 (December):783–91.

1959* Melvin M. Tumin and Roy C. Collins, "Status Mobility and Anomie," *British Journal of Sociology* 10 (September):253–67.

1959   Barbara Wootton, *Social Science and Social Pathology* (London: Allen & Unwin).

1960* Howard Becker, "Normative Reactions to Normlessness," *American Sociological Review* 25 (December):803–10.

1960* Paul Bohannan, ed., *African Suicide and Homicide* (Princeton, NJ: Princeton University Press).

1960* Burton R. Clark, "The 'Cooling-Out' Function in Higher Education," *American Journal of Sociology* 65 (May):569–76.

1960* Richard A. Cloward and Lloyd E. Ohlin, *Delinquency and Opportunity* (New York: Free Press).

1960   Charles D. Farris, "Selected Attitudes of Foreign Affairs as Correlates of Authoritarianism and Political Anomie," *Journal of Politics* 22 (February):50–67.

1960   Roscoe C. Hinkle Jr, "Durkheim in American sociology," in Kurt H. Wolff, ed., *Emile Durkheim, 1858–1917* (Columbus: Ohio University Press), 267–95.

1960   Harry M. Johnson, *Sociology: A Systematic Introduction* (New York: Harcourt, Brace & Co.).

1960   Sister Mary Audrey Kopp, SNJM, "Anomic Pressure and Deviant Behavior," *Sociological Quarterly* 1 (October):226–38.

1960* Gerhard E. Lensky and John C. Leggett, "Caste, Class, and Deference in the Research Interview," *American Journal of Sociology* 65 (March):463–7.

1960   William T. Liu, "The Marginal Catholics in the South," *American Journal of Sociology* 65 (January):383–90.

1960   C. Wright Mills, *Images of Man: The Classical Tradition in Sociological Thinking* (New York: George Braziller).

1960* Ephraim H. Mizruchi, "Social Structure and Anomia in a Small City," *American Sociological Review* 25 (October):645–54.

1960   Joseph Neyer, "Individualism and socialism in Durkheim," in Kurt H. Wolff, ed., *Emile Durkheim, 1858–1917* (Columbus: Ohio University Press), 32–76.

1960   Talcott Parsons, "Durkheim's contribution to the theory of integration of social systems," in Kurt H. Wolff, ed., *Emile Durkheim, 1858–1917* (Columbus: Ohio University Press), 118–53.

1960   Renato Poblete, "Sociological Approach to the Sects," *Social Compass* 7 (5-6):383-406.

1960*   Renato Poblete and Thomas F. O'Dea, "Anomie and the 'Quest for Community,'" *American Catholic Sociological Review* 21 (Spring):18-36.

1960*   Sophia M. Robison, *Juvenile Delinquency: Its Nature and Control* (New York: Holt, Rinehart & Winston).

1960*   Richard L. Simpson, "A Note on Status, Mobility, and Anomie," *British Journal of Sociology* 11 (December):370-2.

1960   Sheldon S. Wolin, *Politics and Vision* (Boston: Little, Brown).

1961*   Dwight G. Dean, "Alienation: Its Meaning and Measurement," *American Sociological Review* 26 (October):753-8.

1961*   Jack P. Gibbs, "Suicide," in Robert K. Merton and Robert A. Nisbet, eds, *Contemporary Social Problems* (New York: Harcourt, Brace & World), ch. 5.

1961*   William J. Goode, "Illegitimacy, Anomie, and Cultural Penetration," *American Sociological Review* 26 (December):910-25.

1961*   Bernard Levenson, "Bureaucratic succession," in Amitai Etzioni, ed., *Complex Organizations* (New York: Holt, Rinehart & Winston), 362-75.

1961*   Seymour Martin Lipset, "Trade Unions and Social Structure: I," *Industrial Relations* 1 (October):75-89.

1961*   Edward McDill, "Anomie, Authoritarianism, Prejudice, and Socio-Economic Status: An Attempt at Clarification," *Social Forces* 39 (March):239-45.

1961   Ephraim H. Mizruchi, "A Reply to Lorna Mui," *American Sociological Review* 26 (April):277-8.

1961*   Joan W. Moore, "Occupational Anomie and Irresponsibility," *Social Problems* 8 (Spring):293-9.

1961   Lorna Holbrook Mui, "Social Structure and Anomia," *American Sociological Review* 26 (April):275-7.

1961   Talcott Parsons, "The point of view of the author," in Max Black, ed., *The Social Theories of Talcott Parsons* (Englewood Cliffs: Prentice-Hall), 311-63.

1961   Gunars Reimanis and S. H. Davol, "Correlates and Predictions of Anomie in a VA Domiciliary," *Journal of Social Psychology* 55 (December):237-44.

1961   A. Lewis Rhodes, "Authoritarianism and Alienation: The F-Scale and the Srole Scale as Predictors of Prejudice," *Sociological Quarterly* 2 (July):193-202.

1961*   A. L. Wood, "Crime and Aggression in Changing Ceylon," *Transactions of the American Philosophical Society* 51 (8):1-132.

1962*   Robert C. Angell, "Preferences for Moral Norms in Three Areas," *American Journal of Sociology* 67 (May):650-60.

1962*   Marshall B. Clinard, "Contributions of Sociology to Understanding Deviant Behaviour," *The British Journal of Criminology* 3 (October):110-29.

1962*   Lewis A. Coser, "Some Functions of Deviant Behavior and

Normative Flexibility," *American Journal of Sociology* 68 (September):172-81

1962* Dwight G. Dean and Jon A. Reeves, "Anomie: A Comparison of a Catholic and a Protestant Sample," *Sociometry* 25 (June):209-12.

1962* Vernon Fox, "Toward an Understanding of Criminal Behavior," *American Journal of Economics and Sociology* 21 (April):145-58.

1962* Everett H. Hagen, *On the Theory of Social Change* (Homewood: Dorsey Press).

1962 H. Hyman, C. Wright and T. Hopkins, *The Applications of Methods of Evaluation* (Berkeley: University of California Press).

1962* Lewis M. Killian and Charles M. Grigg, "Urbanism, Race, and Anomie," *American Journal of Sociology* 67 (May):661-5.

1962 William T. Liu, "Self Concept, Life Goal, and Anomia among Delinquents and Non-Delinquents," *American Catholic Sociological Review* 23 (Spring):41-55.

1962* Edward McDill and J. C. Ridley, "Status, Anomia, Political Alienation, and Political Participation," *American Journal of Sociology* 68 (September):205-13.

1962* Reece McGee, *Social Disorganization in America* (San Francisco: Chandler).

1962 John Madge, *The Origins of Scientific Sociology* (New York: Free Press).

1962* Ephraim H. Mizruchi and Robert Perrucci, "Norm Qualities and Differential Effects of Deviant Behavior: An Exploratory Analysis," *American Sociological Review* 27 (June):391-9.

1962* Dale Ordes and Fred Suffet, "Tendencies Toward Deviance in Competitive Sports," *Graduate Sociological Society Journal* (Columbia University) 2:13-23.

1962* John D. Photiadis and Jeanne Biggar, "Religiosity, Education and Ethnic Distance," *American Journal of Sociology* 67 (May):666-72.

1962 J. A. Ponsioen, *The Analysis of Social Change Reconsidered: A Sociological Study* (The Hague: Mounton).

1962 Elwin H. Powell, "The Evolution of the American City and the Emergence of Anomie," *The British Journal of Sociology* 13 (June):156-68.

1962* Snell Putney and Russell Middleton, "Ethical Relativism and Anomie," *American Journal of Sociology* 67 (January):430-8.

1962 Jetse Sprey, "Sex Differences in Occupational Choice Patterns among Negro Adolescents," *Social Problems* 10 (Summer):11-22.

1963 Piero Amerio, "A proposito di alienazione e anomia tra i lavoratori della Fiat," *Tempi Moderni* 13 (1963):40-4.

1963* Warren Breed, "Occupational Mobility and Suicide Among White Males," *American Sociological Review* 28 (April):179-88.

1963* Lewis A. Coser, ed., *Sociology through Literature: An Introductory Reader* (Englewood Cliffs: Prentice-Hall).

1963 Louis I. Dublin, *Suicide: A Sociological and Statistical Study* (New York: Ronald Press).

1963   John T. Gullahorn and Jeanne E. Gullahorn, "An Extension of the U-Curve Hypothesis," *Journal of Social Issues* 19 (July):33–47.

1963   Lester D. Jaffee, "Delinquency Proneness and Family Anomie," *Journal of Criminal Law, Criminology, and Police Science* 54 (June):146–54.

1963*   Robert J. Kleiner and Seymour Parker, "Goal-Striving, Social Status, and Mental Disorder: A Research Review," *American Sociological Review* 28 (April):189–203.

1963*   William T. Liu and Frank Fahey, "Delinquency, Self Esteem, and Social Control," *American Catholic Sociological Review* 24 (Spring):3–12.

1963*   Alessandro Pizzorno, "Lecture actuelle de Durkheim," *Archives européennes de sociologie* 4 (1):1–36. Also published in Italian: in *Quaderni di sociologia* n.s. 12 (3):272–309.

1963*   Elwin H. Powell, "Reforma, revolución y reacción, como adaptaciones a la anomia," *Revista mexicana de sociologia* 25 (January–April):331–55.

1963*   Hyman Rodman, "The Lower Class Value Stretch," *Social Forces* 42 (December):205–15.

1963*   Richard L. Simpson and H. Max Miller, "Social Status and Anomia," *Social Problems* 10 (Winter):256–64.

1963   Irving Spergel, "Male Young Adult Criminality, Deviant Values, and Differential Opportunities in Two Lower Class Negro Neighborhoods," *Social Problems* 10 (Winter):237–50.

1963   Antonio Tosi, "Anomia, disorganizzazione e comportamento deviato," *Studi di sociologia*, 2 (April–June):173–80.

1963*   F. B. Waisanen, "Stability, Alienation, and Change," *Sociological Quarterly* 4 (Winter):18–31.

1964   Peter Berger and Hansfried Kellner, "Marriage and the Construction of Reality," *Diogenes* 46 (Summer):1–24.

1964*   Roland J. Chilton, "Continuity in Delinquency Area Research," *American Sociological Review* 29 (February):71–83.

1964*   Marshall B. Clinard, "The theoretical implications of anomie and deviant behavior," in *Anomie and Deviant Behavior* (New York: Free Press), 1–56.

1964*   Stephen Cole and Harriet Zuckerman, "Inventory of empirical and theoretical studies of anomie," in Marshall B. Clinard, ed., *Anomie and Deviant Behavior* (New York: Free Press), 243–313.

1964*   Michel Crozier, *The Bureaucratic Phenomenon* (Chicago: University of Chicago Press).

1964*   H. Warren Dunham, "Anomie and mental disorder," in Marshall B. Clinard, ed., *Anomie and Deviant Behavior* (New York: Free Press), 128–57.

1964   S. N. Eisenstadt, ed., *Comparative Social Problems* (New York: Free Press).

1964   Jack P. Gibbs and Walter T. Martin, *Status Integration and Suicide* (Eugene: University of Oregon Books).

1964   Warren O. Hagstrom, "Anomy in Scientific Communities," *Social Problems* 12 (Fall):186–95.

1964   Peter Heintz, "Anomia inter-institucional, anomia individual y anomia colectiva," *Anales de la Facultad Latinoamericana de Ciencias Sociales* 1 (January–December):9–11.

1964   Charles W. Hobart and Nancy Warne, "On Sources of Alienation," *Journal of Existentialism* 5 (Fall):183–98.

1964   Burkart Holzner, "The problem of Anomie and Normative Change," *Archiv für Rechts und Sozialphilosophie* 50:57–86.

1964   John Horton, "The Dehumanization of Anomie and Alienation: A Problem in the Ideology of Sociology," *British Journal of Sociology* 15 (December):283–300.

1964*   Samuel Z. Klausner, *Psychiatry and Religion* (New York: Free Press).

1964*   Edwin M. Lemert, "Social structure, social control, and deviation," in Marshall B. Clinard, ed., *Anomie and Deviant Behavior* (New York: Free Press), 57–97.

1964*   Alfred R. Lindesmith and John Gagnon, "Anomie and drug addiction," in Marshall B. Clinard, ed., *Anomie and Deviant Behavior* (New York: Free Press), 158–88.

1964*   Robert K. Merton, "Anomie, anomia, and social interaction," in Marshall B. Clinard, ed., *Anomie and Deviant Behavior* (New York: Free Press), 213–42.

1964   Mhyra S. Minnis, "Differentials of Isolation, Sex and Suicide," *Proceedings of the Southwestern Sociological Association* 14 (March):77–9.

1964*   Ephraim H. Mizruchi, "Alienation and anomie: Theoretical and empirical perspectives," in Irving L. Horowitz, ed., *The New Sociology* (New York: Oxford University Press), 253–67.

1964   Ephraim H. Mizruchi, *Success and Opportunity: A Study of Anomie* (New York: Free Press).

1964   Benjamin Nelson, "Actors, Directors, Roles, Cues, Meanings, Identities: Further Thoughts on 'Anomie,'" *Psychoanalytic Review* 51 (Spring): 135–60.

1964   Erdman B. Palmore and Phillip E. Hammond, "Interacting Factors in Juvenile Delinquency," *American Sociological Review* 29 (December):848–54.

1964   Elwin H. Powell, "Sources of Anomie in the Urban Community," *Indian Sociological Bulletin* 1 (January):24–7.

1964*   Albert L. Rhodes, "Anomia, Aspiration, and Status," *Social Forces* 42 (May):434–40.

1964*   Hendrik M. Ruitenbeek, *The Individual and the Crowd: A Study of Identity in America* (New York: Nelson & Sons).

1964*   James F. Short, "Gang delinquency and Anomie," in Marshall B. Clinard, ed., *Anomie and Deviant Behavior* (New York: Free Press), 98–127.

1964*   Charles R. Snyder, "Inebriety, alcoholism, and anomie," in

Marshall B. Clinard, ed., *Anomie and Deviant Behavior* (New York: Free Press), 189–212.

1964* Irving Spergel, *Racketville, Slumtown, Haulberg* (Chicago: University of Chicago Press).

1964* Arthur L. Stinchcombe, *Rebellion in a High School* (New York: Quadrangle Books).

1964 Milton J. Yinger, "On Anomie," *Journal for the Scientific Study of Religion* 3 (April): 158–73.

1965 Albert K. Cohen, "The Sociology of the Deviant Act," *American Sociological Review* 30 (February): 5–14.

1965 Franco Crespi, "Anomia senza crisi," *Rivista di sociologia* 3 (September–December):83–155.

· 1965 Jean Duvignaud, *Durkheim* (Paris: Presses universitaires de France).

1965 Alvin W. Gouldner, *Enter Plato: Classical Greece and the Origins of Social Theory* (New York: Basic Books).

1965 Arthur M. Harkins, "Alienation and Related Concepts," *Kansas Journal of Sociology* 1 (Spring):78–89.

1965 Charles W. Hobart, "Types of Alienation: Etiology and Interrelationships," *Canadian Review of Sociology and Anthropology* 2 (May):92–107.

1965 Barclay D. Johnson, "Durkheim's One Cause of Suicide," *American Sociological Review* 30 (December):875–86.

1965 Herbert McClosky and John H. Schaar, "Psychological Dimensions of Anomy," *American Sociological Review* 30 (February):14–40.

1965 Herbert McClosky and John H. Schaar, "Reply to Srole and Nettler," *American Sociological Review* 30 (October):763–7.

1965 S. C. Moon and G. C. McCann, "Anomie scales," in L. Cleland, ed., *Scaling Social Data* (Knoxville: Tennessee Agriculture Experiment Station).

1965 Gwynn Nettler, "A Further Comment on 'Anomy,'" *American Sociological Review* 30 (October):762–3.

1965 Robert A. Nisbet, *Emile Durkheim. With Selected Essays* (Englewood Cliffs: Prentice-Hall).

1965 Marvin E. Olsen, "Alienation and Public Opinions," *Public Opinion Quarterly* 29 (Summer):200–12.

1965 Marvin E. Olsen, "Durkheim's Two Concepts of Anomie," *Sociological Quarterly* 6 (Winter):37–44.

1965 Gunars Reimanis, "Relationship of Childhood Experience Memories to Anomie Later in Life," *Journal of Genetic Psychology* 106 (March):245–52

1965 Sakari Sariola, "Fatalism and Anomie: Components of Rural–Urban Differences," *Kansas Journal of Sociology* 1 (Fall):188–96.

1965 Marvin B. Scott and Roy Turner, "Weber and the Anomic Theory of Deviance," *Sociological Quarterly* 6 (Summer):233–40.

1965   Leo Srole, "A Comment on 'Anomy,'" *American Sociological Review* 30 (October):757–62.

1965   Elmer L. Struening and Arthur H. Richardson, "A Factor Analysis Exploration of the Alienation, Anomia and Authoritarianism Domain," *American Sociological Review* 30 (October):768–76.

1965   Milton J. Yinger, *Toward a Field Theory of Behavior: Personality and Social Structure* (New York: McGraw-Hill).

1966   Tullio Carlo Altan, "Sull'uso del termine di 'anomia' nel campo delle scienze sociali," *Rivista di sociologia* 4 (May–August):77–90.

1966   Peter L. Berger and Thomas Luckmann, *The Social Construction of Reality* (New York: Doubleday).

1966   Albert K. Cohen, *Deviance and Control* (Englewood Cliffs: Prentice-Hall).

1966   Jack P. Gibbs, "The Sociology of Law and Normative Phenomena," *American Sociological Review* 31 (June):315–25.

1966   Frank Harary, "Merton Revisited: A New Classification for Deviant Behavior," *American Sociological Review* 31 (October):693–7.

1966   Robert J. Marx, "Anomie and the Community of the Faithful," *Journal of Religion and Health* 4:291–5.

1966   Curtis R. Miller and Edgar W. Butler, "Anomia and Eunomia: A Methodological Evaluation of Srole's Anomia Scale," *American Sociological Review* 31 (June):400–5.

1966   Charles L. Mulford and Judith B. Murphy, "Selected Correlates of the Stigma Associated with Mental Illness," *Proceedings of the Southwestern Sociological Association* 16:118–29.

1966   Elwin H. Powell, "Crime as a Function of Anomie," *Journal of Criminal Law, Criminology, and Police Science* 57 (June):161–71.

1966   Gunars Reimanis, "Childhood Experience Memories and Anomie in Adults and College Students," *Journal of Individual Psychology* 22 (May):56–64.

1966   Arnold M. Rose, "Prejudice, Anomie, and the Authoritarian Personality," *Sociology and Social Research* 50 (January):141–7.

1966   Gordon Rose, "Anomie and Deviation – A Conceptual Framework for Empirical Studies," *British Journal of Sociology* 17 (March):29–45.

1966   John L. Simmons, "Some Intercorrelations Among 'Alienation' Measures," *Social Forces* 44 (March):370–2.

1967   Erik Allardt, "Emile Durkheim e la sociologia politica," *Rassegna italiana di sociologia* 8 (January–March):47–66.

1967   Christopher Bagley, "Anomie, Alienation and the Evaluation of Social Structures," *Kansas Journal of Sociology* 3 (Summer):110–23.

1967   Alvin L. Bertrand, Quentin L. Jenkins, and Marcial A. Walker, "Anomie and Fatalism," *Proceedings of the Southwestern Sociological Association* 18 (March):109–14.

1967 C. Boef "Politieke Effectiviteit, Homogeniteit en Anomie," *Sociologische Gids* 15 (March–April):112–19.

1967 Charles M. Bonjean, Richard J. Hill, and S. Dale McLemore, *Sociological Measurement: An Inventory of Scales and Indices* (San Francisco: Chandler).

1967 François Bourricaud, "Les regles du jeu en situation d'anomie: le cas peruvien," *Sociologie du travail* 9 (July–September):329–52.

1967 François Chazel, "Considerations sur la nature de l'anomie," *Revue française de sociologie* 8 (April–June):151–68.

1967 Pauline E. Council, "Dysfunction and Alienation in a Small Retirement Village," *Research Reports in Social Science* 10 (February):35–43.

1967 Yalour de Tobar and Margot Romano, *Clase obrera, anomia y cambio social* (Buenos Aires: Tobar).

1967 Richard A. Dodder, "On the Unidimensionality of Srole's Five-Item Anomia Scale," *Kansas Journal of Sociology* 3 (Fall):162–5.

1967 Jack D. Douglas, *The Social Meanings of Suicide* (Princeton: Princeton University Press).

1967 T. M. Elmore and E. D. Chambers, "Anomie, Existential Neurosis, and Personality," *APA Convention Proceedings* 2:341–2.

1967 Michael A. Faia, "Alienation, Structural Strain and Political Deviancy: A test of Merton's Hypothesis," *Social Problems* 14 (Spring):389–413.

1967 Muhammad Fayyaz, "Anomie: A Study in Conceptual Dimensions," *Pakistan Philosophical Congress* 14:35–45.

1967 Robert A. Gordon, "Issues in the Ecological Study of Delinquency," *American Sociological Review* 32 (December):927–44.

1967 Neil W. Henry, "On Anomia and Eunomia," *American Sociological Review* 32 (February):117.

1967 Lawrence K. Hong, "Ordinal Position, Family Size and Anomie," *Research Reports in the Social Sciences* 1 (Spring):61–72.

1967 Mamoru Iga and Kenshiro Ohara, "Suicide Attempts of Japanese Youth and Durkheim's Concept of Anomie," *Human Organization* 26 (Spring–Summer):58–68.

1967 Barry A. Kinsey and Lorne Phillips, "The Influence of Selected Sociocultural Factors Upon Anomie Scores of Alcoholics from an Outpatient Clinic," *Proceedings of the Southwestern Sociological Association* 18 (March):163–6.

1967 Igor S. Kon, "The Concept of Alienation in Modern Sociology," *Social Research* 34 (Autumn):507–28.

1967 Steven Lukes, "Alienation and anomie," in Peter Laslett and W. G. Runciman (eds), *Philosophy, Politics and Society*, third series (New York: Barnes & Noble), 134–56.

1967 C. Paul Marsh, Robert J. Dolan, and William L. Riddick, "Anomia and Communication Behavior," *Rural Sociology* 32 (December):435–45.

1967 Curtis R. Miller and Edgar W. Butler, "Reply to Henry," *American Sociological Review* 32 (February):117–18.

1967 Ephraim H. Mizruchi, "Aspiration and Poverty: A Neglected Aspect of Merton's Anomie," *Sociological Quarterly* 8 (Autumn):439–46.

1967 Authur Neiderhoffer, *Behind the Shield: The Police in Urban Society* (New York: Doubleday).

1967 Gunars Reimanis, "Increase in Psychological Anomie as a Result of Radical and Undesirable Change Expectancy," *Journal of Personality and Social Psychology* 6:454–7.

1967 Lawrence Rosen and Stanley H. Turner, "An Evaluation of the Lander Approach to Ecology of Delinquency," *Social Problems* 16 (Fall):189–200.

1967 Stanton K. Tefft, "Anomy, Values and Culture Change Among Teen-Age Indians," *Sociology of Education* 40 (Spring):145–57.

1967 Jacques Testaniere, "Chahut traditionnel et chahut anomique dans l'enseignement du second degré," *Revue française de sociologie* 8 (Special Issue):17–33.

1967 Jeremy Tunstall, *Old and Alone* (New York: Humanities Press).

1967 W. Y. Wassef, "The Influence of Religion, Socioeconomic Status, and Education on Anomie," *Sociological Quarterly* 8 (Spring):233–8.

1967 Robert W. Winslow, "Anomie and its Alternatives: A Self-Report Study of Delinquency," *Sociological Quarterly* 8 (Autumn):468–80.

1967 Hans L. Zetterberg, "Scientific Acedia," *Sociological Focus* 1 (Fall):34–44.

1968 Raymond Aron, *Progress and Disillusion* (New York: Praeger).

1968 Robert C. Atchley and M. Patrick McCabe, "A new Approach to the Treatment of Offenders," *Sociological Focus* 2 (Winter):41–50.

1968 Dwight G. Dean, "Anomie, Powerlessness, and Religious Participation," *Journal for the Scientific Study of Religion* 7 (Fall):252–4.

1968 Lydia Spaventa De Novellis, "Anomia e suicidio nella società greco-romana," *Revue internationale de sociologie* 4 (1–3):170–9.

1968 Hans Peter Dreitzel, *Die gesellschaftlichen Leiden und das Leiden an der Gesellschaft* (Stuttgart: Enke).

1968 H. P. M. Goddijn, "Het Anomiebegrip bi j Emile Durkheim," *Mens en Maatschappij* 43 (January–February):60–71.

1968 Friso D. Heyt and Karl-Dieter Opp, "Zur Integration von Theorie und Forschung in der Soziologie abweichenden Verhaltens," *Mens en Maatschappij* 43 (January–February):72–99.

1968 Mark Lefton, "Race, Expectations and Anomia," *Social Forces* (March):347–52.

1968 Joel I. Nelson, "Anomie: Comparisons between the Old and the New Middle Class," *American Journal of Sociology* 74 (September):184–92.

1968 P. N. Rastogi, "Polarization, Politics and Anomie in a Rural Locale in East UP," *The Indian Journal of Social Work* 28 (January):371–8.

1968   Ethel Shanas, "A note on Restriction of Life Space," *Journal of Health and Social Behavior* 9 (March):86–90.

1968   Harold Skulsky, "Literature and Philosophy, the Common Ground," *Journal of Aesthetics and Art Criticism* 7 (Winter):183–97.

1968   Robert W. Winslow, "Status Management in the Adolescent Social System: A Reformulation of Merton's Anomie Theory," *British Journal of Sociology* 19 (June):143–59.

1969   Peter L. Berger, *The Sacred Canopy* (New York: Doubleday).

1969   Walter DHondt, "The Criminogenic Social Influences on the Misdemeanor of Swindling," *Tijdschrift voor Sociale Wetenschappen* 14:221–428.

1969   Jean Duvignaud, "Introduction à Emile Durkheim," *Journal Sociologique* (Paris: Presses universitaires de France).

1969   Alan Fox and Allan Flanders, "The Reform of Collective Bargaining," *British Journal of Industrial Relations* 8 (July):151–80. Also published in French, *Sociologie du travail* 11 (July–September):225–40.

1969   Jack P. Gibbs, "Marital Status and Suicide in the United States," *American Journal of Sociology* 74 (March):521–33.

1969   John H. Golthorpe, "Social Inequality and Social Integration in Modern Britain," *The Advancement of Science* 26 (December):190–202.

1969   Laurence J. Gould, "Conformity and Marginality: Two Faces of Alienation," *Journal of Social Issues* 25 (Spring):39–63.

1969   Ann Hartman, "Anomie and Social Casework," *Social Casework* 50 (March):131–7.

1969   Gerhard Hofmann, "Toward an Academic Community," *Research Reports in the Social Sciences* 2 (Fall):55–66.

1969   Eliezer D. Jaffe, "Family Anomie and Delinquency," *British Journal of Criminology* 9 (October):376–88.

1969   Donald F. Krill, "Existential Psychotherapy and the Problem of Anomie," *Social Work* 14 (April):33–49.

1969   Anne Parsons, *Belief, Magic, and Anomie* (New York: Free Press).

1969   Elwin H. Powell, "Anomie and Force: The Case of Rome," *Catalyst* 4 (Spring):79–102.

1969   Leo G. Reeder and Sharon J. Reeder, "Social Isolation and Illegitimacy," *Journal of Marriage and the Family* 31 (3):451–61.

1969   Jose Luis Reyna, "Anomia y participacion simbolica en un area rural," *Revista mexicana de ciencia politica* 15 (October–December):499–518.

1969   Jurgen Ritsert, "Die Antinomien des Anomie Konzepts," *Soziale Welt* 20 (2):145–62.

1969   John P. Robinson, "Alienation and anomie," in John P. Robinson and Phillip R. Shaver, eds, *Measures of Social Psychological Attitudes* (Ann Arbor: Survey Research Center, Institute for Social Research).

1969   Maria Louisa Sala de Gomezgil Rodriguez, "Suicido y status social," *Revista mexicana de sociologia* 31 (January–March):83–92.

1969   Menachem Rosner, "Alienation, Fetichisme, Anomie," *L'Homme et la Société* 11 (January–March):81–108.

1969   Harjit S. Sandhu and Donald E. Allen, "Female Delinquency: Goal Obstruction and Anomie," *Canadian Review of Sociology and Anthropology* 6 (May):107–10.

1969   Dimitrije Sergejev, "Pojam Anomije i Alienacija," *Sociologija* 11 (3):521–9.

1969   Shirley E. Swiggum, "Toward and Extension of Merton's Anomie Theory," *Proceedings of the Southwestern Sociological Association* 19 (April):255–9.

1969   Russell E. Travis, "Theoretical and Empirical Implications of Durkheim's Chronic Anomy," *Proceedings of the Southwestern Sociological Association* 19 (April):55–9.

1969   Leonard Zeitz, Richard J. Medalie, and Paul Alexander, "Anomie, Powerlessness, and Police Interrogation," *Journal of Criminal Law, Criminology and Police Science* 60 (September):314–22.

1970   Neuma Walker Aguiar, "A Model of Change used by Theories of Mobilization and Anomie," *America Latina* 13 (April–September):90–116.

1970   Larry D. Barnett, "Achievement Values and Anomie among Women in a Low-Income Housing Project," *Social Forces* 49 (September):127–33.

1970   Charles M. Bonjean and Michael D. Grimes, "Bureaucracy and Alienation: A Dimensional Approach," *Social Forces* 48 (March):365–73.

1970   Warren Breed, "The Negro and Fatalistic Suicide," *Pacific Sociological Review* 13 (Summer):156–62.

1970   Barbara G. Cashion, "Durkheim's Concept of Anomie and its Relationship to Divorce," *Sociology and Social Research* 55 (October):72–81.

1970   Richard Christie and Stanley Lehmann, "The structure of Machiavellian orientations," in Richard Christie and Florence L. Geis, *Studies in Machiavellianism* (New York: Academic Press), 359–87.

1970   John T. Doby, "Social Change, Conflict and Planning," *Sociological Symposium* 4 (Spring):23–30.

1970   Jean Duvignaud, "Anomie et mutation sociale," in Georges Balandier, ed., *Sociologie des mutations* (Paris: Editions anthropos), 63–81.

1970   D. Stanley Eitzen, "A Study of Voluntary Association Membership among Middle-Class Women," *Rural Sociology* 35 (March):84–91.

1970   Alvin W. Gouldner, *The Coming Crisis of Western Sociology* (New York: Basic Books).

1970   Charles Hampden-Turner, *Radical Man* (Cambridge: Schenkman).

1970　C. T. Husbands, "Some Social and Psychological Consequences of the American Dating System," *Adolescence* 5 (Winter):451–62.

1970　Charles A. S. Hynam, "The Influence of Superstition, Religion and Science upon Anomie in a Modern Western Setting," *Revue internationale de sociologie* 6 (1–3):190–215.

1970　Dean Jaros, "Political Response to New Skills: The Conforming and the Deviant," *Social Science Quarterly* 51 (December):552–60.

1970　Kenneth G. Lutterman and Russell Middleton, "Authoritarianism, Anomia and Prejudice," *Social Forces* 48 (June):485–92.

1970　Simon Marcson, *Automation, Alienation, and Anomie* (New York: Harper & Row).

1970　A. R. Mawson, "Durkheim and Contemporary Social Pathology," *British Journal of Sociology* 21 (September):298–313.

1970　Elwin H. Powell, *The Design of Discord. Studies of Anomie* (New York: Oxford University Press).

1970　Ira L. Reiss, "Premarital Sex as Deviant Behavior," *American Sociological Review* 35 (February):78–87.

1970　Barry Schwartz, "Notes on the Sociology of Sleep," *Sociological Quarterly* 11 (Fall):485–99.

1970　Michael Schwartz and Sheldon Striker, *Deviance, Selves and Others* (Washington, DC: ASA Rose Monograph).

1970　Ethel Shanas, "Aging and Life Space in Poland and the United States," *Journal of Health and Social Behavior* 11 (September):183–90.

1970　Miles E. Simpson, "Social Mobility, Normlessness and Powerlessness in Two Cultural Contexts," *American Sociological Review* 35 (December):1002–13.

1970　Albert E. Tibbs, "Authority versus Anomie," *Southern Journal of Philosophy* 8 (Summer–Fall):191–8.

1971　Ulrich Beck and Elisabeth Gernsheim, "Zu einer Theorie der Studentenunruhen in Fortgeschrittenen Industriegesellschaften," *Kölner Zeitschrift fur Soziologie und Sozialpsychologie* 23 (October):439–77.

1971　Roger Benjamin, *Delinquance juvenile et société anomique* (Paris: Editions du Centre National de la Recherche Scientifique).

1971　P. H. Besanceney, SJ, *Interfaith Marriages: Who and Why* (New Haven: College and University Press Services).

1971　Leslie G. Carr, "The Srole Items and Acquiescence," *American Sociological Review* 36 (April):287–93.

1971　Anthony Giddens, *Capitalism and Modern Social Theory* (Cambridge: Cambridge University Press).

1971　Anthony Giddens, "The 'Individual' in the Writings of Durkheim," *Archives européennes de sociologie* 12 (2):210–28.

1971　Mamoru Iga, "A Concept of Anomie and Suicide of Japanese College Students," *Life-Threatening Behavior* 1 (Winter):232–44.

1971 Joachim Israel, *Alienation from Marx to Modern Sociology* (Boston: Allyn & Bacon).

1971 Jerold E. Levy and Stanley J. Kunitz, "Indian Reservations, Anomie, and Social Pathologies," *Southwestern Journal of Anthropology* 27 (Summer):97–128.

1971 J. Midgley, "Theoretical and Empirical Meanings of Anomie – A Critique," *The South African Journal of Sociology* 3 (September):37–48.

1971 Hart M. Nelsen and Eleanor Frost, "Residence, Anomie and Receptivity to Education among Southern Appalachian Presbyterians," *Rural Sociology* 36 (December):521–32.

1971 William A. Rushing, "Class, Culture, and 'Social Structure and Anomie'," *American Journal of Sociology* 76 (March):857–72.

1971 Robert A. Wilson, "Anomia and Militancy among Urban Negroes," *Sociological Quarterly* 12 (Summer):369–86.

1971 Robert A. Wilson, "Anomie in the Ghetto," *American Journal of Sociology* 77 (July):66–87.

1972 Harry Cohen, "The Anomia of Success and the Anomia of Failure," *British Journal of Sociology* 23 (September):329–43.

1972 Peter Cresswell, "Interpretations of *Suicide*," *British Journal of Sociology* 23 (June):133–45.

1972 Ada W. Finifter, *Alienation and the Social System* (New York: Wiley).

1972 Jose A. Garmendia, "Para una sociologia de la emigracion," *Revista de estudios sociales* 5 (May–August):145–55.

1972 Lawrence K. Hong, "A Comparative Analysis of Extended Kin Visitations, Cohabitations, and Anomia in Rural and Urban Hong Kong," *Sociology and Social Research* 57 (October):43–54.

1972 Gerard J. Hunt and Edgar W. Butler, "Migration, Participation and Alienation," *Sociology and Social Research* 56 (July):440–52.

1972 Dominick La Capra, *Emile Durkheim: Sociologist and Philosopher* (Ithaca: Cornell University Press).

1972 Maria Mies, "Kulturanomie als Folge der westlichen Bildung," *Dritte Welt* 1 (1):23–38.

1972 Hart M. Nelsen, "Sectarianism, World View, and Anomie," *Social Forces* 51 (December):226–33.

1972 Hideaki Omura, "Aspiration and Anomie," *Japanese Sociological Review* 23 (July):25–43.

1972 Dag Osterberg, "Anomi-Begrepet og Historisk Materialisme," *Tidsskrift for samfunnsforskning* 13 (1):69–79.

1972 Gianfranco Poggi, *Images of Society* (Stanford: Stanford University Press).

1972 Duncan W. G. Timms and Elizabeth A. Timms, "Anomia and Social Participation among Surburban Women," *Pacific Sociological Review* 15 (January):123–42.

1972 Ernest Wallwork, *Durkheim. Morality and Milieu* (Cambridge, Mass.: Harvard University Press).

1972 Donald E. Weast, "Patterns of Drinking among Indian Youth:

The Significance of Anomia and Differential Association," *The Wisconsin Sociologist* 9 (Winter):12–28.

1973 M. F. Abraham, "Suicide: The Durkheimian Dilemma and its Resolution," *The Indian Journal of Social Work* 34 (October):209–16.

1973 William P. Anthony and Robert C. Miljus, "Anomie and Vocational–Technical Education," *Journal of Vocational Behavior* 3 (July):357–66.

1973 Philippe Besnard, "Durkheim et les femmes ou le *Suicide* inachevé," *Revue française de sociologie* 14 (January–March):27–61.

1973 Jean Duvignaud, *L'anomie; hérésie et subversion* (Paris: Editions anthropos).

1973 Claude A. Fischer, "On Urban Alienations and Anomie: Powerlessness and Social Isolation," *American Sociological Review* 38 (June):311–26.

1973 William H. Form, "The International Stratification of the Working Class," *American Sociological Review* 38 (December):697–711.

1973 C. A. Garfield, "Psychometric and Clinical Investigation of Frank's Concept of Existential Vacuum and of Anomia," *Psychiatry* 36 (4):396–408.

1973 Alvin W. Gouldner, "Foreword" to Ian Taylor, Paul Walton and Jock Young, *The New Criminology* (New York: Harper Torchbooks), ix–xiv.

1973 Bernard Lacroix, "Regulation et anomie selon Durkheim," *Cahiers internationaux de sociologie* 55 (July–December):265–92.

1973 R. W. Lewis, "Toward an Understanding of Police Anomie," *Journal of Police Science and Administration* 1 (4):484–90.

1973 Steven Lukes, *Emile Durkheim. His Life and Work* (Harmondsworth: Penguin).

1973 J. Munick, "Social Change and Anomia among Age Groups in a Religious Order," *Gerontologist* 13 (3):85.

1973 Deitmar Pfeiffer, "Innovation und Ruckzug: Kritische Ammerkungen zu Klaus Gerdes 'Soziologie der jugenlichen Drogensubkultur,'" *Soziale Welt* 23 (4):497–503.

1973 Wole Soyinka, *Season of Anomy* (London: Rex Collings).

1973 Ian Taylor, Paul Walton and Jock Young, *The New Criminology* (New York: Harper Torchbooks).

1973 Edward A. Thibault and Norman L. Weiner, "The Anomic Cop," *Humboldt Journal of Social Relations* 1 (Fall):36–41.

1973 Milton J. Yinger, "Anomie, alienation, and political behavior," in Jeanne N. Knutson, ed., *Handbook of Political Psychology* (San Francisco: Jossey-Bass).

1974 Hartmut Bohme, *Anomie und Entfremdung* (Kronberg: Scriptor-Verlag).

1074 A. Bourdin, "Jean Duvignaud; L'anomie," *Cahiers internationaux de sociologie* 57 (July):359–67.

1974   Judee K. Burgoon and Michael Burgoon, "Unwillingness to Communicate, Anomia-Alienation, and Communication Apprehension as Predictors of Small Group Communication," *Journal of Psychology* 88 (September):31–8.

1974   Andrzej Celinski, "Analiza i krytyka Mertonowskiej teorii zachowan dewiacyjnych," *Studia Socjologiczne* 54 (3):117–40.

1974   Eva Etzioni-Halevy and R. Shapira, "Semi-Legitimate in Perspective of Anomie," *International Review of History and Political Science* 11 (4):1–24.

1974   Elizabeth Fischer, "Participation and Anomie – Detroit from the 1950s to 1971," *Public Opinion Quarterly* 38 (3):441–2.

1974   William H. Form, "The Political Crisis of Argentine Workers or of American Professors?" *American Sociological Review* 39 (October):759–61.

1974   Lawrence Hynson, Jr, "Anomie: Its History and Research Application," *Free Inquiry* 2 (November):32–8.

1974   R. Jereb, "Anomie and Objection to War," *Sociological Focus* 7 (3):62–80.

1974   Baruch Kimmerling, "Anomie and Integration in Israeli Society," *Studies in Comparative International Development* 9 (Fall):64–89.

1974   Gary R. Lee, "Marriage and Anomie," *Journal of Marriage and the Family* 36 (August):523–32.

1974   Gary R. Lee and Robert W. Clyde, "Religion, Socioeconomic Status, and Anomie," *Journal for the Scientific Study of Religion* 13 (March):35–47.

1974   David D. McCloskey, "What Ever Happened to Anomie?" *Journal for the Scientific Study of Religion* 13 (December):497–502.

1974   Stephen R. Marks, "Durkheim's Theory of Anomie," *American Journal of Sociology* 80 (September):329–63.

1974   Peter A. Munch, "Anarchy and Anomie in an Atomistic Community," *Man* 9 (June):243–61.

1974   Robert H. Orr, "The Additive and Interactive Effects of Powerlessness and Anomie in Predicting Opposition to Pollution Control," *Rural Sociology* 39 (Winter):471–86.

1974   James F. Petras and Robert I. Rhodes, "Comment on 'Internal Stratification of the Working Class,'" *American Sociological Review* 39 (October):757–9.

1974   E. J. Pin, "How to be Saved from Anomie and Alienation," *Social Compass* 21 (3):227–39.

1974   Gunars Reimanis, "Anomie, Crime, Childhood Memories, and Development of Social Interest," *Journal of Individual Psychology* 30 (May):53–8.

1974   Gunars Reimanis, "Psychosocial Development, Anomie, and Mood," *Journal of Personality and Social Psychology* 29 (March):355–7.

1974   Russ Rueger, "The Joy of Anomie," *Human Behavior* 3 (July):64–9.

1974   Prakash C. Sharma, *Social Alienation and Anomie* (Monticello: Council of Planning Librarians).

1974   Nicholas C. Tatsis, "Marx, Durkheim, and Alienation," *Social Theory and Practice* 3 (Fall):223-43.

1974   Edward A. Tiryakian, "Reflections on the Sociology of Civilizations," *Sociological Analysis* (Summer):122-8.

1975   A. Aldestein and C. Mardon, "Suicides – 1974," *Population Trends* 2:13-18.

1975   John Ambler, "Trust in Political and Nonpolitical Authorities in France," *Comparative Politics* 8 (October):31-58.

1975   Jean Baechler, *Les Suicides* (Paris: Calmann-Levy).

1975   Stephen Cole, "The Growth of Scientific Knowledge," in Lewis A. Coser, ed., *The Idea of Social Structure* (New York: Harcourt Brace Jovanovich), 175-220.

1975   Lewis A. Coser, "Merton's uses of the European sociological tradition," *The Idea of Social Structure* (New York: Harcourt Brace Jovanovich), 85-100.

1975   Dennis R. Eckart and Roger Durand, "The Effect of Context in Measuring Anomie," *Public Opinion Quarterly* 39 (Summer):199-206.

1975   Claude S. Fischer, "The City and Political Psychology," *American Political Science Review* 69 (June):559-71.

1975   William H. Form, "The Social Construction of Anomie: A Four-Nation Study of Industrial Workers," *American Journal of Sociology* 80 (March):1165-91.

1975   Klaus Henning Hansen, Mario Nische, and Manfred Walther, "Repetitorbesuch als Strategie Sozialer Anpassung," *Zeitschrift für Soziologie* 4 (July):234-47.

1975   David J. Hanson, "Anomie Theory and Drinking Problems: A Test," *Drinking and Drug Practices Surveyor* 10 (March):23-4.

1975   Lowell L. Hargens, "Anomie und Dissens in wissenschaftlichen Gemeinschaften," *Kölner Zeitschrift für Soziologie und Sozialpsychologie* 18 (Supplement):375-92.

1975   Herbert Hendin, "The New Anomie," *Change* 7 (November):25-9.

1975   Arlie Russell Hochschild, "Disengagement Theory: Critique and Proposal," *American Sociological Review* 40 (October):553-69.

1975   Dean R. Hoge and Carroll W. Jackson, "Christian Beliefs, Nonreligious Factors, and Anti-Semitism," *Social Forces* 53 (June):581-94.

1975   T. Huppes, "Anomie en inflatie," *Mens en Maatschappij* 50 (Summer):238-70.

1975   Eugene Hynes, "Suicide and *Homo Duplex*," *Sociological Quarterly* 16 (Winter):87-104.

1975   L. Laforest, "Strength and Weakness of Theory of Anomie as an Explanation of Alcoholic Deviation," *Toxicomanies* 8 (3):219-38.

1975   Gary R. Lee, "In Defense of 'Normal Science,'" *Journal for the Scientific Study of Religion* 14 (March):57–61.

1975   David M. Rafky, "Police Cynicism Reconsidered," *Criminology* 13 (August):168–92.

1975   Irwin Rosenthal, "Vietnam War Soldiers and the Experience of Normlessness," *Journal of Social Psychology* 96 (June):85–90.

1975   L. J. Siegel, D. G. Pfeiffer and S. A. Rathus, "Anomia and Self-Esteem among Incarcerated Adolescents," *Australian and New Zealand Journal of Criminology* 8 (3–4):235–9.

1975   Alan Swingewood, *Marx and Modern Social Theory* (London: Macmillan).

1975   James J. Teevan, Jr, "On Measuring Anomia: Suggested Modification of the Srole Scale," *Pacific Sociological Review* 18 (April):159–70.

1975   Alex Thio, "A Critical Look at Merton's Anomie Theory," *Pacific Sociological Review* 18 (April):139–58.

1975   Edward A. Tiryakian, "Neither Marx nor Durkheim ... Perhaps Weber," *American Journal of Sociology* 81 (July):1–32.

1975   Stuart H. Traub and Craig B. Little, *Theories of Deviance* (Itasca: F. E. Peacock).

1975   Friedrich V. Wenz, "Anomie and Level of Suicidality in Individuals," *Psychological Reports* 36 (June):817–18.

1976   Peter L. Berger, "In Praise of Particularity: The Concept of Mediating Structures," *Review of Politics* 38 (July):399–410.

1976   Leslie G. Carr and William J. Hauser, "Anomie and Religiosity: An Empirical Re-Examination," *Journal for the Scientific Study of Religion* 15 (March):69–74.

1976   David K. Cohen, "Loss as a Theme in Social Policy," *Harvard Educational Review* 46 (November):553–71.

1976   Werner Cohn, "Jewish Outmarriage and Anomie," *Canadian Review of Sociology and Anthropology* 13 (February):90–105.

1976   Cortarelo Ramon Garcia, "Problemas teoricos de la explicacion del suicidio en Durkheim," *Revista española de la opinion publica* 46 (October–December):65–77.

1976   David J. Gray, "Comment on 'Parachuting' by Gideon Aran," *American Journal of Sociology* 81 (May):1500–2.

1976   K. Groenveld and B. S. Wilpstra, "Anomie en inflatie," *Mens en Maatschappij* 51 (Winter):85–93.

1976   Rodney J. Henningsen and Jerry Cloyd, "Anomie and Alienation," *Human Mosaic* 9 (Spring):13–28.

1976   Richard E. Hilbert, "Anomie as an explanation for Deviance," in Benjamin J. Taylor and Thurman J. White, eds, *Issues and Ideas in America* (Norman: University of Oklahoma Press), 129–60.

1976   René König, "Durkheim. Texts," *Kölner Zeitschrift für Soziologie und Sozialpsychologie* 28 (4):779–91.

1976   Pat Lauderdale, "Deviance and Moral Boundaries," *American Sociological Review* 41 (August):660–76.

1976   David D. McCloskey, "On Durkheim, Anomie, and the Modern Crisis," *American Journal of Sociology* 81 (May):1481-8.

1976   Stephen R. Marks, "Durkheim's Theories of Anomie Reconsidered," *American Journal of Sociology* 81 (May):1488-94.

1976   P. O. Peretti and C. Wilson, "Anomic and Egoistic Theoretical Factors of Contemplated Suicide among Voluntary and Involuntary Retired Aged Males," *Giornale di gerontologia* 24 (2):119-27.

1976   Lorne A. Phillips, "An Application of Anomy Theory to the Study of Alcoholism," *Journal of Studies on Alcohol* 37 (January):78-84.

1976   Whitney Pope, *Durkheim's Suicide: A Classic Analyzed* (Chicago: University of Chicago Press).

1976   Hans Gerd Schutte, "Durkheim vs. Bentham," *Mens en Maatschappij* 51 (4):382-97.

1976   William Simon and John H. Gagnon, "The Anomie of Affluence: A Post-Mertonian Conception," *American Journal of Sociology* 82 (September):356-78.

1976   Robert S. Weiss, "The Emotional Impact of Marital Separation," *Journal of Social Issues* 32 (June):135-45.

1976   Friedrich V. Wenz, "Suicide and Marital Status," *Crisis Intervention* 7 (4):149-61.

1976   Raymond N. Wolfe, "Trust, Anomia, and Locus of Control," *Journal of Social Psychology* 100 (1):151-2.

1976   Elliott R. Worthington, "Vietnam Era Veteran Anomie and Adjustment," *Military Medicine* 141 (3):169-70.

1977   Hein Dieter Basler, "Untersuchungen zur Validitat der Anomia-Skala von Srole," *Kölner Zeitschrift für Soziologie und Sozialpsychologie* 29 (June):335-42.

1977   Donald Carveth, "The Disembodied Dialectic," *Theory and Society* 4 (1):73-102.

1977   Arthur J. Deikman, "Sufism and Psychiatry," *Journal of Nervous and Mental Disease* 165 (November):318-29.

1977   Miriam Dornstein, "Organizational Conflict and Role Stress among Chief Executives in State Business Enterprises," *Journal of Occupational Psychology* 50 (December):253-63.

1977   Jean-Claude Filloux, *Durkheim et le socialisme* (Geneva: Droz).

1977   Samuel T. Gladding, "Psychological Anomie and Religious Identity in Two Adolescent Populations," *Psychological Reports* 41 (October):419-24.

1977   Reuven Kahane, "Patterns of Convergence: Reflections on the Structural Causes of the State of Emergency in India and the 1977 Elections," *Asia Quarterly* 4:257-77.

1977   Martin Killias, "Kriminelle Fremdarbeiter-Kinder?" *Schweizerische Zeitschrift für Soziologie* 3 (June):3-33.

1977   Wilbert M. Leonard, "Sociological and Social-Psychological Correlates of Anomia among a Random Sample of Aged," *Journal of Gerontology* 32 (May):303-10.

1977   Siegwart Lindenberg, "The Direction of Ordering and its Relation to Social Phenomena," *Zeitschrift für Soziologie* 6 (April):203–21.

1977 Bill McKelvey and Uma Sekaran, *Administrative Science Quarterly* 22 (June):281–305.

1977 Czeslaw Matusewicz, "Accepted Values and Juvenile Delinquency" (in Polish), *Przeglad Psychologiczny* 20 (4):707–42.

1977 Eisho Omura, "Anomie in Our Time," *Soshioroji* 22 (November):1–32.

1977 Malcolm R. Parks, "Anomia and Close Friendship Communication Networks," *Human Communication Research* 4 (Fall):48–57.

1977 H. R. Sargent, "Higher Education – Anomie and Apparent Motion," *Educational Forum* 41 (3):359–64.

1977 Adam Schaff, "Anomia a autoalienacja," *Kultura i Spoleczenstwo* 21 (4):35–51.

1977 Rudi Supek, "Problems of Social Integration in Urban Areas," *Sociologija* 19 (1):71–98.

1977 Friedrich V. Wenz, "Marital Status, Anomie, and Forms of Social Isolation," *Diseases of the Nervous System* 38 (November):891–5.

1977 William E. Wilkins, "Longitudinal Differences in Psychological Anomy and Sociological Anomy," *Psychological Reports* 40 (June):866.

1977 Helmut Willke, "Societal Reactions and Engendered Deviation: The Case of Offensive Groups," *Zeitschrift für Soziologie* 6 (October):425–33.

1977 Elliott R. Worthington, "Post-Service Adjustment and Vietnam Era Veterans," *Military Medicine* 142 (November):865–6.

1977 Susan A. Yoder, "Alienation as a Way of Life," *Perspectives in Psychiatric Care* 15 (April–June):66–71.

1978 Ralph Albanese, Jr, "Theatre et anomie: le cas du Misanthrope," *Cahiers internationaux de sociologie* 25 (January–June):113–26.

1978 Daniel Albas, Cheryl Albas, and Ken McCluskey, "Anomie, Social Class and Drinking Behavior of High-School Students," *Journal of Studies on Alcohol* 39 (May):910–13.

1978 Bronislaw Baczko, "Rousseau and Social Marginality," *Daedalus* 107 (Summer):27–40.

1978 R. C. Baum, "Holocaust. Anomic Hobbesian State of Nature," *Zeitschrift für Soziologie* 7 (4):303–26.

1978 Philippe Besnard, "Merton à la recherche de l'anomie," *Revue française de sociologie* 19 (January–March):3–38.

1978 Giampaolo Bonani, "The Slow Demise of the Work Ethic," *International Development Review* 20 (3–4):57–60.

1978 Roberto De Angelis, "Speculazione, trasformazione socioculturale ed anomia in ambiente urbano," *Sociologia* 12 (January–April):67–103.

1978 Charles J. Dudley, "The Division of Labor, Alienation, and Anomie: A Reformulation," *Sociological Focus* 11 (April):97–109.

1978   Leo F. Fay, "Differential Anomic Responses in a Religious Community," *Sociological Analysis* 39 (Spring):62–76.

1978   L. French and F. O. Bryce, "Suicide and Female Aggression: Contemporary Analysis of Anomic Suicide," *Journal of Clinical Psychiatry* 39 (10):761–5.

1978   Kenji Fukazawa, "An Introductory Consideration of Sociology as an Institution – Anomie and Sociologists," *Soshioroji* 23 (November):57–74.

1978   Michael Gilbert, "Neo-Durkheimian Analyses of Economic Life and Strife," *Sociological Review*, n.s. 26 (November):729–54.

1978   Luca Giuliano, "Tentativo di suicidio, gioventù e anomia," *Rassegna italiana di sociologia* 19 (April–June):327–39.

1978   Anthony R. Harris and Randall Stokes, "Race, Self-Evaluation and the Protestant Ethic," *Social Problems* 26 (October):71–85.

1978   L. V. Johnson and Marc Matre, "Anomie and Alcohol Use," *Journal of Studies on Alcohol* 39 (May):894–902.

1978   Robert E. Kapsis, "Black Ghetto Diversity and Anomie: A Sociopolitical View," *American Journal of Sociology* 83 (March):1132–53.

1978   Ruth Rosner Kornhauser, *Social Sources of Delinquency* (Chicago: University of Chicago Press).

1978   Marvin D. Krohn, "A Durkheimian Analysis of International Crime Rates," *Social Forces* 57 (December):654–70.

1978   Peter O. Peretti and Cedric Wilson, "Contemplated Suicide among Voluntary and Involuntary Retirees," *Omega: Journal of Death and Dying* 9 (2):193–201.

1978   David Lewis Smith, Robert Durant and Timothy J. Carter, "Social Integration, Victimization, and Anomia," *Criminology* 16 (November):395–402.

1978   Robert J. Smith and James E. Griffith, "Psychopathy, the Machiavellian, and Anomie," *Psychological Reports* 42 (February):258.

1978   Steven Stack, "Suicide: A Comparative Analysis," *Social Forces* 57 (December):644–53.

1978   Mark Traugott, "Introduction," to *Emile Durkheim on Institutional Analysis* (Chicago: University of Chicago Press), 1–39.

1978   Friedrich V. Wenz, "Economic Status, Family Anomie, and Adolescent Suicide Potential," *Journal of Psychology* 98 (January):45–7.

1978   Charles W. Wright and Susan C. Randall, "Contrasting Conceptions of Deviance in Sociology: Functionalism and Labelling Theory," *British Journal of Criminology* 18 (July):217–31.

1979   Ranbir S. Bhatti and S. M. Channabasavanna, "Social System Approach to Understand Marital Disharmony,"*Indian Journal of Social Work* 40 (April):79–88.

1979   Myron Boor, "Anomie and United States Suicide Rates, 1973–1976," *Journal of Clinical Psychology* 35 (October):703–6.

194

1979   Kenelm Burridge, *Someone, No One: An Essay on Individuality* (Princeton: Princeton University Press).

1979   Patricia W. Clemens and James O. Rust, "Factors in Adolescent Rebellious Feelings," *Adolescence* 14 (Spring):159–73.

1979   Ralf Dahrendorf, *Life Chances* (Chicago: University of Chicago Press).

1979   Nick Danigelis and Whitney Pope, "Durkheim's Theory of Suicide as Applied to the Family," *Social Forces* 57 (June):1081–106.

1979   William de Grove, "A Three-Factor Path Model of Florida Suicide Rates," *Social Science and Medicine* 13A (March):183–5.

1979   Andreas Diekmann and Karl Dieter Opp, "Anomie und Prozesse de Kriminalitatsentwicklung im sozialen Kontext," *Zeitschrift für Soziologie* 8 (October):330–43.

1979   C. Dobson, E. A. Powers, P. M. Keith and W. J. Goudy, "Anomia, Self-Esteem, and Life Satisfaction," *Journal of Gerontology* 34 (4):569–72.

1979   Bruno S. Frey and Karl Dieter Opp, "Anomie, Nutzen und Kosten: Eine Konfrontierung der Anomietheorie mit okonomischen Hypothesen," *Soziale Welt* 30 (3):275–94.

1979   Richard E. Hilbert and Charles W. Wright, "Representations of Merton's Theory of Anomie," *American Sociologist* 14 (August):150–6.

1979   Alton R. Kirk and Robert A. Zucker, "Some Sociopsychological Factors in Attempted Suicide among Urban Black Males," *Suicide and Life-Threatening Behavior* 9 (Summer):76–86.

1979   Guy La France, "Le Concept de moralité dans la sociologie durkheimienne," *Philosophy Research Archives* 5:1174.

1979   D. I. Lasky and J. T. Ziegenfuss, "Anomie and Drug-Use in High-School Students," *International Journal of the Addictions* 14 (6):861–6.

1979   Dag Osterberg, "The Concept of Anomie and Historical Materialism," *International Journal of Sociology* 9 (Winter):63–74.

1979   Paulu A. Saram, "The Significance of Max Weber's Writings to the Study of Deviance," *Archiv für Rechts und Sozialphilosophie* 65:545–71.

1979   Nancy Scheper-Hughes, *Saints, Scholars, and Schizophrenics: Mental Illness in Rural Ireland* (Berkeley: University of California Press).

1979   Welz Rainer, *Selbstmordversuche in stadtischen Lebensumwelten* (Basle: Beltz).

1979   Friedrich V. Wenz, "Self-Injury Behavior, Economic Status and the Family Anomie Syndrome among Adolescents," *Adolescence* 14 (Summer):387–98.

1979   Friedrich V. Wenz, "Sociological Correlates of Alienation among Adolescent Suicide Attempts," *Adolescence* 14 (Winter):19–30.

1980   Mark Abrahamson, "Sudden Wealth, Gratification and Attainment: Durkheim's Anomie of Affluence Reconsidered," *American Sociological Review* 45 (February):49–57.

1980 Robert Samuel Agnew, "Success and Anomie: A Study of the Effect of Goals on Anomie," *Sociological Quarterly* 21 (Winter):53–64.

1980 Nachman Ben-Yehuda, "The European Witch Craze of the 14th to 17th Centuries: A Sociologist's Perspective," *American Journal of Sociology* 86 (July):1–31.

1980 Terry B. Buss, C. Richard Hofstetter, and F. Stevens Redburn, "The Psychology of Mass Unemployment: Some Political and Social Implications," *Political Psychology* 2 (Fall–Winter): 95–113.

1980 Harold Cox, "The Motivation and Political Alienation of Older Americans," *International Journal of Aging and Human Development* 11 (1):1–12.

1980 A. Th. Derksen, "Anomie is niet identiek aan normloosheid bij Durkheim," *Mens en Maatschappij* 55 (June):186–9.

1980 Karen L. de Vogler and Peter Ebersole, "Categorization of College Students' Meaning of Life," *Psychological Reports* 46 (April):387–90.

1980 Richard A. Dodder and Doris J. Astle, "A Methodological Analysis of Srole's Nine-Item Anomia Scale," *Multivariate Behavioral Research* 15 (July):329–34.

1980 Laurence A. French, "Anomie and Violence among Native Americans," *International Journal of Comparative and Applied Criminal Justice* 4 (Spring):75–84.

1980 Ralph B. Ginsberg, *Anomie and Aspirations* (New York: Arno).

1980 Francis Hearn, "Communitas and Reflexive Social Theory," *Qualitative Sociology* 3 (Winter):299–322.

1980 Robert B. Hill, *Merton's Role Types and Paradigm of Deviance* (New York: Arno).

1980 Elizabeth Martin, "The Effects of Item Contiguity and Probing on Measures of Anomia," *Social Psychology Quarterly* 43 (March):116–20.

1980 Allen B. Moore, "An Instrument to Measure Anomia," *Adult Education* 30 (2):82–91.

1980 Gunars Reimanis and Clive F. Posen, "Locus of Control and Anomie in Western and African Cultures," *Journal of Social Psychology* 112 (December):181–9.

1980 Thomas Robbins and Dick Anthony, "The Limits of 'Coercive Persuasion' as an Explanation for Conversion to Authoritarian Sects," *Political Psychology* 2 (Summer):22–34.

1980 Christian Sand, *Anomie und Identitat* (Stuttgart: Akademischer Verlag Heinz).

1980 R. N. Sharma, "Anomie of Economic Deprivation – Merton Re-examined," *Sociological Bulletin* 29 (March):1–32.

1980 Clayton T. Shorkey, "Sense of Personal Worth, Self-Esteem, and

Anomia of Child-Abusing Mothers and Controls," *Journal of Clinical Psychology* 36 (July):817–20.

1980 Robert P. Vecchio, "Individual Differences as a Moderator of the Job Quality–Job Satisfaction Relationship," *Organizational Behavior and Human Performance* 26 (December):305–25.

1980 Susanne P. Wahba, "The Human Side of Banking: Work Attitude and Social Alienation," *Psychological Reports* 47 (October): 391–401.

1980 Linda H. Walters and Alice E. Klein, "A Cross-Validated Investigation of the Crumbaugh Purpose-In Life-Test," *Educational and Psychological Measurement* 40 (Winter):1065–71.

1980 Robert Young, "Autonomy and the 'Inner Self,'" *American Philosophical Quarterly* 17 (January):35–43.

1980 E. Zimmermann, "Anomy, Alienation, Aggression," *Beitrage zür Konfliktforschung* 10 (1):113–29.

1981 Mohamed Cherkaoui, "Changement social et anomie: essai de formalisation de la theorie durkheimienne," *Archives européennes de sociologie* 22 (1):3–39.

1981 Gary J. Felsten, "Current Considerations in Plant Shutdowns and Relocations," *Personnel Journal* 60 (May):369–72.

1981 Franco Ferrarotti, "Social Marginality and Violence in Neourban Societies," *Social Research* 48 (Spring):183–222.

1981 S. Fischer, "Race, Class, Anomie, and Academic Achievement," *Urban Education* 16 (2):149–73.

1981 Lawrence K. Hong, "Anomia and Religiosity," *Review of Religious Research* 22 (March):233–44.

1981 W. G. Jilek, "Anomic Depression, Alcoholism and a Culture-Congenial Indian Response," *Journal of Studies on Alcohol* 42 (2):159–70.

1981 Frederick Koenig, William Swanson, and Carl Harter, "Future Time Orientation, Social Class and Anomia," *Social Behavior and Personality* 9 (2):123–7.

1981 Bernard Lacroix, *Durkheim et le politique* (Paris: Presses de la Fondation nationale des sciences politiques).

1981 A. Martin et al., "Les états mélancoliques de 1900 à1968: étude chez 3000 femmes d'Indre-et-Loire," *Psychopatologie Africaine* 17 (1–3):85–95.

1981 Bruno Montanari, "Cinquanta anni di esperienza giuridica in Italia," *Rivista internazionale di filosofia del diritto* 58 (October–December):643–53.

1981 Dennis L. Peck, "A Comparison of the World View of Older and Younger Persons," *Corrective and Social Psychiatry and Journal of Behavior Technology, Methods and Therapy* 27 (1):62–8.

1981 Robert H. Poresky, Raymond B. Atilano and Kimball Hawkins, "Anomia in Rural Women," *Psychological Reports* 49 (October):480–2.

1981 John Ryan, "Marital Status, Happiness, and Anomia," *Journal of Marriage and the Family* 43 (August):643–9.

1981   Lee Sigelman, "Is Ignorance Bliss? A Reconsideration of the Folk Wisdom," *Human Relations* 34 (November):965–74.

1981   Elida Sigelmann, "Exploratory Study of the Srole Anomia Scale," *Arquivos Brasileiros de Psicologia* 33 (January–June):64–74.

1981   Steven Stack, "Religion and Anomia in America," *Journal of Social Psychology* 114 (August):299–300.

1981   Edward A. Tiryakian, "Sexual Anomie, Social Structure, Societal Change," *Social Forces* 59 (June):1025–53.

1981   C. Trent, J. C. Glass and R. Jackson, "The Impact of a Citizen Affairs Workshop on Anomia, Life Satisfaction and Internal-External Control in a Selected Group of Older Adults," *Educational Gerontology* 6 (2–3):125–33.

1981   Jonathan H. Turner, "Emile Durkheim's Theory of Integration in Differentiated Social Systems," *Pacific Sociological Review* 24 (October):379–91.

1981   Diane Vinokur-Kaplan, Ora Cibulski, Shimon Spero and Shimon Bergman, "Oldster to Oldster," *Journal of Gerontological Social Work* 4 (Fall):75–91.

1981   Lynda H. Walters and Alice E. Klein, "Measures of Anomie and Locus-of-Control for Adolescents," *Educational and Psychological Measurement* 41 (Winter):1203–13.

1982   Philippe Besnard, "L'anomie dans la biographie intellectuelle de Durkheim," *Sociologie et Sociétés* 14 (October):45–53.

1982   Philippe Besnard, "Durkheim and Sexual Anomie: A Comment on Tiryakian," *Social Forces* 61 (September):284–6.

1982   Judith R. Blau and Peter M. Blau, "The Cost of Inequality," *American Sociological Review* 47 (February):114–29.

1982   Myron Boor, "Relationship of Anomia to Perceived Changes in Financial Status, 1973–1980," *Journal of Clinical Psychology* 38 (October):891–2.

1982   K. D. Breault and Karen Barkey, "A Comparative Analysis of Durkheim's Theory of Egoistic Suicide," *Sociological Quarterly* 23 (Summer):321–31.

1982   Paul A. Brinker and Edward F. Crim, "Resignation as a Response to Alienation in a Depressed Rural Area," *American Journal of Economics and Sociology* 41 (April):101–10.

1982   Remi Clignet, "Narcissisme et anomie," *Cahiers internationaux de sociologie* 29 (July–December):197–221.

1982   A. F. Deman, "Autonomy-Control Variation in Child-Rearing and Anomie in Young Adults," *Psychology Reports* 51 (August):7–10.

1982   Dan W. Edwards, "Sex Role Attitudes, Anomy, and Female Criminal Behavior," *Corrective and Social Psychiatry and Journal of Behavior Technology, Methods and Therapy* 28 (1):14–22.

1982   David L. Harvey, "Industrial Anomie and Hegemony," *Current Perspectives in Social Theory* 3:129–59.

1982   Clyde Hendrick, Karen S. Wells and Martin V. Faletti, "Social and Emotional Effects of Geographic Relocation on Elderly

Retirees," *Journal of Personality and Social Psychology* 42 (May):951–62.

1982 F. Hoffmann, "Criminality Theories of Socially-Deviant Behavior and their Common Features," *Kriminalistik* 3 (3):139–40.

1982 Joachim Israel, "Alienation and anomie: A dialectical approach," in S. Giora Shoham, ed., *Alienation and Anomie Revisited* (Tel-Aviv: Ramot), 93–120.

1982 Ellen L. Maher, "Anomic Aspects of Recovery from Cancer," *Social Science and Medicine* 16 (8):907–12.

1982 Carlo Menghi, "Soggettività, diritto, imputabilità: l'anomia nella prospettiva dell'antropoanalisi giuridica," *Rivista internazionale di filosofia del diritto* 59 (October–December):529–76.

1982 Michael Mulkay and Elizabeth Chaplin, "Aesthetics and the Artistic Career: A Study of Anomie in Fine-Art Painting," *Sociological Quarterly* 23 (Winter):117–38.

1982 William W. Philliber and William S. Fox, "Effects of Socioeconomic Status and Perceived Affluence on Anomia," *Sociological Spectrum* 2 (April–June)123–32.

1982 Hallowell Pope and Miller D. Ferguson, "Age and Anomia in Middle and Later Life," *International Journal of Aging and Human Development* 15 (1):51–74.

1982 Gunars Reimanis, "Relationship of Locus of Control and Anomie to Political Interests among American and Nigerian Students," *Journal of Social Psychology* 116 (April):289–90.

1982 Menachem Rosner, "Sociological aspects of alienation and anomie," in S. Giora Shoham, ed., *Alienation and Anomie Revisited* (Tel-Aviv: Ramot), 195–220.

1982 Richard Schacht, "Doubts about anomie and anomia," in S. Giora Shoham, ed., *Alienation and Anomie Revisited* (Tel-Aviv: Ramot), 71–92.

1982 Melvin Seeman, "A prolegomenon on empirical research regarding anomie," in S. Giora Shoham, ed., *Alienation and Anomie Revisited* (Tel-Aviv: Ramot), 121–38.

1982 G. T. Sewall, "Against Anomie and Amnesia," *Phi Delta Kappan* 63 (9):603–6.

1982 Tom W. Smith, "College Dropouts: An Analysis of the Psychological Well-Being and Attitudes of Various Educational Groups," *Social Psychology Quarterly* 45 (March):50–3.

1982 G. J. Stack, "The Concept of Anomie," *Folia Humanistica* 20 (233):395–411.

1982 Cecil L. Willis, "Durkheim's Concept of Anomie: Some Observations," *Sociological Inquiry* 52 (Spring):106–13.

1982 Mallory Wober and Barrie Gunter, "Television and Personal Threat: Fact or Artifact? A British Survey," *British Journal of Social Psychology* 21 (September):239–47.

1983 Philippe Besnard, "Le destin de l'anomie dans la sociologie du suicide," *Revue française de sociologie* 24 (October–December):605–29.

1983 Domenico Campanale, "Antropologia e diritto," *Rivista internazionale di filosofia del diritto* 60 (January–March):28–46.

1983 Frederick J. Deroches, "Anomie: Two Theories of Prison Riots," *Canadian Journal of Criminology* 25 (April):173–90.

1983 R. Thomas Dull, "An Empirical Examination of the Anomie Theory of Drug Use," *Journal of Drug Education* 13 (1):49–62.

1983 R. Eckert, "Are Anomic Processes Institutionalizable?" *Kölner Zeitschrift für Soziologie und Sozialpsychologie* 25:144–55.

1983 Dan W. Edwards, "A Comparison of the Level of Anomie among Fifty Aged Clients Receiving Homemaker Services and Fifty Older Adults in Nursing Homes," *International Journal of Contemporary Sociology* 20 (January–April):61–71.

1983 J. McDonough Figuera, "On the Usefulness of Merton's Anomie Theory," *Youth and Society* 14 (March):259–79.

1983 Barrie Gunter and Mallory Wober, "Television Viewing and Public Trust," *British Journal of Social Psychology* 22 (June):174–6.

1983 Jose Gutierrez, "Programme contre l'anomie de l'exil," *Information psychiatrique* 59 (January):61–4.

1983 S. Hammond, "Alienation, Anomie and Estrangement," *Bulletin of the British Psychological Society* 36 (November):96.

1983 Lawrence A. Troy Lovell, "Anomia among Employed Wives and Housewives: An Exploratory Analysis," *Journal of Marriage and the Family* 45 (May):301–10.

1983 J. Manor, "Anomie in Indian Politics," *Economic and Political Weekly* 18 (19–2):725.

1983 I. Mucha, "Observations on the Anomie Concept," *Heilpädagogische Forschung* 10 (2):217–20.

1983 Marco Orrù, "The Ethics of Anomie: Jean Marie Guyau and Emile Durkheim," *British Journal of Sociology* 34 (December):499–518. Also published in Italian, *Rassegna italiana di sociologia* 24 (July–September):429–51.

1983 E. D. Poole and R. M. Regoli, "Professionalism, Role-Conflict, Work Alienation and Anomia," *Social Science Journal* 20 (1):63–70.

1983 Gunars Reimanis, "Anomie and Interest in Education," *Journal of Social Psychology* 119 (April):243–8.

1983-84 Eugen Schoenfeld, "Integration and Anomia: A Re-examination," *Humboldt Journal of Social Relations* 11 (Fall–Winter):74–85.

1983 Tom W. Smith, "An Experimental Comparison of Clustered and Scattered Scale Items," *Social Psychology Quarterly* 46 (June):163–8.

1983 Steven Stack, "Homicide and Property Crime – the Relationship to Anomie," *Aggressive Behavior* 9 (4):339–44.

1984 Joseph A. Barney, Marcel Fredericks, and Janet Fredericks, "Business Students: Relationship between Social Class, Social Responsibility, Stress Anxiety, and Anomy," *College Student Journal* 18 (Summer):108–12.

1984   Joseph A. Barney, Janet Fredericks and Marcel Fredericks, "Analysis of Academic Achievement and Personality Characteristics of Students in a Business School," *College Student Journal* 18 (Fall):280-3.

1984   Philippe Besnard, "Modes d'emploi du 'suicide'," *L'année sociologique*, 3rd series, 34:127-63.

1984   Francis T. Cullen, *Rethinking Crime and Deviance Theory* (Totowa, NJ: Rowman & Allanheld).

1984   Steve Fenton with Robert Reiner and Ian Hammett, *Durkheim and Modern Sociology* (Cambridge: Cambridge University Press).

1984   Adrian F. Furnham, "Personality, Social Skills, Anomie and Delinquency," *Journal of Child Psychology* 25 (July):409-20.

1984   Adrian F. Furnham, "Value Systems and Anomie in Three Cultures," *Journal of International Psychology* 19 (December):565-79.

1984   Barbara A. Johnson and Jonathan H. Turner, "A Formalization and Reformalization of Anomie Theory," *The South African Journal of Sociology* 15 (November):151-8.

1984   D. A. Nielsen and Charles Manson, "Family of Love: A Case Study of Anomism, Puerilism and Transmoral Consciousness in Civilizational Perspective," *Sociological Analysis* 45 (4):315-37.

1984   M. E. Rozen, "Sabotage, Anomie, and the Economy," *Dissent* 31 (3):362-5.

1984   R. A. Steffenhagen, "Self-Esteem and Anomie," *Deviant Behavior* 5 (1):23-30.

1984   Edward A. Tiryakian, "Sexual Anomy in France Before the Revolution," *Cahiers internationaux de sociologie* 76 (January):161-84.

1984   Edward A. Tiryakian, "From underground to convention: Sexual anomie as an antecedent to the French Revolution," in Scott G. McNall, ed., *Current Perspectives in Social Theory: A Research Annual*, Vol. 5 (Greenwich, Conn.: JAI Press), 289-307.

1984   Gary B. Thom, *The Human Nature of Social Discontent: Alienation, Anomie, Ambivalence* (Totowa, NJ: Rowman & Allanheld).

1985   Manuel Alers-Montalvo, *The Puerto Rico Migrants of New York City: A Study of Anomie* (New York: AMS Press).

1985   R. J. Brym, M. W. Gillespie and A. R. Gillis, "Anomie, Opportunity, and the Density of Ethnic Ties," *Canadian Review of Sociology and Anthropology* 22 (1):102-12.

1985   J. E. B. Hernandez, "Social Indicators Related to Alcoholism in the State of Tabasco, Mexico," *Revista de investigacion clinica* 37 (3):207-17.

1985   Stella P. Huges and Richard A. Dodder, "Anomie as a Correlate of Self-Reported Drinking Behavior," *Journal of Social Psychology* 125 (April):265-6.

1985   Stella P. Huges and Richard A. Dodder, "Student Anomie Levels for Native and Non-Native Samples," *Sociology and Social Research* 70 (1):82-3.

1985   Dennis O. Kaldenberg and William F. Woodman, "General and Specific Measures of Alienation: Is There a Difference?" *Sociological Spectrum* 5 (1–2):155–72.

1985   Donald N. Levine, *The Flight from Ambiguity: Essays in Social and Cultural Theory* (Chicago: University of Chicago Press).

1985   Stjepan G. Meštrović, "Anomia and Sin in Durkheim's Thought," *Journal for the Scientific Study of Religion* 24 (June):119–36.

1985   Stjepan G. Meštrović and Hélène M. Brown, "Durkheim's Concept of Anomie as *Dérèglement*," *Social Problems* 33 (December):81–99.

1985   Lynette J. Olson, Walter R. Schumm, Stephan R. Bollman and Anthony P. Jurich, "Religion and Anomia in the Midwest," *Journal of Social Psychology* 125 (February):131–2.

1985   Marco Orrù, "Anomie and Social Theory in Ancient Greece," *Archives européennes de sociologie* 26 (1):3–28.

1985   R. Peuckert, "Affluent Society and Anomia: The Development of Restlessness Potentials in Western Industrial Societies," *Gegenwartskunde Gesellschaft Staat Erziehung* 34 (3):311–20. In German.

1985   Clayton T. Shorkey and J. Armendar, "Personal Worth, Self-Esteem, Anomia, Hostility and Irrational Thinking of Abusing Mothers," *Journal of Clinical Psychology* 41 (3):414–21.

1985   Steven Stack, "Religion and Anomia: Regional versus National Specifications," *Journal of Social Psychology* 125 (February):133–4.

1985   J. Tobacyk, "Paranormal Beliefs, Alienation and Anomie in College Students," *Psychological Reports* 57 (3):844–6.

1986   Philippe Besnard, "The Americanization of Anomie at Harvard," *Knowledge and Society* 6:138–47.

1986   Robert Alun Jones, *The Sociological Theories of Emile Durkheim* (Beverly Hills, Calif.: Sage).

1986   C. P. M. Knipscheer, "Anomy in the Multigenerational Family: Children and their ·Care for Older Parents," *Zeitschrift für Gerontologie* 19 (1):40–6. In German.

1986   Marco Orrù, "Anomy and Reason in the English Renaissance," *Journal of the History of Ideas* 47 (April–June):177–96.

V Alphabetical Index of Authors, 1885–1986.

This index lists alphabetically the authors of works on anomie contained in the preceding section. For works with more than one author, only the first author is listed.

Allardt, Erik, 1967
Allport, Gordon W., 1954
Alpert, Harry, 1939; 1939
Altan, Tullio Carlo, 1966
Ambler, John, 1975
Amerio, Piero, 1963
Angell, Robert C., 1962
Ansbacher, H. L., 1956
Anthony, William P., 1973
Aron, Raymond, 1968
Aslan, G., 1906
Atchley, Robert C., 1968
Aubert, Vilhelm, 1953

Baczko, Bronislaw, 1978
Baechler, Jean, 1975
Bagley, Christopher, 1967
Baldamus, W., 1955
Barber, Elinor G., 1955
Barnett, Larry D., 1970
Barney, Joseph A., 1984; 1984
Barron, Milton L., 1951; 1954
Basler, Hein Dieter, 1977
Baum, R. C., 1978
Bay, Christian, 1958
Beck, Ulrich, 1971
Becker, Howard, 1938; 1960
Belknap, Ivan, 1949
Bell, Wendell, 1957
Benjamin, Roger, 1971
Bennis, Warren G., 1956
Ben-Yehuda, Nachman, 1980
Berger, Peter L., 1964; 1966; 1969;
    1976
Bertrand, Alvin L., 1967
Besanceney, P. H., 1971
Besnard, Philippe, 1973; 1978; 1982;
    1982; 1983; 1984; 1986
Bhatti, Ranbir S., 1979
Blau, Judith R., 1982
Blondel, Charles, 1933
Blondel, Maurice, 1893
Boef, C., 1967
Bogardus, Emory S., 1940
Bohannan, Paul, 1960
Bohme, Hartmut, 1974
Bonani, Giampaolo, 1978
Bonjean, Charles M., 1967; 1970
Boor, Myron, 1979; 1982
Bordua, David J., 1958
Bourdin, A., 1974
Bourricaud, François, 1967
Breault, K. D., 1982
Breed, Warren, 1958; 1963; 1970

Brinker, Paul A., 1982
Brookes, R. H., 1951; 1952
Brym, R. J., 1985
Burgoon, Judee K., 1974
Burridge, Kenelm, 1979
Buss, Terry B., 1980

Campanale, Domenico, 1983
Campbell, Angus, 1954
Carr, Leslie G., 1971; 1976
Carveth, Donald, 1977
Cary-Lundberg, Isabel, 1959
Cashion, Barbara G., 1970
Celinski, Andrzey, 1974
Chazel, François, 1967
Cherkaoui, Mohamed, 1981
Chilton, Roland J., 1964
Christie, Richard, 1954; 1970
Clark, Burton R., 1960
Clemens, Patricia W., 1979
Clignet, Remi, 1982
Clinard, Marshall B., 1959; 1962;
    1964
Cloward, Richard A., 1956; 1959;
    1960
Cohen, Albert K., 1950; 1955; 1965;
    1966
Cohen, David K., 1976
Cohen, Harry, 1972
Cohn, Werner, 1976
Cole, Stephen, 1964; 1975
Coser, Lewis A., 1962; 1963; 1975
Coser Laub, Rose, 1958
Council, Pauline E., 1967
Cox, Harold, 1980
Crespi, Franco, 1965
Cresswell, Peter, 1972
Crozier, Michel, 1964
Cullen, Francis T., 1984
Cummings, Elaine, 1958

Dahrendorf, Ralf, 1979
Danigelis, Nick, 1979
Davol, Stephen H., 1959
Dean, Dwight G., 1961; 1962; 1968
De Angelis, Roberto, 1978
de Grazia, Sebastian, 1948
de Grove, William, 1979
Deikman, Arthur J., 1977
Deman, A. F., 1982
De Novellis Spaventa, Lydia, 1968
Derksen, A. Th., 1980
Deroches, Frederick J., 1983
de Tobar, Yalour, 1967

de Vogler, Karen L., 1980
DHondt, Walter, 1969
Diekmann, Andreas, 1979
Dobson, C., 1979
Doby, John T., 1970
Dodder, Richard A., 1967; 1980
Dohrenwend, Bruce P., 1959
Dornstein, Miriam, 1977
Douglas, Jack D., 1967
Dreitzel, Hans Peter, 1968
Dubin, Robert, 1959
Dublin, Louis I., 1933; 1963
Dudley, Charles J., 1978
Dull, R. Thomas, 1983
Dunham, H. Warren, 1964
Durkheim, Emile, 1887; 1893; 1897;
    1898; 1902
Duvignaud, Jean, 1965; 1969; 1970;
    1973

Eckart, Dennis R., 1975
Eckert, R., 1983
Edwards, Dan W., 1982; 1983
Eisenstadt, S. N., 1964
Eitzen, D. Stanley, 1970
Elliott, Mabel A., 1934
Elmore, T. M., 1967
Etzioni-Halevy, Eva, 1974

Faia, Michael A., 1967
Farris, Charles D., 1956; 1960
Fay, Leo F., 1978
Fayyaz, Muhammad, 1967
Felsten, Gary J., 1981
Fenton, Steve, 1984
Ferrarotti, Franco, 1981
Figuera McDonough, J., 1983
Filloux, Jean-Claude, 1977
Finifter, Ada W., 1972
Fischer, Claude S., 1973; 1975
Fischer, Elizabeth, 1974
Fischer, S., 1981
Form, William H., 1973; 1974
Fouillée, Alfred, 1906
Fox, Alan, 1969
Fox, Vernon, 1962
Freeman, Howard E., 1958
French, Lawrence A., 1978; 1980
Frey, Bruno S., 1979
Fukazawa, Kenji, 1978
Furnham, Adrian F., 1984; 1984

Garcia Cortarelo, Ramon, 1976
Garfield, C. A., 1973

Garmendia, Jose A., 1972
Gehlke, Charles Elmer, 1915
Gewirth, Alan, 1949
Gibbs, Jack P., 1961; 1964; 1966;
    1969
Giddens, Anthony, 1971; 1971
Gilbert, Michael, 1978
Ginsberg, Ralph B., 1980
Guiliano, Luca, 1978
Gladding, Samuel T., 1977
Glaser, Daniel, 1959
Goddijn, H. P. M., 1968
Gold, Martin, 1958
Golthorpe, John H., 1969
Goode, William J., 1961
Gordon, Robert A., 1967
Gould, Laurence J., 1969
Gouldner, Alvin W., 1958; 1965;
    1970; 1973
Gray, David. J., 1976
Greenwood, Ernest, 1956
Groenveld, K., 1976
Gullahorn, John T., 1963
Gunter, Barrie, 1983
Gutierrez, Jose, 1983
Guyau, Jean Marie, 1885; 1887; 1889

Hagen, Everett H., 1962
Hagstrom, Warren O., 1964
Halbwachs, Maurice, 1930
Hammond, S., 1983
Hampden-Turner, Charles, 1970
Hansen Henning, Klaus, 1975
Hanson, David. J., 1975
Harary, Frank, 1966
Hargens, Lowell L., 1975
Harkins, Arthur M., 1965
Harris, Anthony R., 1978
Hartman, Ann, 1969
Harvey, David L., 1982
Hearn, Francis, 1980
Heintz, Peter, 1964
Hendin, Herbert, 1975
Hendrick, Clyde, 1982
Henningsen, Rodney J., 1976
Henry, Andrew F., 1954
Henry, Neil W., 1967
Hernandez, J. E. B., 1985
Heyt, Friso D., 1968
Hilbert, Richard E., 1976; 1979
Hill, Robert B., 1980
Hinkle, Roscoe C., 1960
Hobart, Charles W., 1964; 1965
Hochschild Russell, Arlie, 1975

Hoffmann, F., 1982
Hofmann, Gerhard, 1969
Hoge, Dean R., 1975
Holzner, Bukart, 1964
Hong, Lawrence K., 1967; 1972; 1981
Horton, John, 1964
Hughes Campbell, Charles, 1958
Hughes, Stella P., 1985; 1985
Hunt, Gerard J., 1972
Huppes, T., 1975
Husbands, C. T., 1970
Hynam, Charles A. S., 1970
Hynam, H., 1962
Hynam, Herbert H., 1953
Hynes, Eugene, 1975
Hynson, Lawrence Jr, 1974

Iga, Mamoru, 1967; 1971
Israel, Joachim, 1971; 1982

Jaco, E. Gartley, 1957
Jaffe, Eliezer D., 1969
Jaffee, Lester D., 1963
Jaros, Dean, 1970
Jeffrey, Clarence Ray, 1959
Jeffreys, M. D. W., 1952
Jereb. R., 1974
Jilek, W. G., 1981
Johnson, Barbara A., 1984
Johnson, Barclay D., 1965
Johnson, Harry M., 1960
Johnson, L. V., 1978
Jones, Robert Alun, 1986

Kahane, Reuven, 1977
Kaldenberg, Dennis O., 1985
Kapsis, Robert E., 1978
Keedy, T. C. Jr., 1958
Kerckhoff, Alan C., 1959
Killian, Lewis M., 1962
Killias, Martin, 1977
Kimmerling, Baruch, 1974
Kinsey, Barry A., 1967
Kirk, Alton R., 1979
Klausner, Samuel Z., 1964
Kleiner, Robert J., 1963
Kobrin, Solomon, 1951
Koenig, Frederick, 1981
Koenig, René, 1958; 1976
Kon, Igor S., 1967
Kopp, Mary Audrey, 1960
Kornhauser, Arthur, 1956
Kornhauser Rosner, Ruth, 1978
Knipscheer, C. P. M, 1986

Krill, Donald F., 1969
Krohn, Marvin D., 1978

LaCapra, Dominick, 1972
Lacroix, Bernard, 1973; 1981
Laforest, L., 1975
La France, Guy, 1979
Lander, Bernard, 1954
Lasky, D. I., 1979
Lasswell, Harold D., 1952
Lauderdale, Pat, 1976
Lazarsfeld, Paul F., 1951
Lee, Gary R., 1974; 1974; 1975
Lefton, Mark, 1968
Lemert, Edwin M., 1964
Lensky, Gerhard E., 1960
Leonard, Wilbert M., 1977
Levenson, Bernard, 1961
Levine, Donald N., 1985
Levy, Jerold E., 1971
Lewis, R. W., 1973
Lindenberg, Siegwart, 1977
Lindesmith, Alfred R., 1964
Lipset, Seymour Martin, 1961
Liu, William T., 1960; 1962; 1963
Lovell Troy, Lawrence A., 1983
Lukes, Steven, 1967; 1973
Lunden, Walter A., 1958
Lutterman, Kenneth G., 1970

McCloskey, David D., 1974; 1976
McClosky, Herbert, 1965; 1965
McDill, Edward, 1961; 1962
McGee, Reece, 1962
MacIver, Robert M., 1950
McKelvey, Bill, 1977
Madge, John, 1962
Maher, Ellen L., 1982
Manor, J., 1983
Marcson, Simon, 1970
Marks, Stephen R., 1974; 1976
Marsh, C. Paul, 1967
Martin, A., 1981
Martin, Elizabeth, 1980
Marx, Robert J., 1966
Matusewicz, Czeslaw, 1977
Mawson, A. R., 1970
Mayo, Elton, 1933
Meier, Dorothy L., 1959
Menghi, Carlo, 1982
Merton, Robert K., 1934; 1938; 1946; 1949; 1956; 1957; 1959; 1964
Mestrović, Stjepan G., 1985; 1985

Midgley, J., 1971
Mies, Maria, 1972
Miller, Curtis R., 1966; 1967
Mills, C. Wright, 1960
Minnis, Mhyra S., 1964
Mizruchi, Ephraim H., 1959; 1960; 1961; 1962; 1964; 1964; 1967
Montanari, Bruno, 1981
Moon, S. C., 1965
Moore, Allen B., 1980
Moore, Joan W., 1961
Mucha, I., 1983
Mui Holbrook, Lorna, 1961
Mulford, Charles L., 1966
Mulkay, Michael, 1982
Munch, Peter A., 1974
Munick, J., 1973

Nelsen, Hart M., 1971; 1972
Nelson, Benjamin, 1964
Nelson, Joel I., 1968
Nettler, Gwynn, 1957; 1959; 1965
Neyer, Joseph, 1960
Niederhoffer, Arthur, 1967
Nielsen, D. A., 1984
Nisbet, Robert A., 1965

Olsen, Marvin E., 1965; 1965
Olson, Lynette J., 1985
Omura, Eisho, 1977
Omura, Hideaki, 1972
Ordes, Dale, 1962
Orr, Robert H., 1974
Orrù, Marco, 1983; 1985; 1986
Osterberg, Dag, 1972; 1979

Palmore, Erdman B., 1964
Parks, Malcolm R., 1977
Parsons, Anne, 1969
Parsons, Talcott, 1937; 1942; 1942; 1951; 1960; 1961
Pfeiffer, Deitmar, 1973
Peck, Dennis L., 1981
Peretti, Peter O., 1976; 1978
Petras, James F., 1974
Peuckert, R., 1985
Philliber, William W., 1982
Phillips, Lorne A., 1976
Photiadis, John D., 1962
Pieris, Ralph, 1952
Pin, E. J., 1974
Pizzorno, Alessandro, 1963
Poblete, Renato, 1960; 1960
Poggi, Gianfranco, 1972

Ponsioen, J. A., 1962
Poole, E. D., 1983
Pope, Hallowell, 1982
Pope, Whitney, 1976
Poresky, Robert H., 1981
Powell, Elwin H., 1958; 1959; 1962; 1963; 1964; 1966; 1969; 1970
Putney, Snell, 1962

Rafky, David M., 1975
Rastogi, P. N., 1968
Reeder, Leo G., 1969
Reimanis, Gunars, 1961; 1965; 1966; 1967; 1974; 1974; 1980; 1982; 1983
Reina, Jose Luis, 1969
Reiss, Ira L., 1970
Rhodes, Albert L., 1961; 1964
Richard, G., 1923
Riesman, David, 1950
Riley White, Matilda, 1951
Ritsert, Jurgen, 1969
Robbins, Thomas, 1980
Roberts, Alan H., 1956
Robinson, John P., 1969
Robison, Sophia M., 1960
Rodman, Hyman, 1963
Rodriguez Sala de Gomezgil, Maria Louisa, 1969
Rokeach, Milton, 1956
Rose, Arnold M., 1959; 1966
Rose, Gordon, 1966
Rosen, Lawrence, 1967
Rosenberg, Morris, 1957
Rosenthal, Irwin, 1975
Rosenthal Stopnicka, Celia, 1954
Rosner, Menachem, 1969; 1982
Rozen, M. E., 1984
Ruitenbeek, Hendrik M., 1964
Rushing, William A., 1971
Russ, Rueger, 1974
Ryan, John, 1981

Sainsbury, P., 1955
Sanada, Makoto, 1957
Sanada, Tadashi, 1957
Sand, Christian, 1980
Sandhu, Harjit S., 1969
Saram, Paulu A., 1979
Sargent, H. R., 1977
Sariola, Sakari, 1965
Schacht, Richard, 1982
Schaff, Adam, 1977
Scheper-Hughes, Nancy, 1979

Schoenfeld, Eugen, 1983
Schutte, Hans Gerd, 1976
Schwartz, Barry, 1970
Schwartz, Michael, 1970
Scott, Marvin B., 1965
Seeman, Melvin, 1959; 1982
Sergejev, Dimitrije, 1969
Sewall, G. T., 1982
Shanas, Ethel, 1968; 1970
Sharma, Prakash C., 1974
Sharma, R. N., 1980
Shorkey, Clayton T., 1980; 1985
Short, James F., 1964
Siegel, L. J., 1975
Sigelman, Lee, 1981
Sigelmann, Elida, 1981
Simmons, John L., 1966
Simon, William, 1976
Simpson, George, 1933; 1951
Simpson, Miles E., 1970
Simpson, Richard L., 1960; 1963
Skulsky, Harold, 1968
Smith, David Lewis, 1978
Smith, Robert J., 1978
Smith, Tom W., 1982; 1983
Snyder, Charles R., 1964
Sorokin, Pitirim A., 1928
Soyinka, Wole, 1973
Spergel, Irving, 1963; 1964
Sprey, Jetse, 1962
Sprott, Walter J. H., 1954
Srole, Leo, 1956; 1956; 1965
Stack, G. J., 1982
Stack, Steven, 1978; 1981; 1982;
    1983; 1985
Steffenhagen, R. A., 1984
Stinchcombe, Arthur L., 1964
Struening, Elmer L., 1965
Supek, Rudi, 1977
Swiggum, Shirley E., 1969
Swingewood, Alan, 1975

Tatsis, Nicholas C., 1974
Taylor, Ian, 1973
Teevan, James J. Jr, 1975
Tefft, Stanton K., 1967
Testaniere, Jacques, 1967
Thibauld, Edward A., 1973
Thio, Alex, 1975
Thom, Gary B., 1984
Tibbs, Albert E., 1970

Timms, Duncan W. G., 1972
Tiryakian, Edward A., 1974; 1975;
    1981; 1984; 1984
Tobacik, T., 1985
Tosi, Antonio, 1963
Tosti, Gustavo, 1898
Traub, Stuart H., 1975
Traugott, Mark, 1978
Travis, Russell E., 1969
Trent, C., 1981
Tumin, Melvin M., 1959
Tunstall, Jeremy, 1967
Turner, Jonathan H., 1981
Turner, Ralph H., 1954

Vecchio, Robert P., 1980
Vinokur-Kaplan, Diane, 1981

Wahba, Susanne P., 1980
Waisanen, F. B., 1963
Wallwork, Ernest, 1972
Walters, Linda H., 1980; 1981
Wassef, W. Y., 1967
Weast, Donald E., 1972
Weiss, Robert S., 1976
Welz, Rainer, 1979
Wendling, Aubrey, 1958
Wenz, Friedrich V., 1975; 1976;
    1977; 1978; 1979; 1979
Wilkins, William E., 1977
Williams, Robin, 1951
Willis, Cecil L., 1982
Willke, Helmut, 1977
Wilson, Robert A., 1971; 1971
Winslow, Robert W., 1967; 1968
Witmer, Helen L., 1955
Wober, Mallory, 1982
Wolfe, Raymond N., 1976
Wolin, Sheldon S., 1960
Wood, A. L., 1961
Wootton, Barbara, 1959
Worthington, Elliott R., 1976; 1977
Wright, Charles W., 1978

Yinger, Milton J., 1964; 1965; 1973
Yoder, Susan A., 1977
Young, Robert, 1980

Zeitz, Leonard, 1969
Zetterberg, Hans L., 1967
Zimmermann, E., 1980.

Index of Names